Julian Hawthorne

United States

From the landing of Columbus to the Signing of the Peace Protocol with Spain, Vol. I

Julian Hawthorne
United States
From the landing of Columbus to the Signing of the Peace Protocol with Spain, Vol. I
ISBN/EAN: 9783743406407

Manufactured in Europe, USA, Canada, Australia, Japa

Cover: Foto ©ninafisch / pixelio.de

Manufactured and distributed by brebook publishing software (www.brebook.com)

Julian Hawthorne

United States

UNITED STATES

*FROM THE LANDING OF COLUMBUS TO
THE SIGNING OF THE PEACE
PROTOCOL WITH SPAIN*

BY

JULIAN HAWTHORNE

IN THREE VOLUMES

ILLUSTRATED

VOL. I

NEW YORK
PETER FENELON COLLIER
MDCCCXCVIII

Copyright, 1898,
BY
PETER FENELON COLLIER.

CONTENTS OF VOLUME ONE

CHAP.		PAGE
	INTRODUCTION	v
	BEFORE DAWN	1
I.	COLUMBUS, RALEIGH AND SMITH	13
II.	THE FREIGHT OF THE "MAYFLOWER"	42
III.	THE SPIRIT OF THE PURITANS	64
IV.	FROM HUDSON TO STUYVESANT	93
V.	LIBERTY, SLAVERY AND TYRANNY	121
VI.	CATHOLIC, PHILOSOPHER AND REBEL	149
VII.	QUAKER, YANKEE AND KING	178
VIII.	THE STUARTS AND THE CHARTER	206
IX.	THE NEW LEAF, AND THE BLOT ON IT	236
X.	FIFTY YEARS OF FOOLS AND HEROES	265
XI.	QUEM JUPITER VULT PERDERE	292
XII.	THE PLAINS OF ABRAHAM AND THE STAMP ACT	320
XIII.	THE PASSING OF THE RUBICON	349

LIST OF ILLUSTRATIONS

VOLUME ONE

POCAHONTAS SAVING THE LIFE OF CAPTAIN JOHN SMITH . . .
A PURITAN'S HOME—RETURNING FROM THE HUNT . . . .
INDIANS ATTACKING NEW ENGLAND SETTLERS . . . . .
SCENE IN NEW AMSTERDAM. 1660 . . . .
"TREPANNING" MEN TO BE SENT TO THE COLONIES . . .
MASSACRE BY INDIANS AT JAMESTOWN, VA., 1644 . . . .
EARLY NEW ENGLAND SCENE—A QUAKER IN THE STOCKS . .
WILLIAM PENN MAKING A TREATY WITH THE INDIANS . . .
AN INCIDENT OF KING PHILIP'S WAR . . . .
ARRESTING A WOMAN CHARGED WITH WITCHCRAFT . . .
DEATH OF GENERAL BRADDOCK—WASHINGTON MOVING THE VIRGINIA
    TROOPS FORWARD . . . .
DEATH OF GENERAL WOLFE, AT QUEBEC, SEPT. 13, 1759 . . .

INTRODUCTION

WHEN we speak of History, we may mean either one of several things. A savage will make picture-marks on a stone or a bone or a bit of wood; they serve to recall to him and his companions certain events which appeared remarkable or important for one or another reason; there was an earthquake, or a battle, or a famine, or an invasion: the chronicler himself, or some fellow-tribesman of his, may have performed some notable exploit. The impulse to make a record of it was natural: posterity might thereby be informed, after the chronicler himself had passed away, concerning the perils, the valor, the strange experiences of their ancestors. Such records were uniformly brief, and no attempt was made to connect one with another, or to interpret them. We find such fragmentary histories among the remains of our own aborigines; and the inscriptions of Egypt and Mesopotamia are the same in character and intention, though more elaborate. Warlike kings thus endeavored, from motives of pride, to perpetuate the memory of their achievements. At the time when they were inscribed upon the rock, or the walls of the tombs, or the

pedestals of the statues, they had no further value than this. But after the lapse of many ages, they acquire a new value, far greater than the original one, and not contemplated by the scribes. They assume their proper place in the long story of mankind, and indicate, each in its degree, the manner and direction of the processes by which man has become what he is, from what he was. Thereby there is breathed into the dead fact the breath of life; it rises from its tomb of centuries, and does its appointed work in the mighty organism of humanity.

In a more complex state of society, a class of persons comes into being who are neither protagonists, nor slaves, but observers; and they meditate on events, and seek to fathom their meaning. If the observer be imaginative, the picturesque side of things appeals to him; he dissolves the facts, and recreates them to suit his conceptions of beauty and harmony; and we have poetry and legend. Another type of mind will give us real histories, like those of Herodotus, Thucydides, Tacitus and Livy, which are still a model in their kind. These great writers took a broad point of view; they saw the end from the beginning of their narratives; they assigned to their facts their relative place and importance, and merged them in a pervading atmosphere of opinion, based upon the organic relation of cause and effect. Studying their works, we are enabled to discern the tendencies and developments of a race, and to note the effects of civilization, character, vice, virtue, and of that sum of them all which we term fate.

During what are called the Dark Ages of Europe, history fell into the hands of that part of the population which alone was conversant with letters—the priestly class;

and the annals they have left to us have none of the value which belongs to the productions of classical antiquity. They were again mere records; or they were mystical or fanciful tales of saints and heroes, composed or distorted for the glorification of the church, and the strengthening of the influence of the priests over the people. But these also, in after times, took on a value which they had not originally possessed, and become to the later student a precious chapter of the history of mankind.

Meanwhile, emerging august from the shadows of antiquity, we have that great body of literature of which our own Bible is the highest type, which purports to present the story of the dealings of the Creator with His creatures. These wonderful books appear to have been composed in a style, and on a principle, the secret of which has been lost. The facts which they relate, often seemingly trivial, and disconnected, are really but a material veil, or symbol, concealing a spiritual body of truth, which is neither trivial nor disconnected, but an organized, orderly and catholic revelation of the nature of man, of the processes of his spiritual regeneration, of his final reconciliation with the Divine. The time will perhaps come when some inspired man or men will be enabled to handle our modern history with the same esoteric insight which informed the Hebrew scribes, when they used the annals of the obscure tribe to which they belonged as a cover under which to present the relations of God with all the human race, past and to come.

Modern history tends more and more to become philosophic: to be an argument and an interpretation, rather than a bald statement of facts. The facts contained in our best histories bear much the same relation to the history itself, that the flesh and bones of the body bear to the person who lives in and by them. The flesh and bones, or the facts, have to exist; but the only excuse for their existence is, that the person may have being, or that the history may trace a spiritual growth or decadence. There was perhaps a time when the historian found a difficulty in collecting facts enough to serve as a firm foundation for his edifice of comment and deduction; but nowadays, his embarrassment is rather in the line of making a judicious selection from the enormous mass of facts which research and the facilities of civilization have placed at his disposal. Not only is every contemporary event recorded instantly in the newspapers and elsewhere; but new light is being constantly thrown upon the past, even upon the remotest confines thereof. Some of the facts thus brought before us are original and vital; others are mere echoes, repetitions, and unimportant variations. But the historian, if he wishes his work to last, must build as does the Muse in Emerson's verse, with

> . . . . "Rafters of immortal pine,
> Cedar incorruptible, worthy her design."

Or he may be sure that the historian who comes after him will sift the wheat from his chaff, and leave him no better reputation than that of the quarry from which the marble of the statue comes. He must tell a consecutive story, but must eschew all redundancy, furnish no more supports for his bridge than its stability requires, prune his tree so severely that it shall bear none but good fruit, forbear to freight the memory of his reader with a cargo so unwieldy as to sink it. On the other hand, of course, he must beware of being too terse; man cannot live by bread alone, and the reader of histories needs to be told the Why as well as the What. But the historical field is so wide that one man, in his one lifetime, can hardly hope by independent and original investigation both to collect all the data from which to build his structure, and so to select his timbers that only the indispensable ones shall be employed. In reality, we find one historian of a given subject or period succeeding another, and refining upon his methods and treatment. With each successive attempt the outlook becomes clearer and more comprehensive, and the meaning of the whole more pronounced. The spirit, for the sake of which the body exists, more and more dominates its material basis, until at last the latter practically vanishes "in the light of its meaning sublime." This is the apotheosis of history, which of course has not yet been attained, and probably can never be more than approximated.

The present work is a very modest contribution toward the desired result. It makes few or no pretensions to original research. There are many histories of the United States, and the fundamental facts thereof are known. But it remains for the student to endeavor to solve and declare the meaning of the familiar events; to state his view of their source and their ultimate issue. In these volumes, I have taken the view that the American nation is the embodiment and vehicle of a Divine purpose to emancipate and enlighten the human race. Man is entering upon a new career of spiritual freedom: he is to enjoy a hitherto unprecedented condition of political, social and moral liberty—as distinguished from license, which in truth is slavery. The stage for this grand evolution was fixed in the Western Continent, and the pioneers who went thither were inspired with the desire to escape from the thralldom of the past, and to nourish their souls with that pure and exquisite freedom which can afford to ignore the ease of the body, and all temporal luxuries, for the sake of that elixir of immortality. This, according to my thinking, is the innermost core of the American Idea; if you go deep enough into surface manifestations, you will find it. It is what differentiates Americans from all other peoples; it is what makes Americans out of emigrants; it is what draws the masses of Europe hither, and makes their rulers fear and hate us. It may often, and uniformly, happen that any given individual is unconscious of the Spirit that moves within him; for it is the way of that Spirit to subordinate its manifestations to its ends, knowing the frailty of humanity. But it is there, and its gradual and cumulative results are seen in the retrospect, and it may perhaps be divined as to the outline of some of its future developments.

Some sort of recognition of the American Idea, and of the American destiny, affords the only proper ground for American patriotism. We talk of the size of our country, of its wealth and prosperity, of its physical power, of its enlightenment; but if these things be all that we have to be proud of, we have little. They are in truth but outward signs of a far more precious possession within. We are the pioneers of the new Day, or we are nothing worth talking about. We are at the threshold of our career. Our record thus far is full of faults, and presents not a few deformities, due to our human frailties and limitations; but our general direction has been onward and upward. At the moment when this book is finished, we seem to be entering upon a fresh phase of our journey, and a vast horizon opens around us. It was inevitable that America should not be confined to any special area on the map of the world; it is of little importance that we fill our own continent with men and riches. We are to teach men in all parts of the world what freedom is, and thereby institute other Americas in the very strongholds of oppression. In order to accomplish this, Americans will be drawn forth and will obtain foothold in remote regions, there to disseminate their genius and inculcate their aims. In Europe and Asia are wars and rumors of wars; but there seems no reason why the true revolution, which Americanism involves, should not be a peaceful and quiet one. Our real enemies may be set in high places, but they are very few, and their power depends wholly on those myriads who are at heart our allies. If we can assure the latter of our good faith and disinterestedness, the battle is won without fighting. Indeed, the day for Mohammedan conquests is gone by, and any such conquest would be far worse than futile.

These are theories and speculations, and so far as they enter into my book, they do so as atmosphere and aim only; they are not permitted to mold the character of the narrative, so that it may illustrate a foregone conclusion. I have related the historical story as simply and directly as I could, making use of the best established authorities. Here and there I have called attention to what seemed to me the significance of events; but any one is at liberty to interpret them otherwise if he will. After all the best use of a history is probably to stimulate readers to think for themselves about the events portrayed; and if I have succeeded in doing that, I shall be satisfied. The history of the United States does mean something: what is it? Are we a decadent fruit that is rotten before it is ripe? or are we the bud of the mightiest tree of time? The materials for forming your judgment are here; form it according as your faith and hope may dictate.

JULIAN HAWTHORNE.

HAWTHORNE'S
HISTORY OF THE UNITED STATES

BEFORE DAWN

WHEN, four centuries ago, adventurers from the Old World first landed on the southern shores of the Western Continent, and pushed their way into the depths of the primeval forest, they found growing in its shadowy fastnesses a mighty plant, with vast leaves radiating upward from the mould, and tipped with formidable thorns. Its aspect was unfriendly; it added nothing to the beauty of the wilderness, and it made advance more difficult. But from the midst of some of them uprose a tall stem, rivaling in height the trees themselves, and crowned with a glorious canopy of golden blossoms. The flower of the forbidding plant was the splendor of the forest.

It was the agave, or American Aloe, sometimes called the Century Plant, because it blooms but once in a lifetime. It is of the family of the lilies; but no other lily rivals its lofty magnificence. From the gloom of the untrodden places it sends its shaft skyward into the sunshine; it is an elemental growth: its simplicity equals its beauty. But until the flower blooms, after its ages of preparation, the plant seems to have no meaning, proportion, or comeliness; only when those golden petals have unfolded upon the summit of their stately eminence do we comprehend the symmetry and significance that had so long waited to avouch themselves.

This Lily of the Ages, native to American soil, may fittingly stand as the symbol of the great Western Republic which, after so many thousand years of spiritual vicissitude and political experiment, rises heavenward out of the wilderness of time, and reveals its golden promise to those who have lost their way in the dark forest of error and oppression. It was long withheld, but it came at last, and about it center the best hopes of mankind. These United States—this America of ours, as we love to call it—is unlike any other nation that has preceded or is contemporary with it. It is the conscious incarnation of a sublime idea—the conception of civil and religious liberty. It is a spirit first, and a body afterward; thus following the true law of immortal growth. It is the visible consummation of human history, and commands the fealty of all noble minds in every corner of the earth, as well as within its own boundaries. There are Americans in all countries; but America is their home.

The seed is hidden in the soil; the germ is shut within the darkness of the womb; the preparation for all birth is obscure. For more than a century after the discovery of Columbus, no one divined the true significance and destiny of the nation-that-was-to-be. Years passed before it was understood even that the coast of the New World was anything more than the western boundaries of the Asiatic continent; Columbus never wavered from this conviction; the Cabots fancied that our Atlantic shores were those of China; and though Balboa, in 1513, waded waist-deep into the Pacific off Darien, and claimed it for Spain, yet the massive immensity of America was not suspected. There was not space for it on the globe as then plotted by geographers; it must be a string of islands, or at best but an attenuated outlying bulwark of the East. News spread slowly in those days; Vasco da Gama had reached India round the Cape of Good Hope before Balboa's exploit; Columbus, on his third voyage, had touched the mainland of South America, and young Sebastian Cabot, sailing from Bristol under the English flag, had driven his prow against Labrador ice in his effort to force a northwest passage; and still the truth was not fully realized. And when, a century later, the English colonies were assigned their boundaries, these were defined north, south and east, but to the west they extended without limit. Panama was but thirty miles across, and no one imagined that three thousand miles of solid land stretched between the Chesapeake and the Bay of San Francisco. Then, as now, orthodoxy fought against the heresy that there could be anything that was not as narrow as itself.

And this physical denial or belittlement of the American continent had its mental complement in the failure to comprehend the destiny of the people which was to inhabit it. Spain thought only of material and theological aggrandizement: of getting gold, and converting heathen, to her own temporal and spiritual glory; and she was as ready to shed innocent blood in the latter cause as in the former. England, without her rival's religious bigotry, was as intent upon winning wealth through territorial and commercial usurpations. Though not a few of the actual discoverers and explorers were generous, magnanimous and kindly men, having in view an honorable renown, based on opening new fields of life and prosperity to future ages, yet the monarchs and the trading Companies that stood behind them exhibited an unvarying selfishness and greed. The new world was to them a field for plunder only. Each aimed to own it all, and to monopolize its produce. The priestly missionaries of the Roman Catholic faith did indeed pursue their ends with a self-sacrifice and courage which deserve all praise; they devoted themselves at the risk and often at the cost of their lives to the enterprise of winning souls, as they believed, to Christ. But the Church dignitaries who sent forth these soldiers of religion sought through them only to increase the credit of their organization; they contemplated but the enlargement of their power. The thought of establishing in the wilderness a place where men might rule themselves in freedom entered not into their calculations. The spirit of the old order survived the birth of the spirit of the new.

But the conflict thus provoked was necessary to the evolution which Providence was preparing. The soul grows strong through hardship; truth conquers by struggling against opposition. It is by resistance, at first instinctive, against restraint that the infant attains self-consciousness. The first settlers who came across the ocean were animated solely by the desire to escape from oppression in their native land; they had as yet no purpose to set up an independent empire. But, as the breath of the forest and the prairie entered into their lungs, and the untrammeled spaciousness of the virgin continent unshackled their minds, they began to resent, though at first timidly, the arrogant pretension to rule them across the waves. Their environment gave them courage, made them hardy and self-dependent, enlightened their intelligence, weaned them from vain traditions, revealed to them the truth that man's birthright is liberty. And gradually, as the reins of tyranny were drawn tighter, these pioneers of the New Day were wrought up to the pitch of throwing off all allegiance, and setting their lives upon the cast. The idea of political freedom is commonplace now; but to conceive it for the first time required a mighty effort, and it could have been accomplished nowhere else than in a vast and untrodden land. The Declaration of Independence, nearly three centuries after Columbus's discovery of America, showed the hitherto blind and sordid world what America was discovered for. Individual men of genius had surmised it many years before; but their hope or forecast had been deemed but an idle vision until in a moment, as it were, the reality was born.

It was essential, however, to the final success of the great revolt, that the men who brought it to pass should be the best of a chosen race. And this requisite also was secured by conflict. It was the inveterate persuasion of many generations that America was the land of gold. Tales told by the Indians stimulated the imagination and the cupidity of the first adventurers; legends of El Dorado kindled the horizons that fled before them as they advanced. Somewhere beyond those savage mountains, amid these pathless forests, was a noble city built and paved with gold. Somewhere flowed a stately river whose waters swept between golden margins, over sands of gold. In some remote region dwelt a barbarian monarch to whom gold and precious stones were as the dross of the wayside. These stories were the offspring of the legends of the alchemists of the Dark Ages, who had professed to make gold in their crucibles; it was as good to pick up gold in armfuls on the earth as to manufacture it in the laboratory. The actual discovery of treasure in Mexico and Peru only whetted the inexhaustible appetite of the adventurers; they toiled through swamps, they cut their way through woods, they scaled precipices, they fought savages, they starved and died; and their eyes, glazing in death, still sought the gleam of the precious metal. Worse than death, to them, would have been the revelation that their belief was baseless. The thirst for wealth is not accounted noble; yet there seems to have been something not ignoble in this romantic quest for illimitable gold. There is a magic in the mere idea of the yellow metal, apart from such practical or luxurious uses as it may subserve; it stood for power and splendor—whatever good the men of that age were prone to appreciate. Howbeit, the strongest and bravest of all lands were drawn together in the search; and inevitably they met and clashed. Foremost among the antagonists were Spain and England. The ambition of Spain was measureless; she desired not only the mastery of America and its riches, but the empire of the world, the leadership in commerce, and the ownership of the very gates of Heaven. England sought land and trade; she was practical and unromantic, but strong and daring; and in her people, unlike the Spanish, were implanted the seeds of human freedom. She had not as yet the prestige of Spain; but men like Francis Drake and Sir Walter Raleigh went far to win it; moreover, the star of Spain had already begun to wane, while that of England was waxing. Whenever, therefore, the strength of the two rivals was fairly pitted, England had the better of the encounter. Spain might dominate, for a while, the southern regions of the continent; and her priests might thread the western wildernesses, and build white-walled missions there; but to England should belong the Atlantic coast from Labrador to Florida: the most readily accessible from Europe, and the best adapted to bring forth that wealth for which gold must be given in exchange. The struggle, as between the Spanish and the English, was temporarily suspended, and it was with France that the latter now found themselves confronted. The French had entered America by way of the St. Lawrence, and down the Mississippi, in expectation, like the others, of finding a passage through to India; they had planted colonies and conciliated the Indians, and were destined to give England much more trouble than her former foe had done. They, like the English, wished to live in the new world; Spain's chief desire was to plunder it and take the booty home with her. In the sequel, England was victorious; and thus approved her right to be the nucleus of the Race of the Future. Finally, it was to be her fate to fight that Race itself, and to be defeated by it; and thus, as the chosen from the chosen, the inhabitants of the Thirteen Colonies were to begin their career.

The birth of America must therefore be dated, not from the discovery of the land, but from the culmination in revolt of the English Colonies. All that preceded this was as the early and ambiguous processes of nature in bringing forth the plant from the seed. Nature knows her work, and its result; but the onlooker sees the result only. The Creator of man knew of what a child America was to be the mother; but the world, intent upon its selfish concerns, recognized it only when the consummation had been reached. And even now she eyes us askance, and mutters doubts as to our endurance and our legitimacy. But America is Europe's best and only friend, and her political pattern must sooner or later, and more or less exactly, be followed by all peoples. Democracy, however unwelcome in its first and outward aspect it may appear, is the logical issue of human experiments in government; it is susceptible of much abuse and open to many corruptions; but these cannot penetrate far below the surface; they are external and obvious, not vital and secret; because at heart the voice of democracy is the voice of God. It may be silent for long, so that some will disbelieve or despair, and say in their haste that democracy is a fraud or a failure. But at last its tones will be heard, and its word will be irresistible and immortal: the word of the Lord, uttering itself through the mouth of His creatures.

The preliminary episodes and skirmishings, therefore, which went before the spiritual self-consciousness of America, will be treated here in outline only; only such events and persons as were the sources of subsequent important conditions will be drawn in light and shadow. This period of adventure and exploration is, it is true, rich in picturesque characters and romantic incident, but they have little organic relation to the history of the true America—which is the tracing of the development and embodiment of an abstract idea. They belong to Europe, whose life was present in them, though the men acted and the incidents occurred in a strange environment. They are attractive subjects of study in themselves, but have small pertinence to the present argument. Our aim will be to maintain an organic coherency.

Still less can we linger in that impressive darkness before

dawn which prevailed upon the continent before the advent of Columbus. The mystery which shrouds the origin and annals of the races which inhabited America previous to the European invasion has been assiduously investigated, but never dispelled. At first it was taken for granted that the "Indians," as the red men were ignorantly called, were the aboriginal denizens of the country. But the mounds, ruined cities, pottery and other remains since found in all parts of the land, concerning which the Indians could furnish no information, and which showed a state of civilization far in advance of theirs, were proof that a great people had existed here in the remote past, who had flourished and disappeared without leaving any trace whereby they could be accounted for or identified. They are an enigma compared with which the archæological problems of the Old World are an open book. We can form no conception of the conditions under which they lived, of their personal characteristics, of their language, habits, or religion. We cannot determine whether these forerunners of the Indians were one people in several stages of development, or several peoples in simultaneous occupation of the land. We can establish no trustworthy connection between them and any Asiatic races, and yet we are reluctant to believe them isolated from the rest of mankind. If they had dwelt here from their creation, why had they not progressed further in civilization?—and if they emigrated hither from another continent, why do their remains not indicate their source? By what agency did they perish, and when? The more keenly we strive to penetrate their mystery, the more perplexing does it appear; the further we investigate them, the more alien from anything we are or have known do they seem. Elusive as mist, and questionable as night, they form a suggestive background on which the vivid and energetic drama of our novel civilization stands out in sharp relief.

Scarcely less mysterious—though living among us still —are the red men whom we found here. They had no written languages or history; their knowledge of their own past was confined to vague and fanciful traditions. They were few in numbers, barbarous in condition, untamable in nature; they built no cities and practiced no industries: their women planted maize and performed all menial labors; their men hunted and fought. Before we came, they fought one another; our coming did not unite them against a common enemy; it only gave each of them one enemy the more. After an intercourse of four hundred years, we know as little of them as we did at first; we have neither educated, absorbed nor exterminated them. The fashion of their faces, and some other indications, seem to point to a northern-Asiatic ancestry; but they cannot tell us even so much as we can guess. There have been among them, now and again, men of commanding abilities in war and negotiation; but their influence upon their people has not lasted beyond their own lives. Amid the roar and fever of these latter ages, they stand silent, useless, and apathetic. They belong to our history only in so far as their savage and treacherous hostility contributed to harden the fortitude of our earlier settlers, and to weld them into a united people.

Posterity may resolve these obscurities; meanwhile they remain in picturesque contrast to the merciless publicity of our own life, and the scientific annihilation of time and distance. They are as the dark and amorphous loam in which has taken root the Flower of the Ages. If extremes must meet, it was fitting that the least and the most highly developed examples of mankind should dwell side by side, at the close of the nineteenth century, in a land to which neither is native: that Europe, the child of Asia, should meet its prehistoric parent here, and work out its destiny before her uncomprehending eyes. The world is an inn of strange meetings; and this encounter is perhaps the strangest of all.

The most dangerous enemy of America has been—not Spain, France, England, or any other nation in arms, but

—our own material prosperity. The lessons of adversity we took to heart, and they brought forth wholesome fruit, purifying our blood and toughening our muscles. So long as the Spirit of Liberty was threatened from without, she was safe and triumphant. But when her foes abroad had ceased to harry her, a foe far more insidious began to plot against her in her own house. The tireless energy and ingenuity which are our most salient characteristics, and which had rendered us formidable and successful on sea and land, were turned by peace into productive channels. The enormous natural resources of the continent began to receive development; men who under former conditions would have been admirals and generals, now became leaders in commerce, manufactures and finance; they made great fortunes, and set up standards of emulation other than patriotism and public spirit. Like the old Spanish and English adventurers, they sought for gold, and held all other things secondary to that. An anomalous oligarchy sprang into existence, holding no ostensible political or social sway, yet influential in both directions by virtue of the power of money. Money can be possessed by the evil as well as by the good, and it can be used to tempt the good to condone evil. The exalted maxim of human equality was interpreted to mean that all Americans could be rich; and the spectacle was presented of a mighty and generous nation fighting one another for mere material wealth. Inevitably, the lower and baser elements of the population came to the surface and seemed to rule; the ordinary citizen, on whom the welfare of the State depends, allowed his private business interest to wean him from the conduct of public affairs, which thereby fell into the hands of professional politicians, who handled them for their personal gain instead of for the common weal. We forgot that pregnant saying, "Eternal vigilance is the price of liberty," and suffered ourselves to be persuaded that because our written Constitution was a wise and patriotic document, we were forever safe even from the effects of our own selfishness and infidelity. As some men are more skillful and persistent manipulators of money than others, it happened that the capital of the country became massed in one place and was lacking in another; the numbers of the poor, and of paupers, increased; and the rich were able to control their political action and sap their self-respect by dominating the employment market. "Do my bidding, or starve," is a cogent argument; it should never be in the power of any man to offer it; but it was heard over the length and breadth of free America. The efforts of laboring men, by organization, to check the power of capitalists, was met by the latter with organizations of their own, which, in the form of vast "trusts" and otherwise, deprived small manufacturers and traders of the power of independent self-support. Strikes and lockouts were the natural outcome of such a situation; and the sinister prospect loomed upon us of labor and capital arrayed against each other in avowed hostility.

Danger from this cause, however, is more apparent than actual. The remedy, in the last resort, is always in ourselves. Laws as to land and contracts may be modified, but the true cure for all such injuries and inequalities is to cease to regard the amassing of "fortunes" as the most desirable end in life. The land is capable of supporting in comfort far more than its present population; ignorance or selfish disregard of the true principles of economy have made it seem otherwise. The proper state of every man is that of a producer; the craving of individuals to own what they have not fairly earned and cannot usefully administer, is vain and disorderly. Men will always be born who have the genius of management; and others who require to have their energies directed; some can profitably control resources which to others would be a mischievous burden. But this truth does not involve any extravagant discrepancy in the private means and establishments of one or the other; each should have as much as his needs, intelligence and taste legitimately warrant, and no more. Such matters will gradually adjust themselves, once the broad underlying principle has been accepted. Meanwhile we may remember that national health is not always synonymous with peace. It was the warning of our Lord—"I am not come to bring peace, but a sword." The war which is waged with powder and ball is often less contrary to true peace than the war which exists while all the outward semblances of peace are maintained. We must not be misled by names. America is perhaps too prone to regard herself in a passive light, as the refuge merely of the oppressed and needy; but she has an active mission too. She stands for so much that is contrary to the ideas that have hitherto ruled the world that she can hardly hope to avoid the hostility, and possibly the attacks, of the representatives of the old order. These, she must be able and ready to repel. We have freely shed our blood for our own freedom; and we should not forget that, though charity begins at home, it need not end there. We should not interpret too strictly the maxims which admonish us to mind our own housekeeping, and to avoid entanglements with the quarrels or troubles of our neighbors. We should not say to the tide of our liberties, Thus far shalt thou go, and no further. America is not a geographical expression, and arbitrary geographical boundaries should not be permitted to limit the area which her principles control. We, who seek to bind the other nations to ourselves by ties of commerce, should recognize the obligations of other ties, whose value cannot be expressed in money.

America wears her faults upon her forehead, not in her heart; her history is just beginning; she herself dreams not yet what her ultimate destiny will be. But so far as her brief past may serve as a key wherewith to open the future, a study of it will not be idle.

CHAPTER FIRST

COLUMBUS, RALEIGH AND SMITH

HE records will have it that America was discovered in consequence of the desire of Europe to profit by the commerce of Cathay, which had hitherto reached them only by the long and expensive process of a journey due west. One caravan had passed on the spices and other valuables to another, until they reached the Mediterranean. It was asked whether the trip could not be more quickly and cheaply made by sea. Assuming, as was generally done, that the earth was flat, why might not a man sail round the southern extremity of Africa, and up the other side to the Orient? It was true that the extremity of Africa might extend to the Southern ice, in which case this plan would not serve; but the attempt might be worth making. This was the view of Henry of Portugal, a scientific and ingenious prince, whose life covered the first sixty years of the Fifteenth Century. And Portuguese mariners did accordingly sail their little ships far down the Atlantic coast of the Dark Continent; but they did not venture quite far enough until long after good Prince Henry was dead, and Columbus had (in his own belief) pioneered a shorter way.

Columbus was a theorist and a visionary. Many men who have been able to show much more plausible grounds for their theories than he could for his have died the laughing-stock of the world. Columbus was a laughing-stock for nearly twenty years; but though the special application of his theory was absurdly wrong, yet in principle it chanced to be right; and he was so fortunate as to be empowered to bring it to a practical demonstration. His notion was that the earth was not flat, but round. Therefore the quickest route to the extreme East must be in exactly the opposite direction; the globe, he estimated, could not be much over fifteen thousand miles in girth; Cathay, by the land route, was twelve thousand miles or so east of Europe; consequently the distance west could not be more than three thousand. This could be sailed over in a month or two, and the saving in time and trouble would be immense.— Thus did he argue—shoving the Atlantic into the Pacific Ocean, subtracting six or seven thousand miles from their united breadth, and obliterating entirely that western continent which he was fated to discover, though he was never to suspect its existence.

The heresy that the earth was a sphere had long been in existence; Aristotle being the earliest source to which it could be traced. Sensible people did not countenance it then, any more than they accept to-day the conjecture that other planets than this may be inhabited. They demonstrated its improbability on historical and religious grounds, and also made the point that, supposing it were round, and that Columbus were to sail down the under side of it, he would never be able to climb back again. But the Genoese was a man who became more firmly wedded to his opinion in proportion as it met with ridicule and opposition; proofs he had none of the truth of his pet idea; but he clung to it with a doggedness which must greatly have exasperated his interlocutors. By dint of sheer persistence, he almost persuaded some men that there might be something in his project; but he never brought any of them to the pitch of risking money on it. It was only upon a woman that he was finally able to prevail; and doubtless the intelligence of Isabella of Castile was less concerned in the affair than was her feminine imagination. Had she known more, she would have done less. But so, for that matter, would Columbus.

Almost as little is known of the personal character of this man as of Shakespeare's; and the portraits of him, though much more numerous than those of the poet, are even less compatible with one another. The estimates and conjectures of historians also differ; some describe a pious hero and martyr, others a dissolute adventurer and charlatan. We are constrained, in the end, to construct his effigy from our own best interpretation of the things he did. Some little learning he had; just enough, probably, to disturb the balance of his judgment. He could read Latin and make maps, and he had ample experience of practical navigation. His life as a mariner got him the habit of meditation, and this favored the espousal of theories, which, upon occasion, he could expound with volubility or defend with passion, as his Italian temperament prompted. His imagination was portentous, and the Fifteenth Century was hospitable to this faculty; there was nothing—except plain but unknown facts —too marvelous to be believed; and that Columbus was even more credulous than his contemporaries is proved by the evidence that even facts were not exempt from his entertainment. An ordinary appetite for the marvelous could swallow stories of chimeras dire, and men whose heads do grow beneath their shoulders; but nothing short of the profligate capacity of a Columbus could digest such a proposition as that the earth was round and could be circumnavigated. The type of half-educated fanatics to which he belonged has always been common; there is nothing exceptional or remarkable in this fanatic except the fortune which finally attended his lifelong devotion to the most improbable hypothesis of his time. It has been our custom to eulogize his courage and his constancy to the truth; but if he had adopted perpetual motion, instead of the rotundity of the earth, as his dogma, he would have deserved our praises just as much. His sole claim to our admiration is, that in the teeth of all precedent and likelihood, he succeeded by one mistake in making another: because he fancied that by sailing west he could find the Indies, he blundered upon a land whose identity he never discovered. Doubtless his blunder was of unspeakable value; but a blunder not the less it was; while as to his courage and perseverance, as much has been shown by a thousand other scientific and philosophical heretics, whose names have not survived, because the thing they imagined turned out an error.

From another point of view, however, Columbus is specially a creature of his age. It was an age which felt, it knew not why, that something new must come to pass. The resources of Europe were exhausted; men had reached the end of their tether, and demanded admittance to some wider pasturage. It was much such a predicament as obtains now, four hundred years later; we feel that changes— enlargements—are due, but know not what or whence. The conception of a voyage across the Atlantic, in that age, seemed as captivating, and almost as fantastic, as a trip to the Moon or Mars would, to an adventurer of our time. Given the vehicle, no doubt many volunteers would offer for the journey; Columbus could get a ship, but the chances of his arriving at his proposed destination must have appeared as problematical to him as the Moon enterprise in a balloon would to a world-weary globe-trotter of to-day. It was not merely that the ship was small and the Atlantic large and stormy; there were legends of vast whirlpools, of abysmal oceanic cataracts, of sea-monsters, malignant genii, and other portents not less terrifying and fatal. Columbus would not have been surprised at falling in with any of these things; but the physical courage which must have been his most prominent trait, added to incorrigible pride of opinion, brought him through.

But the significant feature of his achievement is, not that he sailed or that he arrived, but that he was impelled, irresistibly as it were, to make the attempt. He made it, because it was the one thing left in the world that seemed worth doing; it was the only apparent way of escape from the despair of the familiar and habitual; it was an adventure charged with all unknown possibilities; once conceived, it must be executed at whatever cost. Columbus was fascinated; the unknown drew him like a magnet; he was the involuntary deputy of his period to incarnate its yearnings in act. The hour had struck; and with it, as always, appeared the man. So it has ever been in the history of the world; though we, with characteristic vanity, uniformly put the cart before the horse, and declare that it is the man that brings the hour.

Be that as it may, Columbus was fitted out with three boats by the Spanish king and queen, set sail from Spain on the 3d of August, 1492, and arrived at one of the Caribbean islands on the 12th of October of the same year. He supposed that he had found an East Indian archipelago; and with the easy emotional piety of his time and temperament, he fell on his knees and thanked God, and took possession of everything in sight in the name of Ferdinand and Isabella.

The deed had been done, and Columbus had his reward. It would have been well for him had he recognized this fact, and not tried to get more. He had found land on the other side of the Atlantic; what no other man had believed possible, he had accomplished; he had carried his point, and proved his thesis—or one so much resembling it that he never knew the difference. This, and not a more sordid hope, had been the real motive power of his career up to this time; and the moment when the light from another world gleamed across the water to his hungry eyes had been the happiest that he had ever known, or would know. A mighty hope had been fulfilled; the longing of an age had been gratified in his triumph; a fresh chapter in the world's history had been begun. The thoughts and emotions that surged through the ardent Italian, as he knelt on that coral beach, were lofty and unselfish: as were, in truth, those of the age whose representative he was, when it saw him depart on his adventure. But before the man of destiny had risen from his knees, he had ceased to act as the instrument of God, and had begun to think of personal emoluments. So much he must make over to Spain; so much he might keep for himself; so much was promised to his shipmates. He would be famous—yes: and rich and powerful too; he would be a great vicegerent; his attire should be of silk and velvet, with a gold chain about his neck, and gems on his hands. So adversity set his name among the stars, and prosperity abased his soul to dust. The remaining years of his life were a fruitless struggle to secure what he deemed his rightful wages—to coin his immortal exploit into ducats; and his end was sorrowful and dishonored. The proud self-abnegation of the ancient Roman was lacking in the medieval Genoese.

The white-maned horses of the Atlantic once mastered, there came riders enough. During the next thirty years such men as Amerigo Vespucci (who enjoyed the not singular distinction of having his name associated with the discovery of another man), the Cabots, father and son; Balboa, and Magellan, crossed the sea and visited the new domain. Magellan performed the only unprecedented feat left for mariners by sailing round the earth by way of the South American straits that bear his name; but Vasco da Gama had already entered the Pacific by the Cape of Good Hope. It was by this time beginning to be understood that the new land was really new, and not the other side of the old one; but this only prompted the adventurers to get past or through it to the first goal of their ambition. They had not yet realized the vastness of the Pacific, and took America to be a mere breakwater protecting the precious shores of Cathay. Later, they found that America repaid looting on her own account; but meanwhile there was set on foot that search for the Northwest Passage which resulted in the discovery of almost everything except the Passage itself. To the craze for a Northwest Passage is due the exploration of Baffin's and Hudson's Bays, of the

Gulf and River of St. Lawrence, and of the Great Lakes; the establishment of the English and French fur-trading Companies, which hastened the development of Canada; and the settlement of Oregon and Washington. It led English and Spanish explorers and freebooters up the California coast, and on to Vancouver and Bering Straits; Alaska was circumvented, and the Northwest Passage was found, though the everlasting ice mocked the efforts of the finders. In short, the entire continent was tapped and sounded with a view to forcing a way through or round it; and by the time the attempt was finally given up, the contour, size, and possible value of America had been estimated much more quickly and accurately than they would have been, had not India lain west of it.

All this time Spain had been having the best of the bargain. She had fastened upon the West Indies, Mexico, and Central and South America, and had found gold there in abundance; she bade other nations keep hands off, and was less solicitous than they about the rumored riches of the Orient. Spain, in those days, was held to be invincible on the sea; England's fight with the Spanish Armada was yet to come. But there were already Englishmen of the Drake and Frobisher type who liked nothing better than to capture a Spanish galleon, and "singe the king of Spain's beard"; and these independent sea-rovers were becoming so bold and numerous as to put the Spaniards to serious inconvenience and loss. But the latter could not be ousted from their vantage ground; so the English presently bethought themselves that there might be gold in the more northerly as well as in the central parts of the Continent; and they turned to seek it there. Nothing is more noticeable in every phase of these events than the constant involuntary accomplishment of something other—and in the end beter—than the thing attempted. As Columbus, looking for Indian spices, found America; as seekers of all nations, in their quest for a Northwest Passage, charted and developed the continent:

so Sir Walter Raleigh and his companions, hunting for gold along the northern Atlantic seaboard, took the first steps toward founding the colonies which were in the sequel to constitute the germ of the present United States.

Queen Elizabeth was on the throne of England; more than ninety years had passed since Columbus had landed on his Caribbean island. In 1565 a colony of French Huguenots at St. Augustine had, by a characteristic act of Spanish treachery, been massacred, men, women, and children, at the order of Melendez, and the French thus wiped out of the southern coast of North America forever. While England remained Catholic, the influence of Papal bulls in favor of Spanish authority in America, and matrimonial alliances between the royal families of Spain and England, had restrained English enterprise in the west. Henry VIII. had indeed acted independently both of the Spaniard and of the Pope; but it was not until Elizabeth's accession in 1558, bringing Protestantism with her, that England ventured to assert herself as a nation in the new found world. Willoughby had attempted, in 1553, the preposterous enterprise of reaching India by sailing round Norway and the north of Asia; but his expedition got no further than the Russian port of Archangel. In 1576 and the two succeeding years, Martin Frobisher went on voyages to Labrador and neighboring regions, at first searching for the Northwest Passage, afterward in quest of gold. The only result of his efforts was the bringing to England of some shiploads of earth, which had been erroneously supposed to contain the precious metal. In 1578, Sir Humphrey Gilbert had obtained a patent empowering him to found a colony somewhere in the north; his object being rather to develop the fisheries than to find gold or routes to India. He was stepbrother of Sir Walter Raleigh, and the latter started with him on the first voyage; but they were forced to put back soon after setting out. Gilbert went again in 1583, and reached St. John's, where he erected a pillar commemorating the English occupation; but he was drowned in a storm on the way home. Raleigh, who had stayed in England, and had acquired royal favor and a fortune, remained to carry out, in his own way, the designs which Gilbert's death had left in suspense. In 1584 he began the work.

Raleigh perhaps deserves to be regarded as the greatest English gentleman who ever lived. In addition to the learning of his time, he had a towering genius, indomitable courage and constancy, lofty and generous principles, far-seeing wisdom, Christian humanity, and a charity that gave and forgave to the end. He was a courtier and a statesman, a soldier and a sailor, a merchant and an explorer. His life was one of splendid and honorable deeds; he was not a talker, and found scant leisure to express himself in writing; though when he chose to write poetry he approved himself best in the golden age of English literature; and his "History of the World," composed while imprisonment in the Tower prevented him from pursuing more active employments, is inferior to no other produced up to that time. Such reverses as he met with in life only spurred him to fresh efforts, and his successes were magnificent, and conducive to the welfare of the world. He was a patriot of the highest and purest type; a champion of the oppressed; a supporter of all worthy enterprises, a patron of literature and art. Withal, he was full of the warm blood of human nature; he had all the fire, the tenderness, and the sympathies that may rightly belong to a man. The mind is astonished in contemplating such a being; he is at once so close to us, and so much above the human average. King James I. of England, jealous of his greatness, imprisoned him for twelve years, on a groundless charge, and finally slew him, at the age of sixty-six, broken by disease, and saddened, but not soured, by the monstrous ingratitude and injustice of his treatment. Upon the scaffold, he felt of the edge of the ax which was to behead him, and smiled, remarking, "A sharp medicine to cure me of my diseases!" Such are the exploits of kings.

Raleigh was the first man who perceived that America was to be the home of a white people: that it was to be a dwelling-place, not a mere supply-house for freebooters and home traders. He resolved to do his part toward making it so; he impoverished himself in the enterprise; and though the colony which he planted in what is now North Carolina, but was then called Virginia, in honor of the queen, who was pleased thus to advertise her chastity—though this failed (by no fault of Raleigh's) of its immediate object, yet the lesson thus offered bore fruit in due season, and the colonization of the New World, shown to be a possibility and an advantage, was taken up on the lines Raleigh had drawn, and resulted in the settlement whose heirs we are.

In 1585, after receiving the favorable report of a preliminary expedition, Raleigh sent out upward of a hundred colonists under the command of Sir Richard Grenville, one of the heroic figures of the time, a man of noble nature but fearful passions. They landed on the island of Roanoke, off the mouth of the river of that name, and were well received by the native tribes, who thought they were immortal and divine, because they were without women, and possessed gunpowder. It would have been well had the English responded in kind; but within a few days, Grenville, angry at the non-production of a silver cup which had been stolen from his party during a visit to a village, burned the huts and destroyed the crops; and later, Lane, who had been left by Grenville in command of the colony, invited the principal chief of the region to a friendly conference, and murdered him. This method of procedure would not have been countenanced by the great promoter of the expedition; nor would he have encouraged the hunt for gold that was presently undertaken. This was the curse of the time, and ever led to disaster and blood. Nor did Lane escape the delusion that a passage could be found through the land to the Indies; the savages, humoring his ignorance for their own purposes, assured him that the Roanoke River (which rises some two hundred miles inland) communicated with the Pacific at a distance of but a few days' journey. Lane selected a party and set hopefully forth to traverse fifty degrees of latitude; but ere long his provisions gave out, and he was forced to go starving back again. He arrived at the settlement just in time to save it from annihilation by the Indians.

But there were able men among these colonists, and some things were done which were not foolish. Hariot, who had scientific knowledge, and was a careful observer, made notes of the products of the land, and became proficient in tobacco smoking; he also tested and approved the potato, and in other ways laid the foundation for a profitable export and import trade. John White, an artist, who afterward was put in charge of another colony, made drawings of the natives and their appurtenances, which still survive, and witness his fidelity and skill. Explorations up and down the coast, and for some distance inland, were made; the salubrity of the climate was eulogized, and it was admitted that the soil was of excellent fertility. In short, nothing was lacking, in the way of natural conditions, to make the colony a success; yet the Englishmen grew homesick and despondent, and longed to return to England and English women. The supplies which they were expecting from home had not arrived; and their situation was rendered somewhat precarious by the growing hostility of the natives, who had come to the conclusion that these godlike white men were not persons with whom it was expedient for them to associate.

At this juncture, down upon the coast suddenly swooped a fleet of over twenty sail with the English flag flying, and no less a personage than Sir Francis Drake in command. He was returning from a profitable pirating expedition against the Spaniards in the West Indies, and desired to see for himself how the colony sent out by his friend Raleigh was prospering. Out of his easily-got abundance he generously supplied the needs of the colonists, and presented them with a ship into the bargain, in which they might sail home should circumstances demand it. A couple of his most experienced officers, too, were added to the gift of the generous freebooter; and the outlook was now very different from what it had been a few days before. Yet fate was against them; or, to speak more accurately, they had lost the spirit which should animate pioneers, and when a touch of bad luck was added to their indisposition, they incontinently beat a retreat. A storm arose, which wrecked the ship that Drake had given them, and thus deprived them of the means of escape in case other disasters should arrive. They besought Drake to take them home with him; and he, with inexhaustible good humor, agreed to do so. His fleet, with the slack-souled colonists on board, had scarcely lost sight of the low shores of Roanoke, when the supply ship that had been so long awaited arrived with all the requisites for subduing the wilderness on board. She found the place deserted, and, putting about, sailed for home again. A fortnight later came Sir Richard Grenville with three ships more; and he, being of a persistent nature, would not consent to lose altogether the fruit of the efforts which had been made; he left fifteen of his men on the island, to carry on until fresh colonists could be brought from England. But before this could be done the men were dead, whether by the act of God or of the savages; and the first English experience in colonizing America was at an end.

The story of the second colony, immediately sent out by Raleigh, ends with a mystery that probably hid a tragedy. Seventeen women and two children accompanied the eighty-nine men of the party. Having established the fact that the land was habitable and cultivatable, Raleigh perceived that in order to render it attractive also it was necessary that the colonists should have their helpmeets with them. For the first time in history, therefore, the feet of English women pressed our soil, and the voices of children made music in the woodland solitudes. It had been designed that the more commodious bay of the Chesapeake should be the scene of this settlement; but the naval officer who should have superintended the removal was hungering for a West Indian trading venture, and declined to act. They perforce established themselves in the old spot, therefore, where the buildings were yet standing on the northern end of the little island, which, though deserted now, is for us historic ground. The routine of life began; and before the ship sailed on her return trip to England, the daughter of the governor and artist, John White, who was married to one of his subordinates named Dare, had given birth to a daughter, and called her Virginia. She was the first child of English blood who could be claimed as American; she came into the world, from which she was so soon to vanish, on the 18th of August, 1587. White returned to England with the ship a week or two later. He was to return again speedily with more colonists, and further supplies. But he never saw his daughter and her infant after their farewell in the landlocked bay. He reached England to find Raleigh and all the other strong men of England occupied with plans to repel the invasion that threatened from Spain, and which, in the shape of the Invincible Armada, was to be met and destroyed in the English Channel, almost on the first anniversary of the birth of Virginia Dare. Nothing could be done, at the moment, to relieve the people at Roanoke; but in April of 1588, Raleigh found time, with the defense of a kingdom on his hands, to equip two ships and send them in White's charge to Virginia. All might have been well had White been content to attend with a single eye to the business in hand; but the seas were full of vessels which could be seized and stripped of their precious cargoes, and White thought it would be profitable to imitate the exploits of Drake and Grenville, and take a few prizes to Roanoke with him. But he was the ass in the lion's hide. One of his ships was itself attacked and gutted, and with the other he fled in terror back to London. Raleigh could not help him now; his own fortune was exhausted; and it was not until the Armada had come and gone, and the country had in a measure recovered itself from the shocks of war, that succor could be attempted. The charter which had been granted to Raleigh enabled him to give liberal terms to a company of merchants and others, who on their part could raise the funds for the voyage. But though Raleigh executed this patent in the spring of 1589, it was not until more than a year afterward that the expedition was ready to sail. White went with them, and we may imagine with what straining eyes he scanned the spot where he had last beheld his daughter and grandchild, as the ship glided up the inlet. But no one came forth between the trees to wave a greeting to his long-deferred return; there were no figures on the shore, no smoke of family fires rose heavenward; families and hearths alike were gone. The place was a desert. Little Virginia Dare and the Lost Colony of Roanoke had already passed out of history, leaving no clew to their fate except the single word "CROATAN" inscribed on the bark of a tree. It was the name of an island further down the coast; and had White gone thither, he might even yet have found the lost. But he was a man unfitted in all respects to live in that age and take part in its enterprises. He was a soft, feeble, cowardly and unfaithful creature, yet vain and ambitious, and eager to share the fame of men immeasurably larger and worthier than he. He could draw pictures, but he could not do deeds; and now, after having deserted those to whom he had been in honor bound to cleave, he pleaded the excuse of bad weather and the lateness of the season for abandoning them once more; and, re-embarking on his ship, he went back with all his company to England. It was the dastardly ending of the first effort, nobly conceived, and supported through five years, to engraft the English race in the soil of America.

Tradition hazards the conjecture that the Roanoke colony, or some of them, were cared for by the friendly Indians of Hatteras. There was a rumor that seven of them were still living twenty years after White's departure. But no certain news was ever had of them, though several later attempts to trace them were made. Between the time when their faint-hearted governor had deserted them, and his return, three years had passed; and if they were not early destroyed by the hostile tribes, they must have endured a more lingering pain in hoping against hope for the white sails that never rose above the horizon. Most of them, if not all, were doubtless massacred by the Indians, if not at once, then when it became evident that no succor was to be expected for them. Some, possibly, were carried into captivity; and it may be that Virginia Dare herself grew up to become the white squaw of an Indian brave, and that her blood still flows in the veins of some unsuspected red man. But it is more likely that she died with the others, one of the earliest and most innocent of the victims sacrificed on the altar of a great idea.

White disappears from history at this point; but Raleigh never forgot his colony, and five times, at his own expense, and in the midst of events that might have monopolized the energies of a score of ordinary men, he dispatched expeditions to gain tidings of them. In 1595 he himself sailed for Trinidad, on the northern coast of South America, and explored the river Orinoco, nine degrees above the equator. It was his hope to offset the power of Spain in Mexico and Peru by establishing an English colony in Guiana. Wars claimed his attention during the next few years, and then came his long imprisonment; but in 1616, two years before his execution, he headed a last expedition to the southern coast of the land he had labored so faithfully to unite to England. It failed of its object, and Raleigh lost his head.

But the purpose which he had steadfastly entertained did not die with him; and we Americans claim him to-day as the first friend and father of the conception of a great white people beyond the sea.

As we enter the Seventeenth Century, the figure which looms largest in the foreground is that of Captain John Smith, governor of the colony at Jamestown in 1607. But the way was prepared for him by a man as honorable, though less distinguished, Bartholemew Gosnold by name, who voyaged to the New England coast in 1602, and was the first to set foot on its shores. The first land he sighted was what is now called Maine; thence he steered southward, and disembarked on Cape Cod, on which he bestowed that name. Proceeding yet further south, between the islands off the coast, he finally entered the inclosed sound of Buzzard's Bay, and landed on the island of Cuttyhunk. Gosnold was a prudent as well as an adventurous man, and he was resolved to take all possible precautions against being surprised by the Indians. On Cuttyhunk there was a large pond, and in the pond there was an islet; and Gosnold, with his score of followers, fixed upon this speck of rocky earth as the most suitable spot in the western hemisphere wherein to plant the roots of English civilization. They built a hut and made a boat, and gathered together their stores of furs and sassafras; but these same stores proved their undoing. They could not agree upon an equable division of their wealth; and recognizing that disunion in a strange land was weakness and peril, they all got into their ship and sailed back to England, carrying their undivided furs and sassafras with them. By this mishap, New England missed becoming the scene of the first permanent English colony. For when, five years afterward, Gosnold returned to America with a hundred men and adequate supplies, it was not to Buzzard's Bay, but to the mouth of the James River, that he steered, and on its banks the colony was founded. Gosnold himself seems to have been a man of the type that afterward made the New England whalers famous in all seas; the mariners of New Bedford, New London, Sag Harbor and Nantucket. But the companions of his second voyage were by no means of this stamp; the bulk of them were "gentlemen," who had no familiarity with hard fare and hard work, and expected nature to provide for them in the wilderness as bountifully as the London caterers had done at home. To the accident which brought Gosnold to a southerly instead of a northerly port on this occasion may be due the fact that Virginia instead of Massachusetts became the home of the emigrant cavaliers. Had they, as well as the Puritans, chosen New England for their abiding place, an amalgamation might have taken place which would have vitally modified later American history. But destiny kept them apart in place as well as in sentiment and training; and it is only in our own day that Reconstruction, and the development of means of intercommunication, bid fair to make a homogeneous people out of the diverse elements which for so many generations recognized at most only an outward political bond.

Captain John Smith, fortunately, was neither a cavalier nor a simple mariner, but a man in a class by himself, and just at that juncture the most useful that could possibly have been attached to this adventure. His career even before the present period had been so romantic that, partly for that reason, and partly because he himself was his own chief chronicler, historians have been prone to discredit or modify many of its episodes. But what we know of Smith from other than a Smith source tallies so well with the stories which rest upon his sole authority that there seems to be no sound cause for rejecting the latter. After making all deductions, he remains a remarkable personage, and his influence upon the promotion of the English colonial scheme was wholly beneficial. He was brave, ingenious, indefatigable, prudent and accomplished; he knew what should be done, and was ever foremost in doing it. He took hold of the helpless and slow-witted colonists as a master carpenter handles blocks of wood, and transformed them into an efficient and harmonious structure, strong enough to withstand the first onsets of misfortune, and to endure until the arrival of recruits from home placed them beyond all danger of calamity.

Smith was born in England in 1579, and was therefore only twenty-eight years of age when he embarked with Gosnold. Yet he had already fought in the Netherlands, starved in France, and been made a galley-slave by the Moslem. He had been shipwrecked at one time, thrown overboard at another, and robbed at a third. Thrice had he met and slain Turkish champions in the lists; and he had traversed the steppes of Russia with only a handful of grain for food. He was not a man of university education: the only schooling he had had was in the free schools of Alford and Louth, before his fifteenth year; his father was a tenant farmer in Lincolnshire, and though John was apprenticed to a trade, he ran away while a mere stripling, and shifted for himself ever after. An adventurer, therefore, in the fullest sense of the word, he was; and doubtless he had the appreciation of his own achievements which self-made men are apt to have. But there was sterling pith in him, a dauntless and humane soul, and inexhaustible ability and resource. Such a man could not fail to possess imagination, and imagination and self-esteem combined conduce to highly-colored narrative; but that Smith was a liar is an unwarranted assumption, which will not be countenanced here.

The Gosnold colony had provided itself with a charter, granted by King James, and as characteristic of that monarch as was his treatment of Raleigh. It was the first of many specimens of absentee landlordism from which America was to suffer. It began by setting apart an enormous stretch of territory, bounded on the north by the latitude of the St. Croix River, and on the south by that of Cape Fear, and extending westward indefinitely. To this domain was given the general title of Virginia. It was subdivided into two approximately equal parts, with a neutral zone between them, which covered the space now occupied by the cities of New York, Philadelphia, and Washington, and the land adjoining them. The northern division was given in charge to the "Plymouth Company," and the southern to the "London Company"; they were separate mercantile and colonizing organizations, but the charter applied to both alike.

The colonies were to be under the immediate control of a council composed of residents, but appointed by the king; this council was subordinate to another, meeting in England; and this in its turn was subject to the king's absolute authority. The emigrants were to pay a yearly rent of one-fifth of the gold and silver produced, and a third as much of the copper. A five per cent duty levied on alien traffic was for the first five-and-twenty years to inure to the benefit of the colony, but afterward should be the exclusive perquisite of the Crown. The right to call themselves and their children English was permitted to the emigrants; and they were also allowed to defend themselves against attacks, though it was enjoined upon them to treat the natives with kindness, and to endeavor to draw them into the fold of the Church.

Such was James's idea of what a charter for an American colony should be. He was taking much for granted when he assumed the right to control the emigrants at all; and he was careful to deprive them of any chance to control in the least degree their own affairs. America was to be the abode of liberty; but this monarch thought only of making it a field for his private petty tyranny. The colonists were to be his own personal slaves, and the deputy slaves of the Companies; after discharging all their obligations to him and to them, they might do the best they could for themselves with what was left, provided of course that they strictly observed the laws which his Majesty was kind enough also to draw up for them, the provisions of which included the penalty of death for most offenses above petty larceny. A colony which, amid the hardships and unfamiliar terrors of a virgin wilderness, could enjoy all the benefits of a charter like this, and yet survive, would seem hardy enough for any emergency. But James was king, and kings, in those days, if they pleased no one else, pleased themselves.

As we have seen, the members of the colony, being persons unused to the practice of the useful arts, were little apt to succeed even under the most favoring conditions. But they had Smith, in himself a host, and a few other good heads and able hands; and to speak truth, the provisions of their charter do not seem to have unduly embarrassed them. It could annoy and hamper them occasionally, but only themselves could work themselves serious injury; there were three thousand miles of perilous sea water between their paternal monarch and them, and the wilderness, with all its drawbacks, breeds self-confidence and independence. The mishaps of the colony were due to the shiftlessness of most of its members, and to the insalubrity of the site chosen for their city of Jamestown, whereby more than half of them perished during the first few months. On the voyage out, Smith, who had probably made himself distasteful to the gentlemen adventurers by his unconventional manners and conversation, had been placed under restraint—to what extent is not exactly known; and when the sealed orders under which they had sailed were opened, and it was found that Smith was named a member of the council, he was for some weeks not permitted to exercise his lawful functions in that office. When the troubles began, however, the helpless gentlemen were glad to avail themselves of his services, which he with his customary good humor readily accorded them; and so competent did he show himself that ere long he was in virtual command of them all. The usual search for gold and for the passage through the continent to India having been made, with the usual result, they all set to work to build their fort and town, and to provide food against the not improbable contingency of famine. As crops could not be raised for the emergency, Smith set out to traffic with the natives, and brought back corn enough for the general need. All this while he had been contending with a prevalent longing on the part of the colonists to get back to England; there was no courage left in them but his, which abounded in proportion to their need for it. Prominent among the malcontents was the deposed governor, Wingfield, who tried to bribe the colonists to return; another member of the council was shot for mutiny. In the end, Smith's will prevailed, and he was governor and council and King James all in one; and when, at the beginning of winter, he had brought the settlement to order and safety, he started on a journey of exploration up the Chickahominy. He perceived the immense importance of understanding his surroundings, and at the same time of establishing friendly relations with the neighboring tribes of Indians; and it was obvious that none but he (for the excellent Gosnold had died of fever in the first months of the settlement) was capable of effecting these objects. Accordingly he proceeded prosperously toward the headwaters of the river, a dozen miles above its navigable point; but there, all at once, he found himself in the midst of a throng of frowning warriors, who were evidently resolved to put an end to his investigations, if not to his existence, forthwith.

Another man than Smith would have committed some folly or rashness which would have precipitated his fate; but Smith was as much at his ease as was Julius Cæsar of old on the pirate's ship. His two companions were killed, but he was treated as a prisoner of rank and importance by the brother of the great chief Powhatan, by whom he had been captured. He interested and impressed his captors by his conversation and his instruments; and at the same time he kept his eyes and ears open, and missed no information that could be of use to himself and his colony. Powhatan gave him an audience and seems to have adopted a considerate attitude; at all events he sent him back to Jamestown after a few days, unharmed, and escorted by four Indians, with a supply of corn. But precisely what occurred during those few days we shall never certainly know; since we must choose between accepting Smith's unsupported story, only made public years afterward, and believing nothing at all. Smith's tale has charmed the imagination of all who have heard it; nothing could be more prettily romantic; the trouble with it is, it seems to most people too pretty and romantic to be true. Yet it is simple enough in itself, and not at all improbable; there is no question as to the reality of the dramatis personæ of the story, and their relations one to another render such an episode as was alleged hardly more than might reasonably be looked for.

The story is—as all the world knows, for it has been repeated all over the world for nearly three hundred years, and has formed the subject of innumerable pictures—that Powhatan, for reasons of high policy satisfactory to himself, had determined upon the death of the Englishman, rightly inferring that the final disappearance of the colony would be the immediate sequel thereof. The sentence was that Smith's brains were to be knocked out with a bludgeon; and he was led into the presence of the chief and the warriors, and ordered to lay his head upon the stone. He did so, and the executioners poised their clubs for the fatal blow; but it never fell. For Smith, during his captivity, had won the affection of the little daughter of Powhatan, a girl of ten, whose name was Pocahontas. She was too young to understand or fear his power over the Indians; but she knew that he was a winning and fascinating being, and she could not endure that he should be sacrificed. Accordingly, at this supreme crisis of his career, she slipped into the dreadful circle, and threw herself upon Smith's body, so that the blow which was aimed at his life must kill her first. She clung to him and would not be removed, until her father had promised that Smith should be spared.

So runs the Captain's narrative, published for the first time in 1624, after Pocahontas's appearance in London, and her death in 1617. Why he had not told it before is difficult to explain. Perhaps he had promised Powhatan to keep it secret, lest the record of his sentimental clemency should impair his authority over the tribes. Or it may have been an embellishment of some comparatively trifling incident of Smith's captivity, suggested to his mind as he was compiling his "General History of Virginia." It can never be determined; but certainly his relations with the Indian girl were always cordial, and it seems unlikely that Powhatan would have permitted him to return to Jamestown except for some unusual reason.

Pocahontas's life had vicissitudes such as seldom befall an Indian maiden. Some time between the Smith episode of 1607, and the year 1612, she married one of her father's tributary chiefs, and went to live with him on his reservation. There she was in some manner kidnapped by one Samuel Argall, and held for ransom. The ransom was paid, but Pocahontas was not sent back; and the following year she was married to John Rolfe, a Jamestown colonist, and baptized as Rebecca. He took her to London, where she was a nine days' wonder; and they had a son, whose blood still flows in not a few American veins to-day. If she was ten years old in 1607, she must have been no more than twenty at the time of her death in Gravesend, near London. But her place in American history is secure, as well as in the hearts of all good Americans. She was the heroine of the first American romance; and she is said to have been as beautiful as all our heroines should rightly be.

When Smith, with his Indian escort, got back to Jamestown, he was just in season to prevent the colony from running away in the boat. Soon after a new consignment of emigrants and supplies arrived from England; but again there were fewer men than gentlemen, and Smith sent back a demand for "rather thirty carpenters, husbandmen, gardeners, fishermen, blacksmiths, masons, and diggers up of trees' roots, well provided, than a thousand of such as we have." There spoke the genuine pioneer, whose heart is in his work, and who can postpone "gentility" until it grows indigenously out of the soil. The Company at home were indignant that their colony had not ere now reimbursed them for their expenditure, and much more; and they sent word that unless profits were forthcoming forthwith (one-fifth of the gold and silver, and so forth) they would abandon the colony to its fate. One cannot help admiring Smith for refraining from the obvious rejoinder that to be abandoned was the dearest boon that they could crave; but a sense of humor seems to have been one of the few good qualities which the Captain did not possess. He intimated to the Company that money was not to be picked up ready made in Virginia, but must be earned by hard work with hands and heads in the field and forest. It is his distinction to have been the first man of eminence visiting the new world who did not think more of finding gold, or the passage to India, or both, than of anything else. Smith knew that in this world, new or old, men get what they work for, and in the long run no more than that; and he made his gentlemen colonists take off their coats and blister their gentlemanly hands with the use of the spade and the ax. It is said that they excelled as woodcutters, after due instruction; and they were undoubtedly in all respects improved by this first lesson in Americanism. The American ax and its wielders have become famous since that day; and the gentlemen of Jamestown may enjoy the credit of having blazed the way.

Fresh emigrants kept coming in, of a more or less desirable quality, as is the case with emigrants still. Some of them had been sent out by other organizations than the London Company, and bred confusion; but Smith was always more than equal to the emergency, and kept his growing brood in hand. He had the satisfaction of feeling that he was the right man in the right place; and let the grass grow under neither his feet nor theirs. The abandonment threat of the London Company led him to take measures to make the colony independent so far as food was concerned, and a tract of land was prepared and planted with corn. Traffic for supplies with the Indians was systematized; and by the time Smith's year of office had expired the Jamestown settlement was self-supporting, and forever placed beyond the reach of annihilation—though, the very year after he had left it, it came within measurable distance thereof.

He now returned to England, and never revisited Jamestown; but he by no means relaxed his interest in American colonization, or his efforts to promote it. In 1614 he once more sailed westward with two ships, on a trading and exploring enterprise, which was successful. He examined and mapped the northern coast, already seen by Gosnold, and bestowed upon the country the name of New England. Traditions of his presence and exploits are still told along the shores of Maine, New Hampshire and Massachusetts. In the year following he tried to found a small colony somewhere in these regions, but was defeated by violent storms; and at a subsequent attempt he fell in with French pirates, and his ship and fortune were lost, though he himself escaped in an open skiff: the chains were never forged that could hold this man. Nor was his spirit broken; he took his map and his description of New England, and personally canvassed all likely persons with a view to fitting out a new expedition. In 1617, aided perhaps by the interest which Pocahontas had aroused in London, he was promised a fleet of twenty vessels, and the title of Admiral of New England was bestowed upon him. Admiral he remained till his death; but the fleet he was to command never put forth to sea. A ship more famous than any he had captained was to sail for

New England in 1620, and land the Pilgrims on Plymouth Rock. Smith's active career was over, though he was but eight-and-thirty years of age, and had fifteen years of life still before him. He had drunk too deeply of the intoxicating cup of adventure and achievement ever to be content with a duller draught; and from year to year he continued to use his arguments and representations upon all who would listen. But he no longer had money of his own, and he was forestalled by other men. He was to have no share in the development of the country which he had charted and named. At the time of his death in London in 1632, poor and disappointed, Plymouth, Salem and Boston had been founded, Virginia had entered upon a new career, and Maryland had been settled by the Catholics under Lord Baltimore. The Dutch had created New Amsterdam on Manhattan Island in 1623; and the new nation in the new continent was fairly under way.

Jamestown, as has been said, narrowly escaped extinction in the winter of 1609. The colonists found none among their number to fill Smith's place, and soon relapsed into the idleness and improvidence which he had so resolutely counteracted. They ate all the food which he had laid up for them, and when it was gone the Indians would sell them no more. Squads of hungry men began to wander about the country, and many of them were murdered by the savages. The mortality within the settlement was terrible, and everything that could be used as food was eaten; at length cannibalism was begun; the body of an Indian, and then the starved corpses of the settlers themselves were devoured. Many crawled away to perish in the woods; others, more energetic, seized a vessel and became pirates. In short, such scenes were enacted as have been lately beheld in India and in Cuba. The severity of the famine may be judged from the fact that out of five hundred persons at the beginning of the six months, only sixty diseased and moribund wretches survived. And this in a land which had been described by its discoverers as a very Garden of Eden, flowing with milk and honey.

Meanwhile, great things were preparing in England. Smith's warning that America must be regarded and treated as an agricultural and industrial community, and not as a treasure-box, had borne fruit; and a new charter was applied for, which should more adequately satisfy the true conditions. It was granted in 1609; Lord Salisbury was at the head of the promoters, and with him were associated many hundreds of the lords, commoners and merchants of England. The land assigned to them was a strip four hundred miles in breadth north and south of Old Point Comfort, and across to the Pacific, together with all islands lying within a hundred miles of shore. In respect of administrative matters, the tendency of the new charter was toward a freer arrangement; in especial, the company was to exercise the powers heretofore lodged with the king, and the supreme council was to be chosen by the shareholders. The governor was the appointee of the corporation, and his powers were large and under conditions almost absolute. The liberties of the emigrants themselves were not specifically enlarged, but they were at least emancipated from the paternal solicitude of the stingy and self-complacent pettifogger who graced the English throne.

Lord Delaware was chosen governor; and Newport, Sir Thomas Gates and Sir George Somers were the commissioners who were to conduct the affairs of the colony until his arrival. A large number of emigrants, many of whom contributed in money and supplies to the expedition, were assembled, and the fleet numbered altogether nine vessels. But Newport and his fellow commissioners suffered shipwreck on the Bermudas, and did not reach Jamestown till nine months later, in May, 1610. The calamitous state of things which there awaited them was an unwelcome surprise; and the despairing colonists would be contented with nothing short of exportation to Newfoundland. But before they could gain the sea, Lord Delaware with his ships and provisions was met coming into port; and the intending fugitives turned back with him. The hungry were fed, order was restored, and industry were re-established. A wave of religious feeling swept over the little community; the rule of Lord Delaware was mild, but just and firm; and all would have been well had not his health failed, and compelled him, in the spring of 1611, to return to England. The colony was disheartened anew, and the arrival of Sir Thomas Dale in Delaware's place did not at first relieve the depression; his training had been military, and he administered affairs by martial law. But he believed in the future of the enterprise, and so impressed his views upon the English council that six more ships, with three hundred emigrants, were immediately sent to their relief. Gates, who brought these recruits to Jamestown, assumed the governorship, and a genuine prosperity began. Among the most important of the improvements introduced was an approximation to the right of private ownership in land, which had hitherto been altogether denied, and which gave the emigrants a personal interest in the welfare of the enterprise. In 1612 a third charter was granted, still further increasing the privileges of the settlers, who now found themselves possessed of almost the same political powers as they had enjoyed at home. It was still possible, as was thereafter shown, for unjust and selfish governors to inflict misery and discontent upon the people; but it was also possible, under the law, to give them substantial freedom and happiness; and that was a new light in political conceptions.

More than thirty years had now passed since Raleigh first turned his mind to the colonizing of Virginia. He was now approaching the scaffold; but he could feel a lofty satisfaction in the thought that it was mainly through him that an opportunity of incalculable magnitude and possibilities had been given for the enlargement and felicity of his race. He had sowed the seed of England beyond the seas, and the quality of the fruit it should bear was already becoming apparent to his eyes, soon to close forever upon earthly things. The spirit of America was his spirit. He was for freedom, enlightenment, and enterprise; and whenever a son of America has fulfilled our best ideal of what an American should be, we find in him some of the traits and qualities which molded the deeds and colored the thoughts of this mighty Englishman.

Nor can we find a better example of the restless, practical, resourceful side of the American character than is offered in Captain John Smith; even in his boastfulness we must claim kinship with him. His sterling manhood, his indomitable energy, his fertile invention, his ability as a leader and as a negotiator, all ally him with the traditional Yankee, who carries on in so matter-of-fact a way the solution of the problems of the new democracy. Both these men, each in his degree, were Americans before America.

And with them we may associate the name of Columbus; to him also we must concede the spiritual citizenship of our country; not because of the bare fact that he was the first to reach its shores, but because he had a soul valiant enough to resist and defy the conservatism that will believe in no new thing, and turns life into death lest life should involve labor and self-sacrifice. Columbus, Smith, and Raleigh stand at the portals of our history, types of the faith, success and honor which are our heritage.

CHAPTER SECOND

THE FREIGHT OF THE MAYFLOWER

HE motive force which drove the English Separatists and Puritans to a voluntary exile in New England in 1620 and later, had its origin in the brain of the son of a Saxon slate cutter just a century before. Martin Luther first gave utterance to a mental protest which had long been on the tongue's tip of many thoughtful and conscientious persons in Europe, but which, till then, no one had found the courage, or the energy, or the conviction, or the clear-headedness (as the case might be) to formulate and announce. Once having reached its focus, however, and attained its expression, it spread like a flame in dry stubble, and produced results in men and nations rarely precedented in the history of the world, whose vibrations have not yet died away.

Henry VIII. of England was born and died a Catholic; though of religion of any kind he never betrayed an inkling. His Act of Supremacy, in 1534, which set his will above that of the Pope of Rome, had no religious bearing, but merely indicated that he wanted to divorce one woman in order to marry another. Nevertheless it made it incumbent upon the Pope to excommunicate him, and thus placed him, and England as represented by him, in a quasi-dissenting attitude toward the orthodox faith. And coming as it did so soon after Luther's outbreak, it may have encouraged Englishmen to think on lines of liberal belief.

Passionate times followed in religious—or rather in theological—matters, all through the Sixteenth Century. The fulminations of Luther and the logic of Calvin set England to discussing and taking sides; and when Edward VI. came to the throne, he was himself a Protestant, or indeed a Puritan, and the stimulus of Puritanism in others. But the mass of the common people were still unmoved, because there was no means of getting at them, and they had no stomach for dialectics, if there had been. The new ideas would probably have made little headway had not Edward died and Mary the Catholic come red-hot with zeal into his place. She lost no time in catching and burning all dissenters, real or suspected; and as many of these were honest persons who lived among the people, and were known and approved by them, and as they uniformly endured their martyrdom with admirable fortitude and good-humor, falling asleep in the crackling flames like babes at the mother's breast, Puritanism received an advertisement such as nothing since Christianity had enjoyed before, and which all the unaided Luthers, Melanchthons and Calvins in the world could not have given it.

This lasted five years, after which Mary went to her reward, and Elizabeth came to her inheritance. She was no more of a religion-monger than her distinguished father had been; but she was, like him, jealous of her authority, and a martinet for order and obedience at all costs. A certain intellectual voluptuousness of nature and an artistic instinct inclined her to the splendid forms and ceremonies of the Catholic ritual; but she was too good a politician not to understand that a large part of her subjects were unalterably opposed to the papacy. After some consideration, therefore, she adopted the expedient of a compromise, the substance of which was that whatever was handsome and attractive in Catholicism was to be retained, and only those technical points dropped which made the Pope the despot of the Church. In ordinary times this would have answered very well; human nature likes to eat its cake and have it too; but this time was anything but ordinary. The reaction from old to new ways of thinking, and the unforgotten persecutions of Mary, had made men very fond of their opinions, and preternaturally unwilling to enter into bargains with their consciences. At the same time loyalty to the Crown was still a fetich in England, as indeed it always has been, except at and about the time when Oliver Cromwell and others cut off the head of the First Charles. Consequently when Elizabeth and Whitgift, her Archbishop of Canterbury, set about putting their house in order in earnest, they were met with a mixture of humble loyalty and immovable resistance which would have perplexed any potentates less single-minded. But Elizabeth and Whitgift were not of the sort that sets its hand to the plow and then turns back; they went earnestly on with their banishments and executions, paying particular attention to the Separatists, but keeping plenty in hand for the Puritans also.— The Separatists, it may be observed, were so called because their aim was to dispart themselves entirely from the orthodox communion; the Puritans were willing to remain in the fold, but had it in mind to purify it, by degrees, from the defilement which they held it to have contracted. The former would not in the least particular make friends with the mammon of unrighteousness, or condone the sins of the Scarlet Woman, or of anybody else; they would not inhale foul air, with a view to sending it forth again disinfected by the fragrance of their own lungs. They took their stand unequivocally upon the plain letter of Scripture, and did away with all that leaned toward conciliating the lighter sentiments and emotions; they would have no genuflexions, no altars, no forms and ceremonies, no priestly vestments, no Apostolic Succession, no priests, no confessions, no intermediation of any kind between the individual and his Creator. The people themselves should make and unmake their own "ministers," and in all ways live as close to the bone as they could. The Puritans were not opposed to any of these beliefs; only they were not so set upon proclaiming and acting upon them in season and out of season; they contended that the idolatry of ritual, since it had been several centuries growing up, should be allowed an appreciable time to disappear. It will easily be understood that, at the bottom of these religious innovations and inflammations, was a simple movement toward greater human freedom in all directions, including the political. It mattered little to the zealots on either side whether or not the secret life of a man was morally correct; he must think in a certain prescribed way, on pain of being held damnable, and, if occasion served, of being sent to the other world before he had opportunity to further confirm his damnation. The dissenters, when they got in motion, were just as intolerant and bigoted as the conformists; and toward none was this intolerance more strongly manifested than toward such as were in the main, but not altogether, of their way of thinking. The Quakers and the Independents had almost as hard an experience in New England, at the hands of the Puritans, as the latter had endured from good Queen Bess and her henchmen a few years before. But really, religion, in the absolute sense, had very little to do with these movements and conflicts; the impulse was supposed to be religion because religion dwells in the most interior region of a man's soul. But the craving for freedom also proceeds from an interior place; and so does the lust for tyranny. Propinquity was mistaken for identity, and anything which was felt but could not be reasoned about assumed a religious aspect to the subject of it, and all the artillery of Heaven and Hell, and the vocabulary thereof, were pressed into service to champion it.

But New England had to be peopled, and this was the way to people it. The dissenters perceived that, though they might think as they pleased in England, they could not combine this privilege with keeping clear of the fagot or the gibbet; and though martyrdom is honorable, and perhaps gratifying to one's vanity, it can be overdone.

They came to the conclusion, accordingly, that practical common sense demanded their expatriation; and some of them humbly petitioned her Majesty to be allowed to take themselves off. The Queen did not show herself wholly agreeable to this project; womanlike, and queenlike, she wanted to convince them even more than to be rid of them; or if they must be got rid of, she preferred to dispose of them herself in the manner prescribed for stubborn heretics. But the lady was getting in years, and was not so ardently loved as she had been; and her activity against the heretics could not keep pace with her animosity. She had succeeded in many things, and her reign was accounted glorious; but she had won no glory by the Puritans and Separatists, and her campaign against them had not succeeded. They were stronger than ever, and were to grow stronger yet. It was remembered, too, by her servants, that, when she was dead, some one might ascend the throne who was less averse to nonconformity than she had been; and then those who had persecuted might suffer persecution in their turn. So although the prayer of the would-be colonists was not granted, the severity against them was relaxed; and as Elizabeth's last breath rattled in her throat, the mourners had one ear cocked toward the window, to hear in what sort of a voice James was speaking.

Their fears had been groundless. The new king spoke Latin, and "peppered the Puritans soundly." The walls of Hampton Court resounded with his shrill determination to tolerate none of their nonsense; and he declared to the assembled prelates, who were dissolving in tears of joy, that bishops were the most trustworthy legs a monarch could walk on. The dissenters, who had hoped much, were disappointed in proportion; but they were hardened into an opposition sterner than they had ever felt before. They must help themselves, since no man would help them; and why not—since they had God on their side? They controlled the House of Commons, and made themselves felt there, till

James declared that he preferred a hermitage to ruling such a pack of malcontents. The clergy renewed their persecutions; the government of England was a despotism of the strictest kind; and the fire which had been repressed in Puritan bosoms began to emit sullen sparks through their eyes and lips.

A group of them in the north of England established a church, and called upon all whom it might concern to shake off anti-Christian bondage. John Robinson and William Brewster gave it their support, and their meetings were made interesting by the spies of the government. Finally they were driven to attempt an escape to Holland; and, after one miscarriage, they succeeded in getting off from the coast of Lincolnshire in the spring of 1608, and were transported to Amsterdam. They could but tarry there; their only country now was Heaven; meanwhile they were wandering Pilgrims on the face of the earth, as their Lord had been before them. From Amsterdam they presently removed to Leyden, where they conducted themselves with such propriety as to win the encomiums of the natives. But their holy prosperity did not make them happy, or enable them to be on comfortable terms with the Dutch language; they could not get elbow-room, or feel that they were doing themselves justice; and as the rumors of a fertile wilderness overseas came to their ears, they began to contemplate the expediency of betaking themselves thither. It was now the year 1617; and negotiations were entered into with the London Company to proceed under their charter.

The London Company were disposed to consider the proposition favorably, but the affair dragged, and when it was brought before the government it was quashed by Bacon, who opined that the coat of Christ must be seamless, and that even in a remote wilderness heretics must not be permitted to rend it. The Pilgrims might have replied that if a coat is already torn, it profits not to declare it whole; but they were not students of repartee, and merely relinquished efforts to secure support in that direction. They must go into exile without official sanction, that was all. The king's law enjoined, to be sure, that if any dissenters were discovered abroad they were straightway to be sent to England for discipline; but inasmuch as the threat of exile was, at the same time, held over the same dissenters at home, it would seem a saving of trouble all round to go abroad and trust to God. "If they mean to wrong us," they aptly remarked, "a royal seal, though it were as broad as the house floor, would not protect us." A suggestion that the Dutchmen fit them out for their voyage, and share their profits, fell through on the question of protection against other nations; and when they had prepared their minds to make the venture without any protection at all, it turned out that there was not capital enough in the community to pay for transport. Within three years, however, this difficulty was overcome, and in July of 1620 two ships were hired—the "Speedwell" and the "Mayflower"—and the progenitors of religious and civil liberty in America were ready to set forth.

There was not accommodation for them all on the two vessels, the one of sixty tons, the other of thrice as many; so a division was made, Robinson remaining in Leyden with one party, until means could be had to bring them over; and Brewster accompanying the emigrants, supported by John Carver and Miles Standish. Robinson, one of the finest and purest spirits of the time, died while waiting to join his friends; but most of the others were brought over in due season.

The hymns of praise and hope which were uplifted on the shores of Delft Haven, in the hour of farewell between those who went and those who stayed, though the faith which inspired them was stanch, and the voices which chanted them musical and sweet, could not restrain the tears that flowed at the severing of ties which had been welded by exile, hardship, and persecution for conscience' sake; nor were the two "feasts" which comforted the bellies of the departing ones able to console their hearts. It is different with trips across the Atlantic nowadays: and different, likewise, are the motives which prompt them.

The "Speedwell" turned back at Plymouth, England, and the "Mayflower" went on alone, with her company of one hundred and two, including women, some of whom were soon to be mothers. The Atlantic, though a good friend of theirs, was rough and boisterous in its manners, and tossed them on their way rudely; in that little cabin harrowing discomfort must have been undergone, and Christian forbearance sorely tried. The pitching and tossing lasted more than two months, from the 6th of September till the 7th of December, when they sighted—not the Bay of New York, as they had intended, but the snow-covered sand mounds of Cape Cod. It was at best an inhospitable coast, and the time of their visit could not have been worse chosen.

But indeed they were to be tested to the utmost; their experiences during that winter would have discouraged oak and iron; but it had no such effect upon these English men and women of flesh and blood. The New England winter climate has its reputation still; but these people were not fit for the encounter. They had been living in the moist mildness of Holland for thirteen years, and for more than sixty days had been penned in that stifling "Mayflower" cabin, seasick, bruised and sleepless. It sleeted, snowed, rained and froze, and they could find no place to get ashore on; their pinnace got stove, and the icy waves wet them to the marrow. Standish and some others made explorations on land; but found nothing better than some baskets of maize and a number of Indian graves buried in the snow-drifts. At last they stumbled upon a little harbor, upon which abutted a hollow between low hills, with an icebound stream descending through it to the sea. They must make shift with that or perish. It was the 21st of December.

That date is inscribed on the front page of our history, and the Pilgrim Fathers and their wives and daughters are celebrated persons, though they were only a lot of English farmers in exile for heresy. But no dreams of renown visited them then; they had nothing to uphold them but their amazing faith. What that faith must have been their conduct demonstrates; but it is difficult to comprehend such a spirit; we remember all the persecutions, all the energy of new convictions, and still it seems miraculous. Liberty to think as they pleased, and to act upon their belief: that was all they had to fight with. It seems very thin armor, an ineffective sword: but what a victory they won!

Before they disembarked, a meeting was held in the cabin for the transaction of certain business. Since then, whenever a handful of Yankees have been gathered together, it has been their instinct to organize and pass resolutions. It is the instinct of order and self-government, the putting of each man in his proper place, and assigning to him his function. This meeting of the Pilgrims was the prototype, and the resolutions they passed constitute the model upon which our commonwealth is based. They promised one another, in the presence of God, equal laws and fidelity to the general good: the principles of a free democracy.

They disembarked on the flat bowlder known as Plymouth Rock and set to work to make their home. With the snow under their feet, the dark, naked woods hemming them in, and concealing they knew not what savage perils; with the bitter waves flinging frozen spray along the shore, and immitigable clouds lowering above them—memory may have drawn a picture of the quiet English vales in which they were born, or of the hazy Dutch levels, with the windmills swinging their arms slumberously above the still canals, and the clean streets and gabled façades of the prosperous Holland town which had sheltered and befriended them. They thought of faces they loved and would see no more, and of the secure and tranquil lives they might have led, but for that tooth of conscience at their hearts, which would give them peace only at the cost of almost all that humanity holds dear. Did any of them wish they had not come? did any doubt in his or her heart whether a cold abstraction was worth adopting in lieu of the great, warm, kindly world? Verily, not one!

They got to work at their home-making without delay; but all were ill, and many were dying. That winter they put up with much labor a few log huts; but their chief industry was the digging of clams and of graves. Half of their number were buried before the summer, and there was not food enough for the rest to eat. John Carver, who had been elected governor at landing, died in April, having already lost his son. But those who did survive their first year lived long; it is wonder that they ever died at all, who could survive such an experience.

Spring came, and with it a visitor. It was in March— not a salubrious month in New England; but the trees were beginning to put out brown buds with green or red tips, and grass and shrubs were sprouting in sheltered places, though snow still lay in spots where sunshine could not fall. The trailing arbutus could be found here and there, with a perfume that all the cruelty of winter seemed to have made only more sweet. Birds were singing, too, and the settlers had listened to them with joy; they had gone near to forget that God had made birds. On some days, from the south, came the breathing of soft, fragrant airs; and there were breadths of blue in the sky that looked as if so fresh and tender a hue must have been just created.

The men, in thick jerkins, heavy boots, and sugarloaf hats, were busy about the clearing; some, like Miles Standish, wore a steel plate over their breasts, and kept their matchlocks within reach, for though a pestilence had exterminated the local Indians before they came, and, with the exception of one momentary skirmish, in which no harm was done, nothing had been seen or heard of the red men— still it was known that Indians existed, and it was taken for granted that they would be hostile. Meanwhile the women, in homespun frocks and jackets, with kerchiefs round their shoulders, and faces in which some trace of the English ruddiness had begun to return, sat spinning in the doorways of the huts, keeping an eye on the kettles of Indian meal. The morning sunlight fell upon a scene which, for the first time, seemed homelike: not like the lost homes in England, but a place people could live human lives in, and grow fond of. The hope of spring was with them.

All at once, down the forest glade, treading noiselessly on moccasined feet, came a tall, wild, unfamiliar figure, with feathers in his black hair, and black eyes gleaming above his high cheekbones. An Indian, at last! He had come so silently that he had emerged from the shadow of the forest and was almost amid them before he was seen. Some of the settlers, perhaps, felt a momentary tightening round the heart; for though we are always in the hollow of God's hand, there are times when we are surprised into forgetfulness of that security, and are concerned about carnal perils. Captain Standish, who had taken a flying shot at some of these heathen four or five months ago, caught up a loaded musket leaning against the corner of a hut, and stood on his guard, doubting that more of the savages were lurking behind the trees. He had even thus early in American history come to the view long afterward formulated in the epigram that the only good Indians are the dead ones.

But the keen, spare savage made no hostile demonstration; he paused before the captain, with the dignity of his race, and held out his empty hands. And then, to the vast astonishment of Standish and of the others who had gathered to his support, he opened his mouth and spoke English: "Welcome, Englishmen!" said he. They must have fancied, for an instant, that the Lord had wrought a special miracle for them, in bestowing upon this native of the primeval forest the gift of tongues.

There was, however, nothing miraculous about Samoset, who had picked up his linguistic accomplishment, such as it was, from a fellow savage who had been kidnapped and taken to England, whom he afterward introduced to the colony, where he made himself useful. Samoset's present business was as embassador from the great chief and sachem, Massasoit, lord of everything thereabout, who sent friendly greetings, and would be pleased to confer with the new comers, at their convenience, and arrange an alliance.

These were good words, and they must have taken a weight from every heart there; not only the dread of immediate attack, but the omnipresent and abiding anxiety that the time would come when they would have to fight for their lives, and defend the persecuted church of the Lord against foes who knew nothing of conformist or nonconformist, but who were as proficient as Queen Mary herself in the use of fire and torture. These misgivings might now be dismissed; if the ruler of so many tribes was willing to stand their friend, who should harm them? So they all gathered round Samoset on that sunny spring morning; the women observing curiously and in silence his strange aspect and gestures, and occasionally exchanging glances with one another at some turn of the talk; while the sturdy Miles, and Governor Carver, pale with illness which within a month reunited him with the son he had loved, and Elder Brewster, with his serious mien, and Bradford, who was to succeed Carver, with his strong, authoritative features and thoughtful forehead;—these and more than a score more of the brethren stood eying their visitor, questioning him earnestly and trying to make out his meaning from his imperfect English gruntings. And they spoke one to another of the action that should be taken on his message, or commented with pious exclamations on the mercy of the Lord in thus raising up for them protectors even in the wilderness. Meanwhile a chipmunk flitted along the bole of a fallen tree, a thrush chirped in the brake, a deer, passing airy-footed across an opening in the forest, looked an instant and then turned and plunged fleetly away amid the boughs; and a lean-bellied wolf, prospecting for himself and his friends, stuck his sinister snout through a clump of underbrush, and curled his lips above the long row of his white teeth in an ugly grin. This friendship boded no good to him.

The coming of Samoset was followed after a while by the introduction of Squanto, the worthy savage who had enjoyed the refining influences of distant England, whose services as interpreter were of much value in that juncture; and after a short time Massasoit himself accepted the settlers' invitation to become their guest during the making of the treaty. He was received with becoming honor; the diplomatists proceeded at once to business, and before twilight the state paper had been drawn up, signed and sealed. Its provisions ran that both parties were to abstain from harming each other, were to observe an offensive and defensive alliance, and to deliver up offenders. These terms were religiously kept for half a century; by which time the colonists were able to take care of themselves. Its good effects were illustrated in the case of the chief Canonicus, who was disposed to pick a quarrel with the Englishmen, and sent them, as a symbol of his attitude, a rattlesnake's skin wrapped round a sheaf of arrows. Bradford, to indicate that he also understood the language of emblems, sent the skin back stuffed with powder and bullets. Canonicus seems to have fancied that these substances were capable of destroying him spontaneously, and returned them with pacific assurances. Such weapons, combined with the alliance, were too much for him. Canonicus was chief of the Narragansetts; Massasoit, of the Wampanoags. In 1676 the son of Massasoit, for some fancied slight, made war upon the settlers, and the Narragansetts helped him; in this war, known as King Philip's, the settlers suffered severely, though they were victorious. But had it come during the early years of their sojourn, not one of them would have survived, and New England might never have become what she is now.

Meantime the Pilgrims, pilgrims no longer, settled down to make the wilderness blossom as the rose. At their first landing they had agreed, like the colonists of Virginia, to own their land and work it in common; but they were much quicker than the Jamestown folk to perceive the inexpediency of this plan, and reformed it by giving each man or family a private plot of ground. Agriculture then developed so rapidly that corn enough was raised to supply the Indians as well as the English; and the importation of neat cattle increased the home look as well as the prosperity of the farms. There was also a valuable trade in furs, which stimulated an abortive attempt at rivalry. None could compete with the Pilgrims on their own ground; for were they not growing up with the country, and the Lord—was He not with them? More troublesome than this effort of Weston was the obstruction of the Company in England, and its usurious practices; the colonists finally bought them out, and relied henceforth wholly on themselves, with the best results. As years went by their numbers increased, though but slowly. They did not invite the co-operation of persons not of their way of thinking, and the world was never oversupplied with Separatists. On the other hand, they were active and full of enterprise, and sent out branches in all directions, which shared the vitality of the parent stock. Every man of them was trained to self-government, and where he went order and equity accompanied him. A purer democracy could not be framed; for years the elections were made by the entire body of the assembled citizens; His Dread Majesty, King James, never sent them his royal Charter, but the charter provided by their own love of justice and solid good sense served them far better. Their governors were responsible directly to the people, and were further restrained by a council of seven members. This political basis is that upon which our present form of government rests; but it is strange to see what Daedalian complications, and wheels within wheels, we have contrived to work into the superstructure. A modern ward heeler in New York could have taken up the whole frame of government in Seventeenth Century New England by the butt end, and cracked it like a whip—provided of course the Pilgrim fathers had allowed him to attend the primaries.

But it is more probable that the ward heeler would have found himself promptly in the presence of one of those terrific magistrates whose grim decrees gave New England naughty children the nightmare a century after the stern-browed promulgators of them were dust. The early laws against crime in New England were severe, though death was seldom or never inflicted save for murder. But more irksome to one used to the lax habits of to-day would have been the punctilious rigidity with which they guarded the personal bearing, speech, and dress of the members of their community. Yet we may thank them for having done so; it was a wise precaution; they knew the frailties of the flesh, and how easily license takes an ell if an inch be given it. Nothing less iron than was their self-restraint could have provided material stanch enough to build up the framework of our nation. One might not have enjoyed living with them; but we may be heartily glad that they lived; and we should be the better off if more of their stamp were alive still.

But these iron people had their tender and sentimental side as well, and the self-command which they habitually exercised made the softening, when it came, the more beautiful. One of the love romances of this little colony has come down to us, and may be taken as the substantial truth; it has entered into our literature and poetry, and touches us more nearly even than the tale of Pocahontas. Its telling by our most popular poet has brought it to the knowledge of a greater circle of readers than it could otherwise have reached; but the elaboration of his treatment could add nothing to the human charm of it, or sharpen our conception of the leading characters in the drama. Miles Standish had been a soldier in the Netherlands before joining the Pilgrims, and to him they gave the military guardianship of the colony, with the title of captain. He was then about thirty-six years of age, a bluff, straightforward soldier, whom a life of hardship had made older than his years. He had known little of women's society, but during the long voyage he came to love Priscilla Mullens, and when the spring came to the survivors at Plymouth, he wished to marry her. But he would not trust, as Othello did, to the simple art of a soldier to woo her; and Priscilla was probably no Desdemona. But there was a youth among the colonists, just come of age, whom Standish had liked and befriended, and who, though a cooper and ship-carpenter by trade, was gifted with what seemed to Standish especial graces of person and speech. Alden had not been one of the original pilgrims; he had been hired to repair the "Mayflower" while she lay at Southampton, and decided to sail on her when she sailed; perhaps with the hope of making his fortune in the new world, perhaps because he wished to go where Priscilla went. She was a girl whom any man might rejoice to make his wife; vigorous and wholesome as well as comely, and endowed with a strong character, sweetened by a touch of humor. John had never spoken to her of his love, any more than Miles had; whether Priscilla's clear eyes had divined it, we know not; but it is likely that she saw through the cooper and the soldier both.

The honest soldier was a fool, and saw nothing but Priscilla, and felt nothing but his love for her. He took John Alden by the arm, and, leading him apart into the forest, proposed to him to go to young Mistress Mullens and ask her if she would become the wife of Captain Standish. Alden was honest, too; but he was dominated by his older friend, and lacked the courage to tell him that he had hoped for Priscilla for himself; he let the critical moment for this explanation pass, and then there was nothing for it but to accept the Captain's commission. We can imagine how this situation would be handled by the analytic novelists of our day; how they would spread Alden's heart and conscience out on paper, and dry them, and pick them to pieces. The young fellow certainly had a hard thing to do; he must tread down his own passion, and win the girl for his rival into the bargain. To her he went, and spoke. But the only way he could spur himself to eloquence was to imagine that he was Standish, and then woo her as he would have done had Standish been he.

Maidens of rounded nature, like Priscilla, pay less attention to what a man says than to the tones of his voice, the look in his eyes, and his unconscious movements. As Alden warmed to his work, she glanced at him occasionally, and not only wished that Heaven had made her such a man, but decided that it had. So, when the youth had finished off an ardent peroration, in which the Captain was made to appear in a guise of heroic gallantry that did not suit him in the least, but which was the best John could do for him: there was a pause, while the vicarious wooer wiped his brow, and felt very miserable, remembering that if she yielded, it would be to Miles and not to him. She divined what was in his mind, and sent him to Heaven with one of the womanliest and loveliest things that ever woman said to man: "Why don't you speak for yourself, John?" she asked, gazing straight at him, with a quiver of her lips that was half humor and half the promise of tears.

John still had before him a bad quarter of an hour with the Captain; it was as hard to make him understand that he had not played the traitor to him as it had been to persuade Priscilla to do what she had not done; but the affair ended without a tragedy, which would have spoiled it. Captain Standish, when Priscilla married, went to live in Duxbury; and a year or two later worked off his spleen by slaying the Indian rascals who were plotting to murder the

Weston settlers at Weymouth. He and his men did not wait for the savages to strike the first blow; they made no pretense of exhausting all the resources of diplomacy before proceeding to extremities. They walked up to the enemy, suddenly seized them by the throat, and drove the knives which the Indians themselves wore through their false hearts. There was no more trouble from Indians in that region for a long time; and Captain Standish's feelings were greatly relieved. As for John and Priscilla, they lived long and prospered, John attaining the age of eighty-seven, which indicates domestic felicity. They had issue, and their descendants live among us to this day in comfort and honor.

King James, like other spiteful and weak men, had a long memory, and amid the many things that engaged his attention he did not forget the colonists of Plymouth, who had exiled themselves without a charter from him. In the same year which witnessed their disembarkation at Plymouth Rock, he incorporated a company consisting of friends of his own, and gave them a tract of country between the fortieth and the forty-eighth parallels of north latitude, which of course included the Plymouth colony. In addition to all other possible rights and privileges, it had the monopoly of the fisheries of the coast, and it was from this that revenue was most certainly expected, since it was proposed to lay a tax on all tonnage engaged in it. All the new company had to do was to grant charters to all who might apply, and reap the profits. But the scheme was fated to miscarry, because the pretense of colonization behind it was impotent, and the true object in view was the old one of getting everything that could be secured out of the country, and putting nothing into it. The fisheries monopoly was powerfully opposed in Parliament and finally defeated; small sporadic settlements, with no sound principle or purpose within them, appeared and disappeared along the coast from Massachusetts to the northern borders of Maine. One grant conflicted with another, titles were in dispute, and lawsuits were rife. The king sanctioned whatever injustice or restriction his company proposed, but his decrees, many of them illegal, were ineffective, and produced only confusion. Agriculture was hardly attempted in any of the little settlements authorized by the company, and the only trade pursued was in furs and fishes. The rights of the Indians were wholly disregarded, and the domain of the French at the north was infringed upon. All this while the Pilgrims continued their industries and maintained their democracy, undisturbed by the feeble machinations of the king; and in 1625 the death of the latter temporarily cleared the air. Charles affixed his seal to the famous Massachusetts Charter four years later; and though Gorges and some others continued to harass New England for some time longer, the plan of colonizing by fisheries was hopelessly discredited, and the development of civil and religious liberties among the serious colonists was assured.

The experiments thus far made in dealing with the new country had had a significant result. The Plymouth colony, going out with neither charter nor patronage, and with the purpose not of finding gold or making fortunes, but of establishing a home wherein to dwell in perpetuity—which was handicapped by the abject poverty of its members, and by the severities of a climate till then unknown—this enterprise was found to hold the elements of success from the start, and it steadily increased in power and influence. It suffered from time to time from the tyranny of royal governors and the ignorance or malice of absentee statesmanship; but nothing could extinguish or corrupt it; on the contrary, it went "slowly broadening down, from precedent to precedent," until, when the moment of supreme trial came to the Thirteen Colonies, the descendants of the Pilgrims and the Puritans, and the men who had absorbed their ideas, put New England in the van of patriotism and progress. It is a noble record, and a pregnant example to all friends of freedom.

In suggestive contrast with this was the Jamestown enterprise. As we have seen, this colony was saved from almost immediate extinction solely by the genius and energy of one man, whom his fellow members had at first tried to exclude altogether from their councils and companionship. Belonging to a class socially higher and presumably more intelligent than the Pilgrims, and continually furnished with supplies from the Company in England, they were unable during twelve years to make any independent stand against disaster. In a climate which was as salubrious as that of New England was rigorous, and with a soil as fertile as any in the world, they dwindled and starved, and their dearest wish was to return to England. They were saved at last (as we shall presently see) by two things; first, by the discovery of the value of tobacco as an export, and of its usefulness as a currency for the internal trade of the country; and secondly, and much more, by the Charter of 1618, which gave the people the privilege of helping to make their own laws. That year marked the beginning of civil liberty in America; but what it had taken the Jamestown colonists twelve weary and disastrous years to attain, was claimed by the pious farmers of Plymouth before ever they set foot on Forefather's Rock. Willingness to labor, zeal for the common welfare, indifference to wealth, independence, moral and religious integrity and fervor—these were some of the traits and virtues whose cultivation made the Pilgrims prosperous, and the neglect or lack of which discomfited the Virginia settlers. The latter, man for man, were by nature as capable as the former of profiting by right conditions and training; and as soon as they obtained them they showed favorable results. But in the meantime the lesson was driven home that a virgin country cannot be subdued and rendered productive by selfish and unjust procedure: a homely and hackneyed lesson, but one which can never be too often quoted, since each fresh generation must buy its own experience, and it often happens that a situation essentially old assumes a novel aspect, owing to external modifications of time and place.

The Plymouth Colony, after remaining long separate and self-supporting, consented to a union with the larger and richer settlements of Massachusetts. The charter secured by the latter, and the manner in which it was administered, were alike remarkable. The granting of it was facilitated by the threatened encroachments of other than Englishmen upon the New England domain; it was represented to Charles that it was necessary to be beforehand with these gentry, if they were to be restrained. Charles was on the verge of that rupture with law and order in his own realm which culminated in his dismissal of Parliament, and for ten years attempting the task of governing England without it. He approved the charter without adequately realizing the full breadth and pregnancy of its provisions, which, in effect, secured civil and ecclesiastical emancipation to the settlers under it. But what was quite as important was the consideration that it went into effect at a time incomparably favorable to its success. The Plymouth colony had proved that a godly and self-denying community could flourish in the wilderness, in the enjoyment of spiritual blessings unattainable at home. The power of English prelacy did not extend beyond the borders of England: idolatrous ceremonies could be eschewed in Massachusetts without fear of persecution. Thousands of Puritans were prepared to give up their homes for the sake of liberty, and only waited assurance that it could be obtained. The condition of society and education in England was vicious and corrupt; and though it might become brave and true men to suffer persecution in witness of their faith, yet there was danger that their children might be induced to fall away from the truth, after they were gone. Martyrdom was well, but it must not be allowed to such an extreme as to extirpate the proclaimers of the truth. Many of those who were prepared to take advantage of the charter were of the best stock in

England, men of brains and substance as well as piety; graduates of the Universities, country gentlemen, men of the world and of affairs. A colony made of such elements would be a new thing in the earth; it would comprise all that was strong and wise in human society, and would exclude every germ of weakness and frailty. The sealing of the charter was like the touching of the electric button which, in our day, sets in motion for the first time a vast mechanical system, or fires a simultaneous salute of guns in a hundred cities. King Charles I., who was to lose his anointed head on the block because he tried to crush popular liberty in England, was the immediate human instrument of giving the purest form of such liberty to English exiles beyond the sea.

The charter constituted an organization called the Governor and Company of Massachusetts Bay in New England. The governor, annually elected by the members, was assisted by a deputy and assistants, and was to call a business meeting monthly or oftener, and in addition was to preside four times a year at an assembly of the whole body of the freemen, to make laws and determine appointments. Freedom of Puritan worship was assured, in part explicitly, in part tacitly. The king had no direct relation with their proceedings, beyond the general and vague claims of royal prerogative; and it was an open question whether Parliament had the power to override the authority of the patentees.

It will be seen that this charter was in no respect inharmonious with the system of self-government which had grown up among the Plymouth colonists; it was a more complete and definite formulation of principles which must ever be supported by men who wish so to live as to obtain the highest social and religious welfare. It was the stately flowering of a seed already obscurely planted, and though it was to be now and again checked in its development, would finally bear the fruit of the Tree of Life.

CHAPTER THIRD

THE SPIRIT OF THE PURITANS

AMONG the characteristic figures of this age, none shows stronger lineaments than that of John Endicott. He was, at the time of his coming to Massachusetts, not yet forty years of age; he remained there till his death at six-and-seventy. He was repeatedly elected governor, and died in the governor's chair. In 1645 he was made Major-general of the Colonial troops; nine years before he had headed a campaign against the Pequot Indians. His character illustrated the full measure of Puritan sternness; he was an inflexible persecutor of the Quakers, and was instrumental in causing four of them to be executed in Boston. In his career is found no feeble passage; he was always Endicott. He was a man grown before he attained, under the ministrations of Samuel Skelton of Cambridge, in England, the religious awakening which placed him in the forefront of the Puritan dissenters of his time; and it may be surmised that the force of nature which gave him his self-command would, otherwise directed, have opened still wider the gates of license and recklessness which marked the conduct of many in that period. But, having taken his course, he disciplined himself to the strictest observances, and required them of others. He was a man of perfect moral and physical courage, austere and choleric; yet there was in him a certain cheerfulness and kindliness, like sunshine touching the ruggedness of a granite bowlder. An old portrait of him presents a full and ruddy countenance, without a beard, and with large eyes which gaze sternly out upon the beholder. When the Massachusetts Company was formed, it contained many men of pith and mark, such as Saltonstall, Bellingham, Eaton, and others; but, by common consent, Endicott was chosen as the first governor of the new realm, and he sailed for Boston harbor in June, 1628. He took with him his wife and children, and a small following of fit companions, and landed in September.

Many tales are told of the doings of Endicott in Massachusetts. Like those of all strong men, his deeds were often embellished with legendary ornaments, but the exaggerations, if such there be, are colored by a true conception of his character. At the time of his advent, there was at Merrymount, or Mount Walloston, now within the boundaries of Quincy, near Boston, a colony which was a survival of the one founded by Thomas Weston, through the agency of Thomas Morton, an English lawyer, who was more than once brought to book for unpuritanical conduct. Here was collected, in 1628, a number of waifs and strays, and other persons not in sympathy with the rigorous habits of the Puritans, whose proceedings were of a more or less licentious and unbecoming quality, calculated to disturb the order and propriety of the realm. Endicott, on being apprised of their behavior, went thither with some armed men, and put a summary end to the colony; Morton was sent back to England, and the "revelries" which he had countenanced or promoted were seen no more in Massachusetts. The era for gayeties had not yet come in the new world. Endicott would not be satisfied with crushing out evil; he would also nip in the bud all such lightsome and frivolous conduct as might lead those who indulged in it to forget the dangers and difficulties attending the planting of the reformed faith in the wilderness.

More impressive yet is the story of how he resented the

project of Laud, Archbishop of Canterbury, and the most zealous supporter of the follies and iniquities of King Charles, to force the ritual of the orthodox church upon the people of Massachusetts. When Endicott received from Governor Winthrop the letter containing this news, whose purport, if carried out, would undo all that the Puritans had most passionately labored to establish; for which they had given up their homes and friends, and to the safe-guarding of which they had pledged their lives, their fortunes, and their sacred honor:—he was deeply stirred, and resolved that a public demonstration should be made of the irrevocable opposition of the people to the measure. He was at that time captain of the trained band of Salem, which was used to meet for drill in the square of the little settlement. It had for a long time disquieted Endicott and other Puritan leaders that the banner of England, under which, as Englishmen, they must live and fight, should bear upon it the sign of the red cross, which was the very emblem of the popery which their souls abhorred. It had seemed to them almost a sin to tolerate it; and yet it was treason to take any liberties with the national ensign. But Endicott was now in a mood to encounter any risk; since, if Laud's will were enforced, there would be little left in New England worth fighting for.

Accordingly, on the next training day, when the able men of Salem were drawn up in their breastplates and headpieces, with the Red-Cross flag floating over them, and the rest of the townspeople, with here and there an Indian among them, looking on: Endicott, in his armor, with his sword upon his thigh, spoke in passionate terms to the assembly of the matter which weighed upon his heart. And then, as a symbol of the Puritan protest, and a pledge of his vital sincerity, he took the banner in his hand, and, drawing his sword, cut the cross out of its folds. The unparalleled audacity and rashness of this act, which might have brought upon New England a revocation of her charter and destruction of the liberties which already exceeded those vouchsafed to Englishmen at home, alarmed Winthrop, and sent a thrill throughout the colony. But the deed was too public to be disavowed, and Endicott and they must abide the consequences. Information of the outrage was carried to Charles; but he was fortunately too much preoccupied at the moment with the struggle for his crown at home to be able to take proper action upon the slight put upon his authority in Salem. No punishment was inflicted upon the bold soldier, who thus anticipated by nearly a century and a half the step finally taken by the patriots of 1776.

To return, however, to Endicott's arrival in Boston (as it was afterward named, in honor of that Lincolnshire Boston from which many of the emigrants came). There were already a few settlers there, who had come in from various motives, and one or two of whom were inclined to assert squatter sovereignty. The rights of the Indians were respected, in accordance with the injunctions of the Company; and Sagamore John, who asserted his rights as chief over the neck of land and the hilly promontory of the present city, was so courteously entreated that he permitted the erection of a house there, and the laying out of streets. While these preparations were going forward, the bulk of the first emigration, numbering two hundred persons, with servants, cattle, arms and other provisions, entered the harbor. They had had a prosperous and pious voyage, being much refreshed with religious services performed daily; and it may be recorded as perhaps a unique fact in the annals of ocean navigation that the ship captain and the sailors punctuated the setting of the morning and noon watches with the singing of psalms and with prayer. This sounds apocryphal; but it so stated in the narrative of "New England's Plantation," written and circulated by Mr. Higginson soon after their arrival; and it must be remembered that the ship carried a supply of personages of the clerical profession out of proportion to the number of the rest of the passengers. But palliate the marvel how we may, we cannot help smiling at it, and at the same time regretting that the Puritans themselves probably had no realization of the miracle which was transacting under their noses. They doubtless regarded it as a matter of course, instead of a thing to occur but once in a precession of the equinoxes.

And now, it might be supposed, began the building of the city: the clearing of the forest, the chopping of wood, the sawing of beams, the digging of foundations, the ringing of hammers, and the uprising on every side of the dwellings of civilization. And certainly steps were taken to provide the company with shelter from the present summer heats and from the snows of winter to come; and they had brought with them artisans skilled to do the necessary work. But though the Puritans never could be called remiss in respect of making due provision for the necessities of this life, yet all was done with a view to the conditions of the life to come; and in the annals of the time we read more of the prayers and fasts, the choosing of ministers, and the promotion and practice of godliness in general, than we do of any temporal matters. Men there were, like Endicott, who united the strictest religious zeal with all manner of practical abilities; but there were many, too, who had been no more accustomed to shift for themselves than were the gentlemen of Jamestown. They differed from the latter, however, in an enlightened conception of the work before them, in enthusiasm for the commonweal, and in determination to familiarize themselves as soon as possible with the requirements of their situation. The town did not come up in a night, like the shanty cities of our western pioneers; nor did it contain gambling houses and liquor saloons as its chief public buildings. These men were building a social structure meant to last for all time, and houses in which they hoped to pass the years of their natural lives; and they proceeded with what we would now consider unwarrantable deliberation and with none too much technical skill. They sought neither wealth nor the luxuries it brings; but, rather, welcomed hardship, as apt to chasten the spirit; and never felt themselves so thoroughly about their proper business as when they were assembled in the foursquare little log hut which they had consecrated as the house of God. Boston and Salem grew: they were larger and more commodious at the end of the twelvemonth than they had been at its beginning; but more cannot be said. Sickness, misfortune, and scarcity handicapped the settlers; many died; the yield of their crops was wholly inadequate to their needs; servants whose work was indispensable could not be paid, and were set free to work for themselves, and the outlook was in all respects gloomy. If the enterprise was to be saved, the Lord must speedily send succor.

The Lord did not forget His people. A great relief was already preparing for them, and the way of it was thus.—

The record of the former chartered companies had shown that conducting the affairs of colonists on the other side of the ocean was attended with serious difficulties on both parts. The colonists could not make their needs known with precision enough, or in season, to have them adequately met; and the governing company was unable to get a close knowledge of its business, or to explain and enforce its requirements. Furthermore, there was liable to be continual vexatious interference on the part of the king and his officers, detrimental to the welfare of colonists and company alike.

The men who constituted the Massachusetts Company were not concerned respecting the pecuniary profits of the venture, inasmuch as they looked only for the treasures which moth nor rust can corrupt; their "plantation" was to the glory of God, not to the imbursement of man. Nor were they anxious to impose their will upon the emigrants, or solicitous lest the latter should act unseemly; for the men who were there were of the same character and aim as those who were in England, and there could be no differences between them beyond such as might legitimately arise as to the most expedient way of reaching a given end. But the Company could easily apprehend that the king and his ministers might meddle with their projects and bring them to naught; and since those affairs, unlike mercantile ones, were not of a nature to admit of compromise, they earnestly desired to prevent this contingency.

Debating the matter among themselves, the leaders of the organization conceived the idea of establishing the headquarters of the Company in the midst of the emigrants in America: of becoming, in other words, emigrants themselves, and working side by side with their brethren for the common good. This plan offered manifest attractions; it would remove them from unwelcome propinquity to the Court, would be of great assistance to the work to do which the Company was formed, would give them the satisfaction of feeling that they were giving their hands as well as their hearts to the service of God, and, not least, would give notice to all the Puritans in England, now a great and influential body, that America was the most suitable ground for their earthly sojourning.

These considerations determined them; and it remained only to put the plan into execution. Twelve men of wealth and education, eminent among whom was John Winthrop, the future governor of the little commonwealth, met and exchanged solemn vows that, if the transference could legally be accomplished, they would personally voyage to New England and take up their permanent residence there. The question was shortly after put to the general vote, and unanimously agreed to; a commercial corporation (as ostensibly the Company was) created itself the germ of an independent commonwealth; and on October 20th John Winthrop was chosen governor for the ensuing twelvemonth; money was subscribed to defray expenses; as speedily as possible ships were chartered or purchased; the numbers of the members of the Company were increased, and their resources augmented, by the addition of many outside persons in harmony with the movement, and willing to support it with their fortunes and themselves; and by the early spring of 1630 a fleet of no less than seventeen ships, accommodating nearly a thousand emigrants representing the very best blood and brain of England, was ready to sail.

At the moment of departing, there was a quailing of the spirit on the part of some of the emigrants; but Winthrop comforted them; he told them that they must "keep the unity of the spirit in the bond of peace"; that, in the wilderness, they would see more of God than they could in England; and that their plantation should be of such a quality as that the founders of future plantations should pray that "The Lord make it likely that of New England." These were good words. Nevertheless, there were not a few seceders, and it was not till the year had advanced that the full number of vessels found their way to the port of Boston. But eleven ships, including the Arbella which bore Winthrop, sailed at once, with seven hundred men and women, and every appliance that experience and forethought could suggest for the convenience and furtherance of life in a new country. Their going made a deep impression throughout England.

And well it might! For these people were not unknown and rude, like the Plymouth Pilgrims; they were not fiercely intolerant fanatics, whose sincerity might be respected, but whose company must be irksome to all less extreme than themselves. They were of gentle blood and training; persons whose acquaintance was a privilege; who added to the richness and charm of social life. That people of this kind should remove themselves to the wilderness meant much more, to the average mind, than that religious outcasts like the Pilgrims should do so. For the latter, one place might be as good as another; but that the others should give up their homes and traditions for the hardships and isolation of such an existence seemed incomprehensible; and when no other motive could be found than that which they professed—"the honor of God"—grave thoughts could not but be awakened. The sensation was somewhat the same as if, in our day, a hundred thousand of the most favorably known and highly endowed persons in the country were to remove to Chinese Tartary to escape from the corruption and frivolity of business and social life, and to create an ideal community in the desert. We could smile at such a hegira if Tom, Dick and Harry were concerned in it; but if the men and women of light and leading abandon us, the implied indictment is worth heeding.

The personal character and nature of Winthrop are well known, and may serve as a type for the milder aspect of his companions. He was of a gentle and conciliating temper, affectionate, and prizing the affection of others. There was a certain sweetness about him, a tendency to mild joyousness, a desire to harmonize all conflicts, a disposition to think good, that good might come of it. He was indisposed to violence in opinion as much as in act; he believed that love was the fulfilling of the law, and would dissolve opposition to the law, if it were allowed time and opportunity. His cultivated intellect recognized a certain inevitableness, or preordained growth in mortal affairs, which made him sympathetic even toward those who differed from him, for did they not use the best light they had? He conformed to the English church, and yet he absented himself from England, not being willing to condemn the orthodox ritual, yet feeling that the Gospel in its purity could be more intimately enjoyed in America. He was no believer in the theory of democratic equality; it seemed to him contrary to natural order; there were degrees and gradations in all things, men included; there were those fitted to govern, and those fitted to serve; power should be in the hands of the few, but they should be "the wisest of the best." He had no doubts as to the obligations of loyalty to the King, and yet he gave up home and ease to live where the King was a sentiment rather than a fact. But beneath all

A PURITAN'S HOME—RETURNING FROM THE HUNT

this engaging softness there was strength in Winthrop; the fiber of him was fine, but it was of resolute temper. Simple goodness is one of the mightiest of powers, and he was good in all simplicity. He could help his servants in the humblest household drudgery, and yet preserve the dignity befitting the Governor of the people. He was not a man to be bullied or terrified, but his wisdom and forbearance disarmed an enemy, and thus removed all need of fighting him. He dominated those around him spontaneously and involuntarily; they, as it were, insisted upon being led by him, and commanded him to exact their obedience. His influence was purifying, encouraging, uplifting, and upon the whole conservative; had he lived a hundred years later, he would not have been found by the side of Adams, Patrick Henry, and James Otis. Sympathy and courtesy made him seem yielding; yet, like a tree that bends to the breeze, he still maintained his place, and was less changeable than many whose stubbornness did not prevent their drifting. His insight and intelligence may have enabled him to foresee to what a goal the New England settlers were bound; but though he would have sympathized with them, he would not have been swayed to join them. As it was, he wrought only good to them, for they were in the formative stage, when moderation helps instead of hindering. He mediated between the state they were approaching, and that from which they came, and he died before the need of alienating himself from them arrived. His resoluteness was shown in his resistance to Anne Hutchinson and her supporter, Sir Harry Vane, who professed the heresy that faith absolved from obedience to the moral law; they were forced to quit the colony; and so was Roger Williams, as lovely as and in some respects a loftier character than Winthrop. In reviewing the career of this distinguished and engaging man, we are surprised that he should have found it on his conscience to leave England. Endicott was born to subdue the wilderness, and so was many another of the Puritans; but it seems as if Winthrop might have done and said in King Charles's palace all that he did and said in Massachusetts, without offense. But it is probable that his moderation appears greater in the primitive environment than it would have done in the civilized one; and again, the impulse to restrain others from excess may have made him incline more than he would otherwise have done toward the other side.

But tradition has too much disposed us to think of the Puritans as of men who had thrown aside all human tenderness and sympathy, and were sternly and gloomily preoccupied with the darker features of religion exclusively. Winthrop corrects this judgment; he was a Puritan, though he was sunny and gentle; and there were many others who more or less resembled him. The reason that the somber type is the better known is partly because of its greater picturesqueness and singularity, and partly because the early life of New England was on the whole militant and aggressive, and therefore brought the rigid and positive qualities more prominently forward.

It would be difficult to exaggerate the piety of the dominating powers in Massachusetts during the first years of the colony's existence. It was almost a mysticism. That intimate and incommunicable experience which is sometimes called "getting religion"—the Lord knocking at the door of the heart and being admitted—was made the condition of admission to the responsible offices of government. This was to make God the ruler, through instruments chosen by Himself—theoretically a perfect arrangement, but in practice open to the gravest perils. It not merely paved the way to imposture, but invited it; and the most dangerous imposture is that which imposes on the impostor himself. It created an oligarchy of the most insidious and unassailable type: a communion of earthly "saints," who might be, and occasionally were, satans at heart. It is essentially at variance with democracy, which it regards as a surrender to the selfish license of the lowest range of

INDIANS ATTACKING NEW ENGLAND SETTLERS

unregenerate human nature; and yet it is incompatible with hereditary monarchy, because the latter is based on uninspired or mechanical selection. The writings of Cotton Mather exhibit the peculiarities and inconsistencies of Puritanism in the most favorable and translucent light, for Mather was himself wedded to them, and of a most inexhaustible fertility in their exposition.

Winthrop was responsible for the "Oath of Fidelity," which required its taker to suffer no attempt to change or alter the government contrary to its laws; and for the law excluding from the freedom of the body politic all who were not members of its church communion. The people, however, stipulated that the elections should be annual, and each town chose two representatives to attend the court of assistants. But having thus asserted their privileges, they forbore to interfere with the judgment of their leaders, and maintained them in office. The possible hostility of England, the strangeness and dangers of their surroundings in America, and the appalling prevalence of disease and mortality among them, possibly drove them to a more than normal fervor of piety. Since God was so manifestly their only sword and shield, and was reputed to be so terrible and implacable in His resentments, it behooved them to omit no means of conciliating His favor.

Winthrop found anything but a land flowing with milk and honey, when he arrived at Salem, where the ships first touched. As when, twenty years before, Delaware came to Jamestown, the people were on the verge of starvation, and it was necessary to send a vessel back to England for supplies. There were acute suffering and scarcity all along the New England coast, and though the spirit of resignation was there, it seemed likely that there would be soon little flesh left through which to manifest it. The physical conditions were intolerable. The hovels in which the people were living were wretched structures of rough logs, roofed with straw, with wooden chimneys and narrow and darksome interiors. They were patched with bark and rags; many were glad to lodge themselves in tents devised of fragments of drapery hung on a framework of boughs. The settlement was in that transition state between crude wilderness and pioneer town, when the appearance is most repulsive and disheartening. There is no order, uniformity, or intelligent procedure. There is a clump of trees of the primeval forest here, the stumps and litter of a half-made clearing there, yonder a patch of soil newly and clumsily planted; wigwams and huts alternate with one another; men are digging, hewing, running to head back straying cattle, toiling in with fragments of game on their shoulders; yonder a grave is being dug in the root-encumbered ground, and hard by a knot of mourners are preparing the corpse for interment. There is no rest or comfort anywhere for eye or heart. The only approximately decent dwelling in Salem at this time was that of John Endicott. Higginson was dying of a fever. Lady Arbella, who had accompanied her husband, Isaac Johnson, had been ailing on the voyage, and lingered here but a little while before finding a grave. In a few months two hundred persons perished. It was no place for weaklings—or for evil-doers either; among the earliest of the established institutions were the stocks and the whipping-post, and they were not allowed to stand idle.

Winthrop and most of the others soon moved on down the coast toward Boston. It had been the original intention to keep the emigrants in one body, but that was found impracticable; they were forced to divide up into small parties, who settled where they best could, over an area of fifty or a hundred miles. Nantasket, Watertown, Charlestown, Saugus, Lynn, Malden, Roxbury, all had their handfuls of inhabitants. It was exile within exile; for miles meant something in these times. More than a hundred of the emigrants, cowed by the prospect, deserted the cause and returned to England. Yet Winthrop and the other leaders did not lose heart, and their courage and tranquillity strengthened the others. It is evidence of the indomitable spirit of these people that one of their first acts was to observe a day of fasting and prayer; a few days later the members of the congregation met and chose their pastor, John Wilson, and organized the first Church of Boston. They did not wait to build the house of God, but met beneath the trees, or gathered round a rock which might serve the preacher as a pulpit. There was simplicity enough to satisfy the most conscientious. "We here enjoy God and Jesus Christ," wrote Winthrop: "I do not repent my coming: I never had more content of mind."

After a year there were but a thousand settlers in Massachusetts. Among them was Roger Williams, a man so pure and true as of himself to hallow the colony; but it is illustrative of the intolerance which was from the first inseparable from Puritanism, that he was driven away because he held conscience to be the only infallible guide. We cannot blame the Puritans; they had paid a high price for their faith, and they could not but guard it jealously. Their greatest peril seemed to them to be dissension or disagreements on points of belief; except they held together, their whole cause was lost. Williams was no less an exile for conscience' sake than they; but as he persisted in having a conscience strictly his own, instead of pooling it with that of the church, they were constrained to let him go. They did not perceive, then or afterward, that such action argued feeble faith. They could not, after all, quite trust God to take care of His own; they dared not believe that He could reveal Himself to others as well as to them; they feared to admit that they could have less than the whole truth in their keeping. So they banished, whipped, pilloried, and finally even hanged dissenters from their dissent. We, whose religious tolerance is perhaps as excessive as theirs was deficient, are slow to excuse them for this; but they believed they were fighting for much more than their lives; and as for faith in God, it is surely no worse to fall into error regarding it than to dismiss it altogether.

In a community where the integrity of the church was the main subject of concern, it could not be long before religious conservatism would be reflected in the political field. Representative government was conceded in theory; but in practice, Winthrop and others thought that it would be better ignored; the people could not easily meet for deliberations, and how could their affairs be in better hands than those of the saints, who already had charge of them? But the people declined to surrender their liberties; there should be rotation in office; voting should be by ballot instead of show of hands. Taxation was restricted; and in 1635 there was agitation for a written constitution; and the relative authority of the deputies and the assistants was in debate. Our national predisposition to "talk politics" had already been born.

Among these early inconsistencies and disagreements Roger Williams stood out as the sole fearless and logical figure. Consistency and bravery were far from being his only good qualities; in drawing his portrait, the difficulty is to find shadows with which to set off the lights of his character. The Puritans feared the world, and even their own constancy; Williams feared nothing; but he would reverence and obey his conscience as the voice of God in his breast, before which all other voices must be hushed. He was not only in advance of his time: he was abreast of any times; nothing has ever been added to or detracted from his argument. When John Adams wrote to his son, John Quincy Adams, "Your conscience is the Minister Plenipotentiary of God Almighty placed in your breast: see to it that this minister never negotiates in vain," he did but attire in the diplomatic phraseology which came naturally to him the thought which Williams had avouched and lived more than a century before. Though absolutely radical, Williams was never an extremist; he simply went to the fountain-head of reason and truth, and let the living waters flow whither they might. The toleration which he demanded he always gave; of those who had most evilly entreated him he said, "I did ever from my soul honor and love them, even when their judgment led them to afflict me." His long life was one of the most unalloyed triumphs of unaided truth and charity that our history records; and the State which he founded presented, during his lifetime, the nearest approach to the true Utopia which has thus far been produced.

Roger Williams was a Welshman, born in 1600, and dying, in the community which he had created, eighty-five years later. His school was the famous Charterhouse; his University, Cambridge; and he took orders in the Church of England. But the protests of the Puritans came to his ears before he was well installed; and he examined and meditated upon them with all the quiet power of his serene and penetrating mind. It was not long before he saw that truth lay with the dissenting party; and, like Emerson long afterward, he at once left the communion in which he had thought to spend his life. He came to Massachusetts in 1631, and, as we have seen, was not long in discovering that he was more Puritan than the Puritans. When differences arose, he departed to the Plymouth Colony, and there abode for several useful years.

But though the men of Boston and Salem feared him, they loved him and recognized his ability; indeed, they never could rid themselves of an uneasy sense that in all their quarrels it was he who had the best of the argument; they were often reduced to pleading necessity or expediency, when he replied with plain truth. He responded to an invitation to return to Salem, in 1633, by a willing acceptance; but no sooner had he arrived than a discussion began which continued until he was for the second and final time banished in 1636. The main bone of contention was the right of the church to interfere in state matters. He opposed theocracy as profaning the holy peace of the temple with the warring of civil parties. The Massachusetts magistrates were all church members, which Williams declared to be as unreasonable as to make the selection of a pilot or a physician depend upon his proficiency in theology. He would not admit the warrant of magistrates to compel attendance at public worship; it was a violation of natural right, and an incitement to hypocrisy. "But the ship must have a pilot," objected the magistrates. "And he holds her to her course without bringing his crew to prayer in irons," was Williams's rejoinder. "We must protect our people from corruption and punish heresy," said they. "Conscience in the individual can never become public property; and you, as public trustees, can own no spiritual powers," answered he. "May we not restrain the church from apostasy?" they asked. He replied, "No: the common peace and liberty depend upon the removal of the yoke of soul-oppression."

The magistrates were perplexed, and doubtful what to do. Laud in England was menacing them with episcopacy, and they, as a preparation for resistance, decreed that all freemen must take an oath of allegiance to Massachusetts instead of to the King. Williams, of course, abhorred episcopacy as much as they did; but he would not concede the right to impose a compulsory oath. A deputation of ministers was sent to Salem to argue with him: he responded by counseling them to admonish the magistrates of their injustice. He was cited to appear before the state representatives to recant; he appeared, but only to affirm that he was ready to accept banishment or death sooner than be false to his convictions. Sentence of banishment was thereupon passed against him, but he was allowed till the ensuing spring to depart; meanwhile, however, the infection of his opinions spreading in Salem, a warrant was sent to summon him to embark for England; but he, anticipating this step, was already on his way through the winter woods southward.

The pure wine of his doctrine was too potent for the iron-headed Puritans. But it was their fears rather than their hearts that dismissed him; those who best knew him praised him most unreservedly; and even Cotton Mather admitted that he seemed "to have the root of the matter in him."

Williams's journey through the pathless snows and frosts of an exceptionally severe winter is one of the picturesque and impressive episodes of the times. During more than three months he pursued his lonely and perilous way; hollow trees were a welcome shelter; he lacked fire, food and guides. But he had always pleaded in behalf of the Indians; he had on one occasion denied the validity of a royal grant unless it were countersigned by native proprietors; and during his residence in Plymouth he had learned the Indian language. All this now stood him in good stead. The man who was outcast from the society of his white brethren, because his soul was purer and stronger than theirs, was received and ministered unto by the savages; he knew their ways, was familiar in their wigwams, championed their rights, wrestled lovingly with their errors, mediated in their quarrels, and was idolized by them as was no other of his race. Pokanoket, Massasoit and Canonicus were his hosts and guardians during the winter and spring; and in summer he descended the river in a birch-bark canoe to the site of the present city of Providence, so named by him in recognition of the Divine mercies; and there he pitched his tent beside the spring, hoping to make the place "a shelter for persons distressed for conscience."

His desire was amply fulfilled. The chiefs of the Narragansetts deeded him a large tract of land; oppressed persons flocked to him for comfort and succor, and never in vain; a republic grew up based on liberty of conscience, and the civil rule of the majority: the first in the world. Orthodoxy and heresy were on the same footing before him; he trusted truth to conquer error without aid of force. Though he ultimately withdrew from all churches, he founded the first Baptist church in the new world; he twice visited England, and obtained a charter for his colony in 1644. Williams from first to last sat on the Opposition Bench of life; and we say of him that he was hardly used by those who should most have honored him. Yet it is probable that he would have found less opportunity to do good at either an earlier or a later time. Critics so keen and unrelenting as he never find favor with the ruling powers; he would have been at least as "impossible" in the Nineteenth Century as he was in the Seventeenth; and we would have had no Rhode Island to give him. We can derive more benefit from his arraignment of society two hundred and fifty years ago than we should were he to call us to account to-day, because no resentment mingles with our intellectual appreciation: our withers seem to be unwrung. The crucifixions of a former age are always denounced by those who, if the martyr fell into their hands, would be the first to nail him to the cross.

But the Puritanism of Williams, and that of those who banished him, were as two branches proceeding from a single stem; their differences, which were the type of those that created two parties in the community, were the inevitable result of the opposition between the practical and the theoretic temperaments. This opposition is organic; it is irreconcilable, but nevertheless wholesome; both sides possess versions of the same truth, and the perfect state arises from the contribution made by both to the common good—not from their amalgamation, or from a compromise between them. Williams's community was successful, but it was successful, on the lines he laid down, only during its minority; as its population increased, civil order was assured by a tacit abatement of the right of individual independence, and by the insensible subordination of particular to general interests. In Massachusetts, on the other hand, which from the first inclined to the practical view—which recognized the dangers surrounding an organization weak in physical resources, but strong in spiritual conviction, and which, by reason of the radical nature of those convictions, was specially liable to interference from the settled power of orthodoxy:—in Massachusetts there was a diplomatic tendency in the work of building up the commonwealth. The integrity of Williams's logic was conceded, but to follow it out to its legitimate conclusions was deemed inconsistent with the welfare and continuance of the popular institutions. The condemnation of dissenters from dissent sounded unjust; but it was the alternative to the more far-reaching injustice of suffering the structure which had been erected with such pains and sacrifice to fall to pieces just when it was attaining form and character. The time for universal toleration might come later, when the vigor and solidity of the nucleus could no longer be vitiated by fanciful and transient vagaries. The right of private judgment carried no guarantee comparable with that which attached to the sober and tested convictions of the harmonious body of responsible citizens.

When, therefore, the young Henry Vane, coming to Boston with the prestige of aristocratic birth and the reputation of liberal opinions, was elected Governor in 1635, and presently laid down the principle that "Ishmael shall dwell in the presence of his brethren," he at once met with opposition; and he and Anne Hutchinson, and other visionaries and enthusiasts, were made to feel that Boston was no place for them. Yet at the same time there was a conflict between the body of the freemen and the magistrates as to the limits and embodiments of the governing power; the magistrates contended that there were manifest practical advantages in life appointments to office, and in the undisturbed domination of men of approved good life and intellectual ability; the people replied that all that might be true, but they would still insist upon electing and dismissing whom they pleased. Thus was inadvertently demonstrated the invincible security of democratic principles; the masses are always willing to agree that the best shall rule, but insist that they, the multitude, and not any Star Chamber, no matter how impeccable, shall decide who the best are. Herein alone is safety. The masses, of course, are not actuated by motives higher than those of the select few; but their impartiality cannot but be greater, because, assuming that each voter has in view his personal welfare, their ballots must insure the welfare of the majority. And if the welfare of the majority be God's will, then the truth of the old Latin maxim, Vox Populi vox Dei, is vindicated without any recourse to mysticism. The only genuine Aristocracy, or Rule of the Best, must in other words be the creation not of their own will and judgment, but of those of the subjects of their administration.

The political experiments and vicissitudes of these early times are of vastly greater historical importance than are such external episodes, as, for example, the Pequot war in 1637. A whole tribe was exterminated, and thereby, and still more by the heroic action of Williams in preventing, by his personal intercession, an alliance between the Pequots and the Narragansetts, the white colonies were preserved. But beyond this, the affair has no bearing upon the development of the American idea. During these first decades, the most profound questions of national statesmanship were discussed in the assemblies of the Massachusetts Puritans, with an acumen and wisdom which have never been surpassed. The equity and solidity of most of their conclusions are extraordinary; the intellectual ability of the councilors being purged and exalted by their ardent religious faith. The "Body of Liberties," written out in 1641 by Nathaniel Ward, handles the entire subject of popular government in a masterly manner. It was a Counsel of Perfection molded, by understanding of the prevailing conditions, into practical form. The basis of its provisions was the primitive one which is traced back to the time when the Anglo-Saxon tribes met to choose their chiefs or to decide on war or other matters of general concern. It was the basis suggested by nature; for, as the chief historian of these times has remarked, freedom is spontaneous, but the artificial distinctions of rank are the growth of centuries. Lands, according to this instrument, were free and alienable; the freemen of a corporation held them, but claimed no right of distribution. There should be no monopolies: no wife-beating: no slavery "Except voluntary": ministers as well as magistrates should be chosen by popular vote. Authority was given to approved customs; the various towns or settlements constituting the commonwealth were each a living political organism. No combination of churches should control any one church:—such were some of the provisions. The colonies were availing themselves of the unique opportunity afforded by their emancipation, in the wilderness, from the tyranny and obstruction of old-world traditions and licensed abuses.

By the increasing body of their brethren in England, meanwhile, New England was looked upon as a sort of New Jerusalem, and letters from the leaders were passed from hand to hand like messages from saints. Up to the time when Charles and Laud were checked by Parliament, the tide of emigration set so strongly toward the American shores that measures were taken by the King to arrest it; by 1638, there were in New England more than twenty-one thousand colonists. The rise of the power of Parliament stopped the influx; but the succeeding twenty years of peace gave the much-needed chance for quiet and well-considered growth and development. The singular prudence and foresight of Winthrop and others in authority, during this interregnum, was showed by their declining to accept certain apparent advantages proffered them in love and good faith by their English friends. A new patent was offered them in place of their royal charter; but the colonists perceived that the reign of Parliament was destined to be temporary, and wisely refused. Other suggestions, likely to lead to future entanglements, were rejected; among them, a proposition from Cromwell that they should all come over and occupy Ireland. This is as curious as that other alleged incident of Cromwell and Hampden having been stopped by Laud when they had embarked for New England, and being forced to remain in the country which soon after owed to them its freedom from kingly and episcopal tyranny.

Material prosperity began to show itself in the new country, now that the first metaphysical problems were in the way of settlement. In Salem they were building ships, cotton was manufactured in Boston; the export trade in furs and other commodities was brisk and profitable. The English Parliament passed a law exempting them from taxes. After so much adversity, fortune was sending them a gleam of sunshine, and they were making their hay. But something of the arrogance of prosperity must also be accredited to them; the Puritans were never more bigoted and intolerant than now. The persecution of the Quakers is a blot on their fame, only surpassed by the witchcraft cruelties of the concluding years of the century. Mary Dyar, and the men Robinson, Stephenson and Leddra were executed for no greater crime than obtruding their unwelcome opinions, and outraging the propriety of the community. The fate of Christison hung for a while in the balance; he was not less guilty than the others, and he defied his judges; he told them that where they murdered one, ten others would arise in his place; the same words that had been heard many a time in England, when the Puritans themselves were on their trial. Nevertheless the judges passed the sentence of death; but the people were disturbed by such bloody proceedings, and Christison was finally set free. It must not be forgotten that the Quakers of this period were very different from those who afterward populated the City of Brotherly Love under Penn. They were fanatics of the most extravagant and incorrigible sort; loudmouthed, frantic and disorderly; and instead of observing modesty in their garb, their women not seldom ran naked through the streets of horrified Boston, in broad daylight. They thirsted for persecution as ordinary persons do for wealth or fame, and would not be satisfied till they had provoked punishment. The granite wall of Puritanism seemed to exist especially for them to dash themselves against it. Such persons can hardly be deemed sane; and it is of not the slightest importance what particular creed they profess. They are opposed to authority and order because they are authority and order; in our day, we group such folk under the name, Anarchists; but, instead of hanging them as the Puritans did, we let them froth and threaten, according to the policy of Roger Williams, until the lack of echoes leads them to hold their peace.

Although slavery, or perpetual servitude, was forbidden by the statute, there were many slaves in New England, Indians and whites as well as negroes. The first importation of the latter was in 1619, by the Dutch, it is said. No slave could be kept in bondage more than ten years; it was stipulated that they were to be brought from Africa, or elsewhere, only with their own consent; and when, in 1638, it appeared that a cargo of them had been forcibly introduced, they were sent back to Africa. Prisoners of war were condemned to servitude; and, altogether, the feeling on the subject of human bondage appears to have been both less and more fastidious than it afterward became. There was no such indifference as was shown in the Southern slave trade two centuries later, nor was there any of the humanitarian fanaticism exhibited by the extreme Abolitionists of the years before the Civil War. It may turn out that the attitude of the Puritans had more common-sense in it than had either of the others.

The great event of 1643 was the natural outcome of the growth and expansion of the previous time. It was the federation of the four colonies of Massachusetts, Plymouth,

New Haven, and Connecticut. Connecticut had been settled in 1630, but it was not till six years afterward that a party headed by the renowned Thomas Hooker, the "Son of Thunder," and one of the most judicious men of that age, journeyed from Boston with the deliberate purpose of creating another commonwealth in the desert. Connecticut did not offer assurances of a peaceful settlement; the Indians were numerous there, and not well-disposed; and in the south, the Dutch of New Amsterdam were complaining of an infringement of boundaries. These ominous conditions came to a head in the Pequot war; after which peace reigned for many years. A constitution of the most liberal kind was created by the settlers, some of the articles of which led to a correspondence between Hooker and Winthrop as to the comparative merits of magisterial and popular governments. Unlearned men, however religious, if elected to office, must needs call in the assistance of the learned ministers, who, thus burdened with matters not rightly within their function, might err in counseling thereon. Of the people, the best part was always the least, and of that best, the wiser is the lesser.—This was Winthrop's position. Hooker replied that to allow discretion to the judge was the way to tyranny. Seek the law at its mouth; it is free from passion, and should rule the rulers themselves; let the judge do according to the sentence of the law. In high matters, business should be done by a general council, chosen by all, as was the practice of the Jewish and other well-ordered states. —This is an example of the political discussions of that day in New England; both parties to it concerned solely to come at the truth, and free from any selfish aim or pride. The soundness of Hooker's view may be deduced from the fact that the constitution of Connecticut (which differed in no essential respect from those of the other colonies) has survived almost unchanged to the present day. Statesmanship, during two and a half centuries, has multiplied details and improved the nicety of adjustments; but it has not discerned any principles which had not been seen with perfect distinctness by the clear and venerable eyes of the Puritan fathers.

Eaton, another man of similar caliber, was the leading spirit in the New Haven settlement, assisted by the Reverend Mr. Davenport; many of the colonists were Second-Adventists, and they called the Bible their Statute-Book. The date of their establishment was 1638. The incoherent population of Rhode Island caused it to be excluded from the federation; but Williams, journeying to London, obtained a patent from the exiled but now powerful Vane, and took as the motto of his government, "Amor Vincet Omnia." New Hampshire, which had been united to Massachusetts in 1641, could have no separate part in the new arrangement; and Maine, an indeterminate region, sparsely inhabited by people who had come to seek not God, but fish in the western world, was not considered. The articles of federation of the four Calvinist colonies aimed to provide mutual protection against the Indians, against possible encroachment from England, against Dutch and French colonists: they declared a league not only for defense and offense, but for the promotion of spiritual truth and liberty. Nothing was altered in the constitutions of any of the contracting parties; and an equitable system of apportioning expenses was devised. Each partner sent two delegates to the common council; all affairs proper to the federation were determined by a three-fourths vote; a law for the delivery of fugitive slaves was agreed to; and the commissioners of the other jurisdictions were empowered to coerce any member of the federation which should break this contract. The title of The United Colonies of New England was bestowed upon the alliance. The articles were the work of a committee of the leading men in the country, such as Winthrop, Winslow, Haynes and Eaton; and the confederacy lasted forty years, being dissolved in 1684.

It was a great result from an experiment begun only

about a dozen years before. It was greater even than its outward seeming, for it contained within itself the forces which should control the future. This country is made up of many elements, and has been molded to no small extent by circumstances hardly to be foreseen; but it seems incontestable that it would never have endured, and continued to be the goal of all pilgrims who wish to escape from a restricted to a freer life, had not its corner-stone been laid, and its outline fixed, by these first colonists of New England. It has been calculated that in two hundred years the physical increase of each Puritan family was one thousand persons, dispersed over the territory of the United States; and the moral influence which this posterity exerted on the various communities in which they fixed their abode is beyond computation. But had the Puritan fathers been as ordinary men: had they come hither for ends of gain and aggrandizement: had they not been united by the most inviolable ties that can bind men—community in religious faith, brotherhood in persecution for conscience' sake, and an intense, inflexible enthusiasm for liberty—their descendants would have had no spiritual inheritance to disseminate. Many superficial changes have come upon our society; there is an absence of a fixed national type; there are many thousands of illiterate persons among us, and of those who are still ignorant of the true nature of democratic institutions; all the tongues of Europe and of other parts of the world may be heard within our boundaries; there are great bodies of our citizens who selfishly pursue ends of private enrichment and power, indifferent to the patent fact that multitudes of their fellows are thereby obstructed in the effort to earn a livelihood in this most productive country in the world; there are many who have prostituted the name of statesmanship to the gratification of petty and transient ambitions: and many more who, relieved by the thrift of their ancestors from the necessity to win their bread, have renounced all concern in the welfare of the state, and live trivial and empty lives: all this, and more, may be conceded. But such evil humors, be it repeated, are superficial, attesting the vigor, rather than the decay, of the central vitality. America still stands for an idea; there is in it an immortal soul. It was by the Puritans of Massachusetts Bay that this soul was implanted; to inspire it was their work. They experienced the realities, they touched the core of things, as few men have ever done; for they were born in an age when the world was awakening from the spiritual slumber of more than fifteen hundred years, and upon its bewildered eyes was breaking the splendor of a great new light. The Puritans were the immediate heirs of the Reformation (so called; it might more truly have been named the New Incarnation, since the outward modifications of visible form were but the symptoms of a freshly-communicated informing intelligence). It transfigured them; from men sunk in the gross and sensual thoughts and aims of an irreligious and priest-ridden age—an age which ate and drank and slept and fought, and kissed the feet of popes, and maundered of the divine right of kings—from this sluggish degradation it roused and transfigured the Englishmen who came to be known as Puritans. It was a transfiguration, though its subjects were the uncouth, almost grotesque figures which chronicle and tradition have made familiar to us. For a people who were what the Puritans were before Puritanism, cannot be changed by the Holy Ghost into angels of light; their stubborn carnality will not evaporate like a mist; it clings to them, and being now so discordant with the impulse within, an awkwardness and uncouthness result, which suggest some strange hybrid: to the eye and ear, they are unlovelier and harsher than they were before their illumination; but Providence regards not looks; it knew what it was about when it chose these men of bone and sinew to carry out its purposes. Once enlisted, they never could be quelled, or seduced, or deceived, or wearied; they were in fatal earnest, and faithful unto death, for they believed that

God was their Captain. They had got a soul; they put it into their work, and it is in that work even to this day.

It does not manifestly appear to our contemporary vision; it is overloaded with the rubbish of things, as a Greek statue is covered with the careless debris of ages; but, as the art of the sculptor is vindicated when the debris has been removed, so will the fair proportions of the State conceived by the Puritans, and nourished and defended by their sons, declare themselves when in the maturity of our growth we have assimilated what is good in our accretions, and disencumbered ourselves of what is vain. It is the American principle, and it will not down; it is a solvent of all foreign substances; in its own way and time it dissipates all things that are not harmonious with itself. No lesser or feebler principle would have survived the tests to which this has been subjected; but this is indestructible; even we could not destroy it if we would, for it is no inalienable possession of our own, but a gift from on High to the whole of mankind. But let us piously and proudly remember that it was through the Puritans that the gift was made. Other nations than the English have contributed to our substance and prosperity, and have yielded their best blood to flow in our veins. They are dear to us as ourselves, as how should they not be, since what, other than ourselves, are they? None the less is it true that what was worthiest and most unselfish in the impulse that drove them hither was a reflection of the same impulse that actuated the Puritans when America was not the most powerful of republics, but a wilderness. None of us all can escape from their greatness—from the debt we owe them: not because they were Englishmen, not because they made New England; but because they were men, inspired of God to make the earth free that was in bondage.

CHAPTER FOURTH

FROM HUDSON TO STUYVESANT

THERE are two scenes in the career of Henry Hudson which can never be forgotten by Americans. One is in the first week in September, 1609. A little vessel, of eighty tons, is lying on the smooth waters of a large harbor. She has the mounded stern and bluff bows of the ships of that day; one of her masts has evidently been lately stepped; the North American pine of which it is made shows the marks of the ship-carpenter's ax, and the whiteness of the fresh wood. The square sails have been rent, and mended with seams and patches; the sides and bulwarks of the vessel have been buffeted by heavy seas off the Newfoundland coast; the paint and varnish which shone on them as she dropped down the reaches of the Zuyder Zee from Amsterdam, five months ago, have become whitened with salt and dulled by fog and sun and driving spray. Across her stern, above the rudder of massive oaken plank clamped with iron, is painted the name "HALF MOON," in straggling letters. On her poop stands Henry Hudson, leaning against the tiller; beside him is a young man, his son; along the bulwark lounge the crew, half Englishmen, half Dutch; broad-beamed, salted tars, with pigtails and rugged visages, who are at home in Arctic icefields and in Equatorial suns, and who now stare out toward the low shores to the north and west, and converse among themselves in the nameless jargon—

the rude compromise between guttural Dutch and husky English—which has served them as a medium of communication during the long voyage. It is a good harbor, they think, and a likely country. They are impatient for the skipper to let them go ashore, and find out what grows in the woods.

Meanwhile the great navigator, supporting himself, with folded arms, against the creaking tiller, absorbs the scene through his deep-set eyes in silence. Many a haven had he visited in his time; he had been within ten degrees of the North Pole; he had seen the cliffs of Spitzbergen loom through the fog, and had heard the sound of Greenland glaciers breaking into vast icebergs where they overhung the sea; he had lain in the thronged ports of the Netherlands, where the masts cluster like naked forests, and the commerce of the world seethes and murmurs continually; he had dropped anchor in quiet English harbors, under cool gray skies, with undulating English hills in the distance, and prosperous wharfs and busy streets in front. He had sweltered, no doubt, beneath the heights of Hong-Kong, amid a city of swarming junks; and further south had smelled the breeze that blows through the straits of the Spice Islands. He knew the surface of the earth, as a farmer knows his farm; but never, he thought, had he beheld a softer and more inviting prospect than this which spread before him now, mellowed by the haze of the mild September morning.

On all sides the shores were wooded to the water's edge: a giant forest, unbroken, dense and tall, flourishing from its own immemorial decay, matted with wild grape vine, choked with brush, wild as when the Creator made it; untouched, since then. It was as remote—as lost to mankind—as it was beautiful. The hum and turmoil of the civilized world was like the memory of a dream in this tranquil region, where untrammeled nature had worked her teeming will for centuries upon silent centuries. Here were such peace and stillness that the cry of the blue jay seemed audacious; the dive of a gull into the smooth water was a startling event. To the imaginative mind of Hudson this spot seemed to have been set apart by Providence, hidden away behind the sandy reaches of the outer coast, so that irreverent man, who turns all things to gain, might never discover and profane its august solitudes. Here the search for wealth was never to penetrate; the only gold was in the tender sunshine, and in the foliage of here and there a giant tree, which the distant approach of winter was lulling into golden slumber. But then, with a sigh, he reflected that all the earth was man's, and the fullness thereof; and that here too, perhaps, would one day appear clearings in the primeval forest, and other vessels would ride at anchor, and huts would peep out from beneath the overshadowing foliage on the shores. But it was hard to conjure up such a picture; it was difficult to imagine so untamed a wilderness subdued, in ever so small a degree, by the hand of industry and commerce.

Northwestward, across the green miles of whispering leaves, the land appeared to rise in long, level bluffs, still thronged with serried trees; a great arm of the sea, a mile or two in breadth, extended east of north, and thither, the mariner dreamed, might lie the long-sought pathway to the Indies. A tongue of land, broadening as it receded, and swelling in low undulations, divided this wide strait from a narrower one more to the east. All was forest; and eastward still was more forest, stretching seaward. Southward, the land was low—almost as low and flat as the Netherlands themselves; an unexplored immensity, whose fertile soil had for countless ages been hidden from the sun by the impervious shelter of interlacing boughs. No—never had Hudson seen a land of such enduring charm and measureless promise as this: and here, in this citadel of loneliness, which no white man's foot had ever trod, which, till then, only the eyes of the corsair Verrazano had seen, near a century before—here was to arise, like Aladdin's Palace, the metropolis of the western world; enormous, roaring, hurrying, trafficking, grasping, swarming with its millions upon millions of striving, sleepless, dauntless, exulting, despairing, aspiring human souls; the home of unbridled luxury, of abysmal poverty, of gigantic industries, of insolent idleness, of genius, of learning, of happiness and of misery; of far-reaching enterprise, of political glory and shame, of science and art; here human life was to reach its intensest, most breathless, relentless and insatiable expression; here was to stand a city whose arms should reach westward over a continent, and eastward round the world; here were to thunder the streets and tower the buildings and reek the chimneys and arch the bridges and rumble the railways and throb the electric wires of American New York, the supreme product of Nineteenth Century civilization, radiant with the virtues and grimy with the failings that mankind has up to this time developed.

On the 23d of June, two years later, Henry Hudson was the central figure in another scene. He sat in a small, open boat, hoary with frozen spray; he was muffled in the shaggy hide of a white bear, roughly fashioned into a coat; a sailor's oilskin hat was drawn down over his brow, and beneath its rim his eyes gazed sternly out over a wide turbulence of gray waters, tossing with masses of broken ice. His dark beard was grizzled with frost; his cheeks were gaunt with the privations of a long, arctic winter spent amid endless snows, in darkness unrelieved, smitten by storms, struggling with savage beasts and harried by more inhuman men. He sat with his hand at the helm; against his other shoulder leaned his son, his inseparable companion, now sinking into unconsciousness; the six rowers—the stanch comrades who, with him, had been thrust forth to perish by the mutineers—plied their work heavily and hopelessly; their rigid jaws were set; no words nor complaints broke from them, though death was slowly settling round their valiant hearts. Overhead brooded a somber vault of clouds; the circle of the horizon, which seemed to creep in upon them, was one unbroken sweep of icy dreariness, save where, to the southeast, the dark hull of the "Discovery," and her pallid sails, rocked and leaned across the sullen heave of the waters. She was bound for Europe; but whither is Hudson bound?

His end befitted his life; he vanished into the unknown, as he had come from it. There is no record of the time or place of his birth, or of his early career, nor can any tell where lie his bones; we only know that his limbs were made in England, and that the great inland sea, called after him, ebbs and flows above his grave. He first comes into the ken of history, sailing on the seas, resolute to discover virgin straits and shores; and when we see him last, he is still toiling onward over the waves, peering into the great mystery. Possibly, as has been suggested, he may have been the descendant of the Hudson who was one of the founders of the Muscovy Company, in whose service the famous navigator afterward voyaged on various errands. It matters not; he lived, and did his work, and is no more; his strong heart burned within him; he saw what none had seen; he triumphed, and he was overcome. But the doubt that shrouds his end has given him to legend, and the thunder that rolls brokenly among the dark crags and ravines of the Catskills brings his name to the hearer's lips.

The Dutch had had many opportunities offered to them to discover New York, before they accepted the services of Henry Hudson, who was willing to go out of his own country to find backers, so only that he might be afloat. Almost every year, from 1581 onward, the mariners of the Netherlands strove, by east and by west, to pass the barrier that America interposed between them and the Eastern trade they coveted. The Dutch East India Company was the first trading corporation of Europe; and after the war with Spain, during the twelve years' truce, the little country was overflowing with men eager to undertake any enterprise, and with money to fit them out. The Netherlands suddenly bloomed out the most prosperous country in the world.

They would not be hurried; they took their time to think it over, as Dutchmen will; but at length they conceived an immense project for acquiring all the trade, or the best part of it, of both the West and the East. They studied the subject with the patient particularity of their race; they outclassed Spain on the seas, and they believed they could starve out her commerce. Some there were, however, who feared that in finding new countries they would lose their own; Europe was again in a turmoil, and they were again fighting Spain before New Amsterdam was founded. But meanwhile, in 1609, quite inadvertently, Henry Hudson discovered it for them at a moment when they supposed him to be battling with freezing billows somewhere north of Siberia. When he was stopped by Nova Zembla ice, he put about and crossed the Atlantic to Nova Scotia, and so down the coast, as we have seen, to the Chesapeake, the Delaware, and finally the Hudson. He told his tale in glowing words when he got back; but the Dutch merchants perhaps fancied he was spinning sailors' yarns, and heeded not his report till long after.

Hudson, after passing the Narrows, anchored near the Jersey shore, and received a visit from some Indians with native commodities to exchange for knives and beads. They presented the usual Indian aspect as regarded dress and arms; but they wore ornaments of red copper under their feather mantles, and carried pipes of copper and clay. They were affable, but untrustworthy, stealing what they could lay their hands on, and a few days later shooting arrows at a boatload of seamen from the ship, and killing one John Colman. Hudson went ashore, and was honored with dances and chants; upon the whole, the impression mutually created seems to have been favorable. An abundance of beans and

SCENE IN NEW AMSTERDAM, 1660

oysters was supplied to the crew; and no doubt trade was carried on to the latter's advantage; we know that years afterward the whole of Manhattan Island was purchased of its owners for four-and-twenty dollars. The present inhabitants of New York City could not be so easily overreached.

Hudson now began the first trip ever made by white men up the great river. How many millions have made it since! But he, at this gentlest time of year, won with the magic not only of what he saw, but of the unknown that lay before him—what must have been his sensations! As reach after reach of the incomparable panorama spread itself out quietly before him, with its beauty of color, its majesty of form, its broad gleam of placid current, the sheer lift of its brown cliffs, its mighty headlands setting their titanic shoulders across his path, its toppling pinnacles assuming the likeness of giant visages, its swampy meadows and inlets, lovely with flowers and waving with rushes, its royal eagles stemming the pure air aloft, its fish leaping in the ripples—and then, as he sailed on, mute with enchantment, the blue magnificence of the mountains soaring heavenward and melting into the clouds that hung about their summits—as all this multifarious beauty unfolded itself, Hudson may well have thought that the lost Eden of the earth was found at last. And ere long, he dreamed, the vast walls through which the river moved would diverge and cease, like another Pillars of Hercules, and his ship would emerge into another ocean. It was verily a voyage to be remembered; and perhaps it returned in a vision to his dimming eyes, that day he steered his open boat through the arctic surges of Hudson's Bay.

For ten days or more he pressed onward before a southerly breeze, until, in the neighborhood of what now is Albany, it became evident that the Pacific was not to be found in northern New York. He turned, therefore, and drifted slowly downward with the steady current, while the matchless hues of the American autumn glowed every day more sumptuously from the far-billowing woods. What sunrises and what sunsets dyed the waters with liquid splendor: what moons, let us hope, turned the glories of day into the spiritual mysteries of fairyland! Hudson was not born for repose; his fate was to sail unrestingly till he died; but as he passed down through this serene carnival of opulent nature, he may well have wished that here, after all voyages were done, his lot might finally be cast; he may well have wondered whether any race would be born so great and noble as to merit the gift of such a river and such a land.

He landed at various places on the way, and was always civilly and hospitably welcomed by the red men, who brought him their wild abundance, and took in return what he chose to give. The marvelous richness of the vegetation, and the vegetable decay of ages, had rendered the margins of the stream as deadly as they were lovely; fever lurked in every glade and bower, and serpents whose bite was death basked in the sun or crept among the rocks. All was as it had always been; the red men, living in the midst of nature, were a part of nature themselves; nothing was changed by their presence; they altered not the flutter of a leaf or the posture of a stone, but stole in and out noiseless and lithe, and left behind them no trace of their passage. It is not so with the white man: before him, nature flies and perishes; he clothes the earth in the thoughts of his own mind, cast in forms of matter, and contemplates them with pride; but when he dies, another comes, and refashions the materials to suit himself. So one follows another, and nothing endures that man has made; for this is his destiny. And at length, when the last man has dressed out his dolls and built his little edifice of stones and sticks, and is gone: nature, who was not dead, but sleeping, awakes, and resumes her ancient throne, and her eternal works declare themselves once more; and she dissolves the bones in the grave, and the grave itself vanishes, with its record of what man had been. What says our poet?—

> "How am I theirs,
>   When they hold not me,
>   But I hold them?"

In 1613, or thereabout, Christianson and Block visited the harbor and got furs, and also a couple of Indian boys to show the burghers of Amsterdam, since they could not fetch the great river to Holland. In 1614 they went again with five ships—the "Fortune of Amsterdam," the "Fortune of Hoorn," and the "Tiger of Amsterdam" (which was burned), and two others. Block built himself a boat of sixteen tons, and explored the Sound, and the New England coast as far as Massachusetts Bay; touched at the island known by his name, and forgathered with the Indian tribes all along his route. The explorers were granted a charter in the same year, giving them a three years' monopoly of the trade, and in this charter the title New Netherland is bestowed upon the region. The Dutch were at last bestirring themselves. Two years after, Schouten of Hoorn saw the southernmost point of Tierra del Fuego, and gave it the name of his home port as he swept by; and three other Netherlanders penetrated to the wilds of Philadelphia that was to be. A fortified trading post was built at Albany, where now legislation instead of peltries is the subject of barter. At this juncture internal quarrels in the Dutch government led to tragic events, which stimulated plans of western colonization, and the desire to start a commonwealth on Hudson River to forestall the English—for the latter as well as the Dutch and Spanish claimed everything in sight. The Dutch East India Company began business in 1621 with a twenty-four year charter, renewable. It was given power to create an independent nation; the world was invited to buy its stock, and the States-General invested a million guilders in it. Its field was the entire west coast of Africa, and the east coast of North and South America. Such schemes are of planetary magnificence; but of all this realm, the Dutch now hold the little garden patch of Dutch Guiana only, and the pleasant records of their sojourn on Manhattan Island between the years 1623 and 1664.

Indeed, the Dutch episode in our history is in all respects refreshing and agreeable; the burghers set us an example of thrift and steadiness too good for us to follow it; and they deeded to us some of our best citizens, and most engaging architectural traditions. But it is not after all for these and other material benefits that we are indebted to them; we thank them still more for being what they were (and could not help being): for their character, their temperament, their costume, their habits, their breadth of beam, their length of pipes, the deliberation of their courtships, the hardness of their bargains, the portentousness of their tea-parties, the industrious decorum of their women, the dignity of their patroons, the strictness of their social conduct, the soundness of their education, the stoutness of their independence, the excellence of their good sense, the simplicity of their prudence, and above all, for the wooden leg of Peter Stuyvesant. In a word, the humorous perception of the American people has made a pet of the Dutch tradition in New York and Pennsylvania; as, likewise, of the childlike comicalities of the plantation negro; the arch waggishness of the Irish emigrants, and the cherubic shrewdness of the newly-acquired German. The Dutch gained much, on the sentimental score, by transplantation; their old-world flavor and rich coloring are admirably relieved against the background of unbaked wilderness. We could not like them so much or laugh at them at all, did we not so thoroughly respect them; the men of New Amsterdam were worthy of their national history, which recounts as stirring a struggle as was ever made by the love of liberty against the foul lust of oppression. The Dutch are not funny anywhere but in Seventeenth Century Manhattan; nor can this singularity be explained by saying that Washington Irving made them so. It inheres in the situation; and the delightful chronicles of Diedrich Knickerbocker owe half their enduring fascination to their sterling veracity—the veracity which is faithful to the spirit and gambols only with the letter. The humor of that work lies in its sympathetic and creative insight quite as much as in the broad good-humor and imaginative whimsicality with which the author handles his theme. The caricature of a true artist gives a better likeness than any photograph.

The first ship containing families of colonists went out early in 1623, under the command of Cornelis May; he broke ground on Manhattan, while Joris built Fort Orange at Albany, and a little group of settlers squatted round it. May acted as director for the first year or two; the trade in furs was prosecuted, and the first Dutch-American baby was born at Fort Orange.

Fortune was kind. King Charles, instead of discussing prior rights, offered an alliance; at home, the bickerings of sects were healed. Peter Minuit came out as director-general and paid his twenty-four dollars for the Island—a little less than a thousand acres for a dollar. At all events, the Indians seemed satisfied from Albany to the Narrows. The Battery was designed, and there was quite a cluster of houses on the clearing back of it. An atmosphere of Dutch homeliness began to temper the thin American air. The honest citizens were pious, and had texts read to them on Sundays; but they did not torture their consciences with spiritual self-questionings like the English Puritans, nor dream of disciplining or banishing any of their number for the better heavenly security of the rest. The souls of these Netherlanders fitted their bodies far better than was the case with the colonists of Boston and Salem. Instead of starving and rending them, their religion made them happy and comfortable. Instead of settling the ultimate principles of theology and government, they enjoyed the consciousness of mutual good-will, and took things as they came. The new world needed men of both kinds. It must, however, be admitted that the people of New Amsterdam were not wholly harmonious with those of Plymouth. Minuit and Bradford had some correspondence, in which, while professions of mutual esteem and love were exchanged, uneasy things were let fall about clear titles and prior rights. Minuit was resolute for his side, and the attitude of Bradford prompted him to send for a company of soldiers from home. But there was probably no serious anticipation of coming to blows on either part. There was space enough in the continent for the two hundred and seventy inhabitants of New Amsterdam and for the Pilgrim Fathers, for the present.

Spain was an unwilling contributor to the prosperity of the Dutch colonists, by the large profits which the latter gained from the capture of Spanish galleons; but in 1629 the charter creating the order of Patroons laid the foundation for abuses and discontent which afflicted the settlers for full thirty years. Upon the face of it, the charter was liberal, and promised good results; but it made the mistake of not securing popular liberties. The Netherlands were no doubt a free country, as freedom was at that day understood in Europe; but this freedom did not involve independence for the individual. The only recognized individuality was that of the municipalities, the rulers of which were not chosen by popular franchise. This system answered well enough in the old home, but proved unsuited to the conditions of settlers in the wilderness. The American spirit seemed to lurk like some subtle contagion in the remotest recesses of the forest, and those who went to live there became affected with it. It was longer in successfully vindicating itself than in New England, because it was not stimulated on the banks of the Hudson by the New England religious fervor: it was supported on grounds of practical expediency merely. Men could not prosper unless they received the rewards of industry, and were permitted to order their private affairs in a manner to make their labor pay. They were not content to have the Patroon devour their profits, leaving them enough only for a bare subsistence. The Dutch families scattered throughout the domain could not get ahead, while yet they could not help feeling that the bounty of nature ought to benefit those whose toil made it available, at least as much as it did those who toiled not, but simply owned the land in virtue of some documentary transaction with the powers above, and therefore claimed ownership also over the poor emigrant who settled on it—having nowhere else to go. The emigrants were probably helped to comprehend and formulate their own misfortunes by communications with stragglers from New England, who regaled them with tales of such liberties as they had never before imagined. But the seed thus sown by the Englishmen fell on fruitful soil, and the crop was reaped in due season.

The charter intended, primarily, the encouragement of emigration, and did not realize that it needed very little encouragement. The advantages offered were more alluring than they need have been. Any person who, within four years, could establish a colony of fifty persons, was given privileges only comparable to those of independent princes. They were allowed to take up tracts of land many square miles in area, to govern them absolutely (according to the laws of the realm), to found and administer cities, and in a word to drink from Baucis's pitcher to their hearts' content. In return, the home administration expected the benefit of their trade. Two stipulations only restrained them: they were to buy titles to their land from the Indians, and they were to permit, on penalty of removal, no cotton or woolen manufactures in the country. That was a monopoly which was reserved to the weavers in the old country.

This was excellent for such as could afford to become patroons; but what about the others? The charter provided that any emigrant who could pay for his exportation might take up what land he required for his needs, and cultivate it independently. Other emigrants, unable to pay their fare out, might have it paid for them, but in that case, of course, incurred a mortgage to their benefactors. In effect, they could not own the product of the work of their hands, until it had paid their sponsors for their outlay, together with such additions in the way of interest on capital as might seem to the sponsors equitable.

The Company further undertook to supply slaves to the colony, should they prove to be a paying investment; and it was chiefly because the climate of New York was less favorable to the Guinea Coast negro than was that further south, that African slavery did not take early and firm root in the former region. Philosophers have long recognized the influence of degrees of latitude upon human morality. The patroon planters could dispense with black slaves, since they had white men enough who cost them no more than their keep, and would, presumably, not involve the expense of overseers. Everything, therefore, seemed harmonious and sunshiny, and the Company congratulated itself.

But the patroons, through their agents, began buying up all the land that was worth having, and found it easy to evade the stipulation restricting them to sixteen miles apiece. One of them had an estate running twenty-four miles on either bank of the Hudson, below Albany (or Fort Orange as it was then), and forty-eight miles inland. It was superb; but it was as far as possible from being democracy; and the portly Van Rensselaer of Rensselaerwyck would have shuddered to his marrow, could he have cast a prophetic eye into the Nineteenth Century.

The Company at home presently discovered that its incautious liberality had injured its own interests, as well as those of poor settlers; for the estates of the patroons covered the trading posts where the Indians came to traffic, and all the profits from the latter swelled the pockets of the patroons. But the charter could not be withdrawn; the directors must be content with whatever sympathetic benefits might be conferred by the increasing wealth of the colony. The patroons were becoming more powerful than their creators, and took things more and more into their own lordly hands. Neither patroons nor Company concerned themselves about the people. The charter had, indeed, mentioned the subjects of schools and religious instructors for the emigrants, but had made no provision for the maintenance of such; and the patroons conceived that such luxuries were deserving of but the slightest encouragement. The more a poor man knows, the less contented is he. Such was the argument then, and it is occasionally heard to-day, when our trusts and corporations are annoyed by the complaints and disaffections of their only half ignorant employés.

Governor Minuit was not held to be the best man in the world for his position, and he was recalled in 1632, and Wouter Van Twiller, who possessed all of his predecessor's faults and none of his virtues, took his place. A governor with the American idea in him would have saved Manhattan a great deal of trouble, and perhaps have enabled the Dutch to keep their hold upon it; but no such governor was available, and worse than Van Twiller was yet to come. A colony had already been planted in Delaware, but unjust dealings with the Indians led to a massacre which left nothing of the Cape Henlopen settlement but bones and charred timbers. The English to the south were led to renew the assertion of their never-abandoned claim to the region; there were encroachments by the English settlers on the Connecticut boundary, and the Dutch, deprived by the wars in Europe of the support of their countrymen at home, were too feeble to do more than protest. But protests from those unable to enforce them have never been listened to with favor—not even by the English. Besides, the Dutch, though amenable to religious observances, were far from making them the soul and end of all thought and action; and this lack of aggressive religious fiber put them at a decided political disadvantage with their rivals. Man for man, they were the equals of the English, or of any other people; as they magnificently demonstrated, forty years afterward, by defeating allied and evil-minded Europe in its attempt to expunge them as a nation. But the indomitable spirit of Van Tromp and De Ruyter was never awakened in the New Netherlands; commercial considerations were paramount; and though the Dutch settlers remained, and were always welcome, the colony finally passed from the jurisdiction of their own government, with their own expressed consent.

Van Twiller vanished after eight years' mismanagement, and the sanguinary Kieft took the reins. But before his incumbency, Sweden, at the instance of Gustavus Adolphus, and by the agency of his chancellor Oxenstiern, both men of the first class, lodged a colony on Delaware Bay, which subsisted for seventeen years, and was absorbed, at last, without one stain upon its fair record. Minuit, being out of a job, offered his experienced services in bringing the emigrating Swedes and Finns to their new abode, and they began their sojourn in 1638. They were industrious, peaceable, religious and moral, and they declared against any form of slavery. They threw out a branch toward Philadelphia. But Gustavus Adolphus had died at Luetzen before the Swedes came over, and Queen Christina had not the ability to carry out his ideas, even had she possessed the power. The Dutch began to dispute the rights of the Scandinavians; Rysingh took their fort Casimir in 1654, and Peter Stuyvesant with six hundred men received their submission in the same year. But this success was of no benefit to the Dutch; the tyrannous monopolies which the Company tried to establish in Delaware, instead of creating revenues, caused the country to be deserted by the settlers, who betook themselves to the less oppressive English administrations to the southward; and it was not until the English took possession of both Delaware and the rest of the New Netherlands that it began to yield a fair return on the investment.

But we must return to the ill-omened Kieft. It was

upon the Indian question that he made shipwreck, not only incurring their deadly enmity, but alienating from himself the sympathies and support of his own countrymen. The Algonquin tribe, which inhabited the surrounding country, had been constantly overreached in their trade with the Dutchmen; the principle upon which barter was carried on with the untutored savage being, "I'll take the turkey, and you keep the buzzard: or you take the buzzard, and I'll keep the turkey." This sounded fair; but when the Indian came to examine his assets, it always appeared that a buzzard was all he could make of it. Partly, perhaps, by way of softening the asperities of such a discovery, the Dutch merchant had been wont to furnish his victim with brandy (not eleemosynary, of course); but the results were disastrous. The Indians, transported by the alcohol beyond the anything-but-restricted bounds which nature had imposed upon them, felt the insult of the buzzard more keenly than ever, and signified their resentment in ways consistent with their instincts and traditions. In 1640 an army of them fell upon the colony in Staten Island, and slaughtered them, man, woman and child, with the familiar Indian accessories of tomahawk, scalping-knife and torch. The Staten Islanders, it should be stated, had done nothing to merit this treatment; but Indian logic interprets the legal maxim "Qui facit per alium, facit per se," as meaning that if one white man cheats him, he can get his satisfaction out of the next one who happens in sight. Staten Island was a definite and convenient area, and when its population had been exterminated, the Indians could feel relieved from their obligation. Not long afterward an incident such as romancers love to feign actually took place; an Indian brave who, as a child years before, had seen his uncle robbed and slain, and had vowed revenge, now having become of age, or otherwise qualified himself for the enterprise, went upon the warpath, and returned with the long-coveted scalp at his girdle. Evidently the time had come for Governor Kieft to assert himself.

It was of small avail to invade the wilds of New Jersey, or to offer rewards for Raritans, dead or alive. The sachems were willing to express their regret, but they would not surrender the culprits, and declared that the Dutchmen's own brandy was the really guilty party. Kieft would not concede the point, and the situation was strained. At this juncture, the unexpected happened. The Mohawks, a kingly tribe of red men, who claimed all Northeast America from the St. Lawrence to the Delaware, and who had already driven the Algonquins before them like chaff, sent down a war party from northern New York, and demanded tribute from them. There were more Algonquins than there were Mohawks; but one eagle counts for more than many kites. The kites came fluttering to Fort Orange for protection: not so much that they feared death or torture, but they were overawed by the spirit of the Mohawk, and could not endure to face him. Kieft fancied that he saw his opportunity. He would teach the red scoundrels a lesson they would remember. There was a company of soldiers in the Fort, and in the river were moored some vessels with crews of Dutch privateers on board. Kieft made up his party, and when night had fallen he sent them on their bloody errand, guided by one who knew all the camps and hiding-places of the doomed tribe. It was a revolting episode; a hundred Indians were unresistingly murdered. They would have made a stronger defense had they not been under the impression that it was the Mohawks who were upon them; and to be killed by a Mohawk was no more than an Algonquin should expect. But when it transpired that the Dutch were the perpetrators, the whole nation gave way to a double exasperation: first, that their friends had been killed, and secondly that they had suffered under a misapprehension. The settlers, in disregard of advice, were living in scattered situations over a large territory, and they were all in danger, and defenseless, even if New Amsterdam itself could escape. Kieft was heartily cursed by all impartially; he was compelled to make overtures for peace, and a pow-wow was held in Rockaway woods, in the spring of 1643. Terms were agreed upon, and, according to Indian usage, gifts were exchanged. But those of the chiefs so far exceeded in value the offerings of Kieft that these were regarded as a fresh insult; war was declared, and dragged along for two years more. It was not until 1645 that the grand meeting of the settlers and the Five Nations took place at Fort Amsterdam, and the treaty of lasting peace was ratified. Kieft sailed from New Amsterdam with the consciousness of having injured his countrymen more than had any enemy; but he was drowned off the Welsh coast, without having brought forth fruits meet for repentance.

Peter Stuyvesant is a favorite character in our history because he was a manly and straightforward man, faithful to his employers, fearless in doing and saying what he thought was right, and endowed with a full share of obstinate, homely, kindly human nature. He was not in advance of his age, or superior to his training; he was the plain product of both, but free from selfishness, malice, and unworthy ambitions. He was born in 1602, and came to America a warrior from honorable wars, seamed and knotty, with a famous wooden leg which all New Yorkers, at any rate, love to hear stumping down the corridors of time. His administration, the last of the Dutch regime, wiped out the stains inflicted by his predecessors, and resisted with equal energy encroachments from abroad and innovations at home. He was a true Dutchman, with most of the limitations and all the virtues of his race; fond of peace and of dwelling in his own "Bowery," yet not afraid to fight when he deemed that his duty. His tenure of office lasted from 1647 till 1664, a period of seventeen active years; after the English took possession of the town and called it New York, Peter went back to Holland, unwilling to live in the presence of new things; but he found that, at the age of sixty-three, he could not be happy away from the home that he had made for himself in the new world; so he returned to Manhattan Island, and completed the tale of his eighty years on the farm which is now the most populous and democratic of New York's thoroughfares. There he smoked his long-stemmed pipe and drank his schnapps, and thought over old times, and criticised the new. After two and a half centuries, the memory of him is undimmed; and it is to be wished that some fitting memorial of him may be erected in the city which his presence honored.

The very next year after his arrival, free trade was established in New Amsterdam. There had been a strict monopoly till then; but in one way or another it was continually evaded, and the New Amsterdam merchants found themselves so much handicapped by the restrictions, that their inability reacted upon the managers at home. There were not at that time any infant industries in need of protection, and the colony was large and capacious enough to take what the mother country sent it, and more also. But in order to prevent loss, an export duty was enforced, which pressed lightly on those who paid it, and comforted those to whom it was paid. Commerce was greatly stimulated, and the merchants of old Amsterdam sent compliments and prophesies of future greatness to their brethren across the sea. Every new-hatched settlement that springs up on the borders of the wilderness is liable to be "hailed" by its promoters as destined to become the Queen City of its region; the wish fathers the word, and the word is an advertisement. But the merchant princes of Amsterdam spoke by the card; they perceived the almost unique advantages of geographical position and local facilities of their American namesake; with such a bay and water front, with such a river, with such a soil and such openings for trade, what might it not become! Yes: but—"Sic vos non vobis ædificatis!" The English reaped what the Dutch had sown, and New York inherits the glory and power predicted for New Amsterdam.

The soil of Manhattan Island being comparatively poor,

the place was destined to be used as a residence merely, and the houses of prosperous traders and burghers began to assemble and bear likeness to a town. The primeval forest still clothed the upper part of the island; but the visible presence of a municipality in the southern extremity prompted the inhabitants to suggest a remodeling of the government somewhat after the New England pattern, where patroons were unknown and impossible. It is not surprising that suggestions to this effect from the humbler members of the community were not cordially embraced by either the patroons or their creators at home; in fact, it was still-born. That the people should rule themselves was as good as to say that the horse should loll in the carriage while his master toiled between the shafts. The thing was impossible, and should be unmentionable. The people, however, continued to mention it, and even to neglect paying the taxes which had been imposed with no regard to their reasonable welfare. A deputation went to Holland to tell the directors that they could neither farm nor trade with profit unless the burdens were lightened; the directors thought otherwise, and the consequence was that devices were practiced to lighten them illicitly. This added to the interest of life, but subverted the welfare of the state. Where political rights are not secured to all men by constitutional right, those who are unable to get them by privilege, intrigue to steal what such rights would guarantee. At this rate, there would presently be a Council of Ten and an Inquisition in New Amsterdam. In 1653, the Governor was constrained to admit the deputies from the various settlements to an interview, in which they said their say, and he his. "We have come here at our own expense," they observed, "from various countries of Europe, expecting to be given protection while earning our living; we have turned your wilderness into a fruitful garden for you, and you, in return, impose on us laws which disable us from profiting by our labor. We ask you to repeal these laws, allow us to make laws to meet our needs, and appoint none to office who has not our approbation." Thus, in substance, spoke the people; and we, at the end of the Nineteenth Century, may think they were uttering the veriest axioms of political common sense. What sturdy Peter Stuyvesant thought is perfectly expressed in what he replied.

"The old laws will stand. Directors and council only shall be law-makers: never will they make themselves responsible to the people. As to officers of government, were their election left to the rabble, we should have thieves on horseback and honest men on foot." And with that, we may imagine, the Governor stamped his wooden toe.

The people shrugged their shoulders. "We aim but at the general good," said they. "All men have a natural right to constitute society, and to assemble to protect their liberties and property."

"I declare this assembly dissolved," Peter retorted. "Assemble again at your peril! The authority which rules you is derived not from the whim of a few ignorant malcontents." Alas! the seed of the American Idea had never germinated in Peter's soldierly bosom; and when the West India Company learned of the dialogue, they spluttered with indignation. "The people be d——d!" was the sense of their message. "Let them no longer delude themselves with the fantasy that taxes require their assent." With that, they dismissed the matter from their minds. Yet even then, the Writing was on the wall. The flouted people were ripe to welcome England; and England, in the shape of Charles II., who had come at last to his own, meditated wiping the Dutch off the Atlantic seaboard. It availed not to plead rights: Lord Baltimore snapped his fingers. Lieutenant-governor Beekman, indeed, delayed the appropriation of Delaware; but Long Island was being swallowed up, and nobody except the government cared. The people may be incompetent to frame laws: but what if they decline to fight for you when called upon? If they cannot make taxes to please themselves, at all events they will not make war to please anybody else. If they are poor and ignorant, that is not their fault. The English fleet was impending: what was to be done? Could Stuyvesant but have multiplied himself into a thousand Stuyvesants, he knew what he would do; but he was impotent. In August, 1664, here was the fleet actually anchored in Gravesend Bay, with Nicolls in command. "What did they want?" the Governor inquired. "Immediate recognition of English sovereignty," replied Nicolls curtly; and the gentler voice of Winthrop of Boston was heard, advising surrender. "Surrender would be reproved at home," said poor Stuyvesant, refusing to know when he was beaten. He was doing his best to defeat the army and navy of England single-handed. But the burgomasters went behind him, and capitulated, and —Peter to the contrary for four days more notwithstanding— New Amsterdam became New York.

The English courted favor by liberal treatment of their new dependents on the western shore of the Hudson; whatever the Dutch had refused to do, they did. The Governor and Council were to be balanced by the people's representatives; no more arbitrary taxation; citizens might think and pray as best pleased them; land tenure was made easy, and seventy-five acres was the bounty for each emigrant imported, negroes included. By such inducements the wilderness of New Jersey, assigned to Berkeley and Carteret, was peopled by Scots, New Englanders and Quakers. Settlement proceeded rapidly, and in 1668 a colonial legislature met in the town named after Elizabeth Carteret. There were so many Puritans in the assembly, and their arguments were so convincing, that New Jersey law bore a strong family resemblance to that of New England. This had its effect, when, in 1670, the rent question came up for settlement. The Puritans contended that the Indians held from Noah, and as they were lawful heirs of the Indians, they declined to pay rents to the English proprietors. There was no means of compelling them to do so, and they had their way. The Yankees were already going ahead.

Manhattan did not get treated quite so well. The Governor had everything his own way, the council being his creatures, and the justices his appointees. The people were permitted no voice in affairs, and might as well have had Stuyvesant back again. After Nicolls had strutted his term, Lord Lovelace came, and outdid him. His idea of how to govern was formulated in his instructions to an agent: "Lay such taxes," said he, "as may give them liberty for no thought but how to discharge them." Lord Lovelace was an epigrammatist; but in the end he had to pay for his wit. He attempted to levy a tax for defense, and was met with refusal; the towns of Long Island had not one cent either for tribute or defense; his lordship swore at them heartily, but they heeded him not; and he found himself in the shoes of the ousted Dutch Governor in another sense than he desired. And then was poetical justice made complete; for who should appear before the helpless forts but Evertsen with a Dutch fleet! New York, New Jersey and Delaware surrendered to him almost with enthusiasm, and the work of England seemed to be all undone.

But larger events were to control the lesser. France and England combined in an iniquitous conspiracy to destroy the Dutch Republic, and swooped down upon the coast with two hundred thousand men. The story has often been told how the Dutch, tenfold outnumbered, desperately and gloriously defended themselves. They finally swept the English from the seas, and patroled the Channel with a broom at the masthead. By the terms of the treaty of peace which Charles was obliged by his own parliament to make, all conquests were mutually restored, and New York consequently reverted to England. West Jersey was bought by the Quakers; the eastern half of the province was restored to the rule of Carteret. The Atlantic coast, from Canada down to Florida, continuously, was English ground, and so remained until, a century later, the transplanted spirit of liberty, born in England, threw down the gauntlet to the spirit of English tyranny, and won independence for the United States.

When we remember that the Dutch maintained their government in the new world for little more than fifty years, it is surprising how deep a mark they made there. It is partly because their story lends itself to picturesque and graphic treatment; it is so rich in character and color, and telling in incident. Then, too, it has a beginning, middle and end, which is what historians as well as romancers love. But most of all, perhaps, their brief chronicles as a distinct political phenomenon illustrate the profound problem of self-government in mankind. The Netherlanders had proved, before any of them came hither, with what inflexible courage they could resent foreign tyranny; and the municipalities, as well as the nation, had grasped the principles of independence. But it was not until they erected their little commonwealth amid the forests of the Hudson that they awakened to the conception that every man should bear his part in the government of all. To attain this, it was necessary to break through a crust of conservatism almost as stubborn as that of Spain. The authority of their upper classes had never been questioned; the idea had never been entertained that a citizen in humble life could claim any right to influence the conditions under which his life should be carried on. That innate and inalienable right of the individual to life, liberty, and the pursuit of happiness, which Jefferson asserted, and which has become an axiom to every American school-boy, does not appear, upon investigation, to be either inalienable or innate. The history of mankind shows that it has been constantly alienated from them; and if we pass in review the population of the world, from the oldest to contemporary times, and from savage tribes to the most highly civilized nations, we find the plebeian bowing before the patrician, the poor man serving the wealthy. The conception of human equality before the law is not a congenital endowment, but an accomplishment, arduously acquired and easily forfeited. The first impulse of weakness in the presence of strength is to bow down before it; it is the impulse of the animal, and of the unspiritual, the unregenerate nature in man. The ability to recognize the solidarity of man, and therefore the equality of spiritual manhood, involves an uplifting of the mind, an illumination of the soul, which can be regarded as the result of nothing less than a revelation. It is not developed from below—it is received from above; it is a divine whisper in the ear of fallen man, transfiguring him, and opening before him the way of life. It postulates no loss of humility; it does not disturb the truth that some must serve and some must direct; that some shall have charge over many things, and some over but few. It does not supersede the outward order of society. But it affirms that to no man or body of men, no matter how highly endowed by nature or circumstance with intellect, position or riches, shall be accorded the right to dispose arbitrarily of the lives and welfare of the masses. Not elsewhere than in the hands of the entire community shall be lodged the reins of government. The administration shall be with the chosen ones whose training and qualifications fit them for that function; but the principles on which their administration is conducted shall be determined by the will and vote of all.

This is not lightly to be believed or understood; Peter Stuyvesant voiced the unenlightened thought when he said that, should the rabble rule, order and honesty must be overthrown. This is the inevitable conclusion of materialistic logic. Like produces like; evil, evil; ignorance, ignorance. Only by inspired faith will the experiment be tried of trusting the Creator to manifest His purposes, not by the conscious wisdom of any man or men, but through the unconscious, organic tendency, mental and moral, of universal man. We may call it "the tendency, not ourselves, which makes for righteousness"; or we may analyze it into the resultant of innumerable forces, taking a direction independent of them all; or we may say simply that it is the Divine method of leading us upward; it is all one. Universal suffrage is an act of faith; and, faithfully carried out, it brings political and religious emancipation to the people. How far it has been carried out in this country is a question we shall have to answer hereafter; we may say here that our forefathers realized its value, and gave to us in our Constitution the mechanism whereby to practice it. To it they added the memory of their courage and their sacrifices in its behalf; and more than this was not theirs to give.

The English Puritans received their revelation in one way; the Dutch traders and farmers in another; but it was the same revelation. To neither could it be imparted in Europe, but only in the virgin solitudes of an untrodden continent. There man, already civilized, was enabled to perceive the inefficiency and distortion of his civilization, and to grasp the cure. Hudson, an Englishman, but at the moment in Dutch service, opened the gates to the Netherlanders, and thus enabled their emigrants to perfect the work of emancipation which had been brought to the highest stage it could reach at home. They were opposed by the directors in Amsterdam, by their own governors and patroons, and by the errors which immemorial usage had ingrained in them as individuals. They overcame these forces, not by their own strength, nor by any violent act of revolution, but by the slow, irresistible energy of natural law, with which, as with a gravitative force, they had placed themselves in harmony. Thus they exemplified one of the several ways in which freedom comes to man, and took their place as a component element in the limitless cosmopolitanism of our population.

Their subsequent history shows that nothing truly valuable is lost in democracy. The high behavior and dignified manners which belonged to their patroons may be observed among their descendants in contemporary New York; the men whose ancestors controlled a thousand tenants have not lost the power of handling large matters in a large spirit; but they exercise it now for worthier ends than of old. Similarly, the Dutch stolidity which amuses us in the chronicles, reappears to-day in the form of steadiness and judgment; the obstinacy of headstrong Peter, as self-confidence and perseverance; the physical grossness of the old burghers, as constitutional vigor. Many of their customs too have come down to us; their heavy afternoon teas are recalled in our informal receptions; their New Year's Day sociability in our calls, their Christmas celebrations in our festival of Santa Claus. Much of our domestic architecture reflects their influence: the gabled fronts, the tiled fireplaces, the high "stoops," and the custom of sitting on them in summer evenings. In general it is seen that the effect of democratic institutions is to save the grain and reject the chaff, because criticism becomes more close and punctual, abuses and license are not chartered, and the individual is bereft of artificial supports and disguises, and must appear more nearly as God made him.

CHAPTER FIFTH

LIBERTY, SLAVERY, AND TYRANNY

WE LEFT the colony at Jamestown emerging from thick darkness and much tribulation toward the light. Some distance was still to be traversed before full light and easement were attained; but fortune, upon the whole, was kinder to Virginia than to most of the other settlements; and though clouds gathered darkly now and then, and storms threatened, and here and there a bolt fell, yet deliverance came beyond expectation. Something Virginia suffered from Royal governors, something from the Indians, something too from the imprudence and wrong-headedness of her own people. But her story is full of stirring and instructive passages. It tells how a community chiefly of aristocratic constitution and sympathies, whose loyalty to the English throne was deep and ardent, and whose type of life was patrician, nevertheless were won insensibly and inevitably to espouse the principles of democracy. It shows how, with honest men, a king may be loved, and the system which he stands for reverenced and defended, while yet the lovers and apologists choose and maintain a wholly different system for themselves. The House of Stuart had none but friends in Virginia; when the son of Charles the First was a fugitive, Virginia offered him a home; and the follies and frailties of his father, and the grotesque chicaneries of his grandfather, could not alienate the colonists' affection.

Yet, from the moment their Great Charter was given them, they never ceased to defend the liberties which it bestowed against every kingly effort to curtail or destroy them; and on at least one occasion they fairly usurped the royal prerogative. They presented, in short, the striking anomaly of a people acknowledging a monarch and at the same time claiming the fullest measure of political liberty till then enjoyed by any community in modern history. They themselves perceived no inconsistency in their attitude; but to us it is patent, and its meaning is that the sentiment of a tradition may be cherished and survive long after intelligence and experience have caused the thing itself to be consigned to the rubbish-heap of the past.

So long as Sir Thomas Smythe occupied the president's chair of the London Company, there could be no hope of substantial prosperity for the Jamestown emigrants. He was a selfish and conceited satrap, incapable of enlightened thought or beneficent action, who knew no other way to magnify his own importance than by suffocating the rights and insulting the self-respect of others. He had a protege in Argall, a disorderly ruffian who was made deputy-governor of the colony in 1617. His administration was that of a freebooter; but the feeble and dwindling colony had neither power nor spirit to do more than send a complaint to London. Lord Delaware had in the meantime sailed for Virginia, but died on the trip; Argall was, however, dismissed, and Sir George Yeardley substituted for him—a man of gracious manners and generous nature, but somewhat lacking in the force and firmness that should build up a state. He had behind him the best men in the company if not in all England: Sir Edward Sandys, the Earl of Southampton, and Nicolas Ferrar. Smythe had had resignation forced upon him, and with him the evil influences in the management retired to the background. Sandys was triumphantly elected governor and treasurer, with Ferrar as corporation coun-

"TREPANNING" MEN TO BE SENT TO THE COLONIES

sel; Southampton was a powerful supporter. They were all young men, all royalists, and all unselfishly devoted to the cause of human liberty and welfare. Virginia never had better or more urgent friends.

Yeardley, on his arrival, found distress and discouragement, and hardly one man remaining in the place of twenty. The colonists had been robbed both by process of law and without; they had been killed and had died of disease; they had deserted and been deported; they had been denied lands of their own, or the benefit of their own labor; and they had been permitted no part in the management of their own affairs. The rumor of these injuries and disabilities had got abroad, and no recruits for the colony had been obtainable; the Indians were ill-disposed, and the houses poor and few. Women too were lamentably scanty, and the people had no root in the country, and no thought but to leave it. Like the emigrants to the Klondike gold-fields in our own day, they had designed only to better their fortunes and then depart. The former hope was gone; the latter was all that was left.

Yeardley's business, in the premises, was agreeable and congenial; he had a letter from the company providing for the abatement of past evils and abuses, and the establishment of justice, security and happiness. He sent messengers far and wide, summoning a general meeting to hear his news and confer together for the common weal.

Hardly venturing to believe that any good thing could be in store for them, the burgesses and others assembled, and crowded into the place of meeting. Twenty-two delegates from the eleven plantations were there, clad in their dingy and dilapidated raiment, and wide-brimmed hats; most of them with swords at their sides, and some with rusty muskets in their hands. Their cheeks were lank and their faces sunburned; their bearing was listless, yet marked with some touch of curiosity and expectation. There were among them some well-filled brows and strong features, announcing men of ability and thoughtfulness, though they had lacked the opportunity and the cue for action. Their long days on the plantations, and their uneasy nights in the summer heats, had given them abundant leisure to think over their grievances and misfortunes, and to dream of possible reforms and innovations. But of what profit was it? Their governors had no thought but to fill their own pockets, the council was powerless or treacherous, and everything was slipping away.

It was in the depths of summer—the 30th of July, 1619. More than a year was yet to pass before the "Mayflower" would enter the wintry shelter of Plymouth harbor. In the latitude of Jamestown the temperature was almost tropical at this season, and exhausting to body and spirit. The room in which they met, in the governor's house in Jamestown, was hardly spacious enough for their accommodation: four unadorned walls, with a ceiling that could be touched by an upraised hand. It had none of the aspect of a hall of legislature, much less of one in which was to take place an event so large and memorable as the birth of liberty in a new world. But the delegates thronged in, and were greeted at their entrance by Yeardley, who stood at a table near the upper end of the room, with a secretary beside him and a clergyman of the Church of England on his other hand. The colonists looked at his urbane and conciliating countenance, and glanced at the document he held in his hand, and wondered what would be the issue. Nothing of moment, doubtless; still, they could scarcely be much worse off than they were; and the new governor certainly had the air of having something important to communicate. They took their places, leaning against the walls, or standing with their hands clasped over the muzzles of their muskets, or supporting one foot upon a bench; and the gaze of all was concentrated on the governor. As he opened the paper, a silence fell upon the assembly.

Such, we may imagine, were the surroundings and circumstances of this famous gathering, the transactions of which fill so bright a page in the annals of the early colonies. The governor asked the clergyman for a blessing, and when the prayer was done suggested the choosing of a chairman, or speaker. The choice fell upon John Pory, a member of the former council. Then the governor read his letter from the company in London.

The letter, in few words, opened the door to every reform which could make the colony free, prosperous and happy, and declared all past wrongs at an end. It merely outlined the scope of the improvements, leaving it to the colonists themselves to fill in the details. "Those cruel laws were abrogated, and they were to be governed by those free laws under which his majesty's subjects in England lived." An annual grand assembly, consisting of the governor and council and two burgesses from each plantation, chosen by the people, was to be held; and at these assemblies they were to frame whatever laws they deemed proper for their welfare. These concessions were of the more value and effect, because they were advocated in England by men who had only the good of the colony at heart, and possessed power to enforce their will.

It seemed almost too good to be true: it was like the sun rising after the long arctic night. Those sad faces flushed, and the moody eyes kindled. The burgesses straightened their backs and lifted their heads; they looked at one another, and felt that they were once more men. There was a murmur of joy and congratulation; and thanks were uttered to God, and to the Company, for what had been done. And forthwith they set to work with life and energy, and with a judgment and foresight which were hardly to have been looked for in legislators so untried, to construct the platform of enactments upon which the commonwealth of Virginia was henceforth to stand.

From the body of the delegates, two committees were selected to devise the new laws and provisions, while the governor and the rest reviewed the laws already in existence, to determine what part of them, if any, was suitable for continuance. Among the articles agreed upon were regulations relating to distribution and tenure of land, which replaced all former patents and privileges, and set all holders on an equal footing: the recognition of the Church of England as governing the mode of worship in Virginia, with a good salary for clergymen and an injunction that all and sundry were to appear at church every Sunday, and bring their weapons with them—thus insuring Heaven a fair hearing, while at the same time making provision against the insecurity of carnal things. The wives of the planters as well as their husbands were capacitated to own land, because, in a new world, a woman might turn out to be as efficient as the man. This sounds almost prophetic; but it was probably intended to operate on the cultivation of the silkworm. Plantations of the mulberry had been ordered, and culture of the cocoon was an industry fitting to the gentler sex, who were the more likely to succeed in it on account of their known partiality for the product. On the other hand, excess in apparel was kept within bounds by a tax. The planting of vines was also ordered; but as a matter of fact the manufacture of neither wine nor silk was destined to succeed in the colony; tobacco and cotton were to be its staples, but the latter had not at this epoch been attempted. Order and propriety among the colonists were assured by penalties on gaming, drunkenness, and sloth; and the better to guard against the proverbial wiles of Satan, a university was sketched out, and direction was given that such children of the heathen as showed indications of latent talent should be caught, tamed and instructed, and employed as missionaries among their tribes. Finally, a fixed price of three shillings for the best quality of tobacco, and eighteen pence for inferior brands, was appointed; thus giving the colony a currency which had the double merit of being a sound medium for traffic, and an agreeable consolation and incense when the labors of the day were past.

It was a good day's work; and the assembly dissolved with the conviction that their time had never before been passed to such advantage. Yeardley, knowing the disposition of the managers in London, opposed no objection to the immediate practical enforcement of the new enactments; and indeed Sandys, when he had an opportunity of examining the digest, expressed the opinion that it had been "well and judiciously formed." The colonists, for their part, dismissed all anxieties and shadows from their minds, and fell to putting in crops and putting up dwellings as men will who have a stake in their country, and feel that they can live in it. Their confidence was not misplaced; within a year from this time the number of the colonists had been more than doubled, and all troubles seemed at an end.

So long, however, as James I. disgraced the throne of England, popular liberties could never be quite sure of immunity; and during the five or six years that he still had to live, he did his best to disturb the felicity of his Virginian subjects. He was unable to do anything very serious, and what he did do, was in contravention of law. He got Sandys out of the presidency; but Southampton was immediately put in his place; he tried to get away the patent which he himself had issued, and finally did so; but the colony kept its laws and its freedom, though the Throne thenceforward appointed the governors. He put a heavy tax on tobacco, which he professed to regard as an invention of the enemy; and he countenanced an attempt by Lord Warwick, in behalf of Argall, to continue martial law in the colony instead of allowing trial by Jury; but in this he was defeated. He sent out two commissioners to Virginia to discover pretexts for harassing it, and took the matter out of the hands of Parliament; but the Virginians maintained themselves until death stepped in and put a final stop to his majesty's industry, and Charles I. came to the throne.

The climate of Virginia does not predispose to exertion; yet farming involves hard physical work; and, beyond anything else, the wealth of Virginia was derived from farming. Manufactures had not come in view, and were discouraged or forbidden by English decree. But, as we saw in the early days of Jamestown, the settlers there were unused to work, and averse from it; although, under the stimulus of Captain John Smith, they did learn how to chop down trees. After the colony became popular, and populous, the emigrants continued to be in a large measure of a social class to whom manual labor is unattractive. A country in which laborers are indispensable, and which is inhabited by persons disinclined to labor, would seem to stand no good chance of achieving prosperity. How, then, is the early prosperity of Virginia to be explained? The charter did not make men work.

It was due to the employment of slave labor. Slaves in the Seventeenth Century were easily acquired, and were of several varieties. At one time, there were more white slaves than black. White captives were often sold into slavery; and there was also a regular trade in indentured slaves, or servants, sent from England. These were to work out their freedom by a certain number of years of labor for their purchaser. Convicts from the prisons were also utilized as slaves. In the same year that the Virginia charter bestowed political freedom upon the colonists, a Dutch ship landed a batch of slaves from the Guinea coast, where the Dutch had a footing. They were strong fellows, and the ardor of the climate suited them better than that of the regions further north. Negroes soon came to be in demand therefore; they did not die in captivity as the Indians were apt to do, and a regular trade in them was presently established. A negro fetched in the market more than twice as much as either a red or a white man, and repaid the investment. There was no general sentiment against traffic in human beings, and it was not settled that negroes were human, exactly. Slavery at all events had been the normal condition of Guinea negroes from the earliest times, and they undoubtedly were worse treated by their African than by their European and American owners. They were born slaves, or at least in slavery. There had of course been enlightened humanitarians as far back as the Greek and Roman eras, who had opined that the principle of slavery was wrong; and such men were talking still; but ordinary people regarded their deliverances as being in the nature of a counsel of perfection, which was not intended to be observed in practice. There are fashions in humanitarianism, as in other matters, and multitudes who denounced slavery in the first half of this Nineteenth Century, were in no respect better practical moralists than were the Virginians two hundred years before. But the time had to come, in the course of human events, when negro slavery was to cease in America; and those whose business interests, or sentimental prejudices, were opposed to it, added the chorus of their disapproval to the inscrutable movements of a Power above all prejudices. Negro slavery, as an overt institution, is no more in these States; but he would be a bold or a blind man who should maintain that slavery, both black and white, has no existence among us to-day. Meanwhile the Seventeenth Century planters of Virginia bought and sold their human chattels with an untroubled conscience; and the latter, comprehending even less of the ethics of the question than their masters did, were reasonably happy. They were not aware that human nature was being insulted and degraded in their persons: they were transported by no moral indignation. When they were flogged, they suffered, but when their bodies stopped smarting, no pain rankled in their minds. They were treated like animals, and became like them. They had no anxieties; they looked neither forward nor backward; their physical necessities were provided for. White slavery gradually disappeared, but the feeling prevailed that slavery was what negroes were intended for. The planters, after a few generations, came to feel a sort of affection for their bondsmen who had been born on the estates and handed down from father to son. Self-interest, as well as natural kindliness, rendered deliberate cruelties rare. The negroes, on the other hand, often loved their masters, and would grieve to leave them. The evils of slavery were not on the surface, but were subtle, latent, and far more malignant than was even recently realized. The Abolitionists thought the trouble was over when the Proclamation of Emancipation was signed. "We can put on our coats and go home, now," said Garrison; and Wendell Phillips said, "I know of no man to-day who can fold his arms and look forward to his future with more confidence than the negro." We shall have occasion to investigate the intelligence of these forecasts by-and-by. But there is something striking in the fact that that country which claims to be the freest and most highly civilized in the world should be the last to give up "the peculiar institution." How can devotion to liberty co-exist in the mind with advocacy of servitude? This, too, is a subject to which we must revert hereafter. At the period we are now treating, there were more white than black slaves, and the princely estates of later times had not been thought of. Indeed, in spite of their marriage to liberty, the colonists did not yet feel truly at home. Marriage of a more concrete kind was needed for that.

This defect was understood in England, and the Company took means to remedy it. A number of desirable and blameless young women were enlisted to go out to the colony and console the bachelors there. The plan was discreetly carried out; the acquisition of the young ladies was not made too easy, so that neither was their self-respect wounded, nor were the bachelors allowed to feel that beauty and virtue in female form were commonplace commodities. The romance and difficulty of the situation were fairly well preserved. There stood the possible bride; but she was available only with her own consent and approval; and before entering the matrimonial estate, the bridegroom elect must pay all charges—so many pounds of tobacco. And how many pounds of tobacco was a good wife worth? From one point of view, more than was ever grown in Virginia; but the sentimental aspect of the transaction had to be left out of consideration, or the enterprise would have come to an untimely conclusion. From one hundred to one hundred and fifty pounds of the weed was the average commercial figure; it paid expenses and gave the agents a commission; for the rest, the profit was all the colonist's. Many a happy home was founded in this way, and, so far as we know, there were no divorces and no scandals. But it must not be forgotten that, although tobacco was paid for the wife. there was still enough left to fill a quiet pipe by the conjugal fireside. They were the first Christian firesides where this soothing goddess had presided: no wonder they were peaceful!

Charles I. was a young man, with a large responsibility on his shoulders; and two leading convictions in his mind. The first was that he ought to be the absolute head of the nation; Parliament might take counsel with him, but should not control him when it came to action. The same notion had prevailed with James I., and was to be the immediate occasion of the downfall of James II.; as for Charles II., his long experience of hollow oak trees, and secret chambers in the houses of loyalists, had taught him the limitations of the kingly prerogative before he began his reign; and the severed head of his father clinched the lesson. But the Stuarts, as a family, were disinclined to believe that the way to inherit the earth was by meekness, and none of them believed it so little as the first Charles.

The second conviction he entertained was that he must have revenues, and that they should be large and promptly paid. His whole pathetic career—tragic seems too strong a word for it, though it ended in death—was a mingled story of nobility, falsehood, gallantry and treachery, conditioned by his blind pursuit of these two objects, money and power.

Upon general principles, then, it was to be expected that Charles would be the enemy of Virginian liberties. But it happened that money was his more pressing need at the time his attention first was turned on the colony; he saw that revenues were to be gained from them; he knew that the charter recently given to them had immensely increased their productiveness; and as to his prerogative, he had not as yet felt the resistance which his parliament had in store for him, and was therefore not jealous of the political privileges of a remote settlement—one, too, which seemed to be in the hands of loyal gentlemen. "Their liberties harm me not," was his thought, "and they appear to be favorable to the success of the tobacco crop; the tobacco monopoly can put money in my purse; therefore let the liberties remain. Should these planters ever presume to go too far, it will always be in my power to stop them." Thus it came about that tobacco, after procuring the Virginians loving wives, was also the means of securing the favor of their king. But they, naturally, ascribed the sunshine of his smile to some innate merit in themselves, and their gratitude made them his enthusiastic supporters as long as he lived. They mourned his death, and opened their arms to all royalist refugees from the power of Cromwell. When Cromwell sent over a man-of-war, however, they accepted the situation. Virginia had by that time grown to so considerable an importance that they could adopt a somewhat conservative attitude toward the affairs even of the mother country.

The ten years following Charles's accession were a period of peace and growth in the colony; of great increase in population and in production, and of a steady ripening of political liberties. But the conditions under which this development

MASSACRE BY INDIANS AT JAMESTOWN, VA., 1644

went on were different from those which existed in New England and in New York. The Puritans were actuated by religious ideals, the Dutch by commercial projects chiefly; but the Virginia planters were neither religious enthusiasts nor tradesmen. Their tendency was not to huddle together in towns and close communities, but to spread out over the broad and fertile miles of their new country, and live each in a little principality of his own, with his slaves and dependents around him. They modeled their lives upon those of the landed gentry in England; and when their crops were gathered, they did not go down to the wharfs and haggle over their disposal, but handed them over to agents, who took all trouble off their hands, and after deducting commissions and charges made over to them the net profits. This left the planters leisure to apply themselves to liberal pursuits; they maintained a dignified and generous hospitality, and studied the art of government. A race of gallant gentlemen grew up, well educated, and consciously superior to the rest of the population, who had very limited educational facilities, and but little of that spirit of equality and independence which characterized the northern colonies. Towns and cities came slowly; the plantation system was more natural and agreeable under the circumstances. Orthodoxy in religion was the rule; and though at first there was a tendency to eschew narrowness and bigotry, yet gradually the church became hostile to dissenters, and Puritans and Quakers were as unwelcome in Virginia as were the latter in Massachusetts, or Episcopalians anywhere in New England. All this seems incompatible with democracy; and probably it might in time have grown into a liberal monarchical system. The slaves were not regarded as having any rights, political or personal; their masters exercised over them the power of life and death, as well as all lesser powers. The bulk of the white population was not oppressed, and was able to get a living, for Virginia was "the best poor man's country in the world"; there was little or none of the discontent that embarrassed the New Amsterdam patroons; the charter gave them representation, and their manhood was not undermined. Had Virginia been an island, or otherwise isolated, and free from any external interference, we can imagine that the planters might at last have found it expedient to choose a king from among their number, who would have found a nobility and a proletariat ready made.

But Virginia was not isolated. She was loyal to the Stuarts, because they did not bring to bear upon her the severities which they inflicted upon their English subjects; but when she became a royal colony, and had to put up with corrupt and despotic favorites of the monarch, who could do what they pleased, and were responsible to nobody but the monarch who had made them governor, loyalty began to cool. Moreover, men whose ability and advanced opinions made them distasteful to the English kings, fled to the colonies, and to Virginia among the rest, and sowed the seeds of revolt. Calamity makes strange bedfellows: the planters liked outside oppression as little as did the common people, and could not but make common cause with them. The distance between the two was diminished. Social equality there could hardly be; but political and theoretic equality could be acknowledged. The English monarchy made the American republic; spurred its indolence, and united its parts. Man left to himself is lax and indifferent; from first to last it is the pressure of wrong that molds him into the form of right. George I. gave the victory to the Americans in the Revolution as much as Washington did. And before George's time, the colonies had been keyed up to the struggle by years of injustice and outrage. And this injustice and outrage seemed the more intolerable because they had been preceded by a period of comparative liberality. It needs powerful pressure to transform English gentlemen with loyalist traditions and sympathies into a democracy; but it can be done, and the English kings were the men to do it.

Until the period of unequivocal tyranny arrived, the chief shadow upon the colony was cast by its relations with the Indians. Powhatan, the father of Pocahontas, and chief over tribes whose domains extended over thousands of square miles, kept friendship with the whites till his death in 1618. His brother, Opechankano, professed to inherit the friendship along with the chieftainship; but the relations between the red men and the colonists had never been too cordial, and the latter, measuring their muskets and breastplates against the stone arrows and deerskin shirts of the savages, fell into the error of despising them. The Indians, for their part, stood in some awe of firearms, which they had never held in their own hands, and the penalty for selling which to them had been made capital years before. But they had their own methods of dealing with foes; and since neither side had ever formally come to blows, they had received no object lesson to warn them to keep hands off. Opechankano was intelligent and far-seeing; he perceived that the whites were increasing in numbers, and that if they were not checked betimes, they would finally overrun the country. But he did not see so far as his brother, who had known that the final domination of the English could not be prevented, and had therefore adopted the policy of conciliating them as the best. Opechankano, therefore, quietly planned the extermination of the settlers; the familiar terms on which the white and red men stood played into his hands. Indians were in the habit of visiting the white settlements, and mingling with the people. Orders for concerted action were secretly circulated among the savages, who were to hold themselves ready for the signal.

It might after all never have been given, but for an unlooked for incident. A noisy and troublesome Indian, who imagined that bullets could not kill him, fell into a quarrel with a settler, and slew him; and was himself shot while attempting to escape from arrest. "Sooner shall the heavens fall," devoutly exclaimed Opechankano, when informed of this mishap, "than I will break the peace of Powhatan." But the waiting tribes knew that the time had come.

On the morning of March 22, 1622, the settlers arose as usual to the labors of the day; some of them took their hoes and spades and went out into the fields; others busied themselves about their houses. Numbers of Indians were about, but this excited no remark or suspicion; they were not formidable; a dog could frighten them; a child could hold them in check. Indians strolled into the cabins, and sat at the breakfast-tables. No one gave them a second thought. No one looked over his shoulder when an Indian passed behind him.

But, miles up the country from Jamestown lived a settler who kept an Indian boy, whom he instructed, and who made himself useful about the place; and of all the Indians in Virginia that day he was the only one whose heart relented. His brother had lain with him the night before, and had given him the word: he was to kill the settler and his family the next morning. The boy seemed to assent, and the other went on his way. The boy lay till dawn, his savage mind divided between fear of the great chief and compassion for the white man who had been kind to him and taught him. In the early morning he arose and stood beside his benefactor's bed. The man slept: one blow, and he would be dead. But the boy did not strike; he wakened him and told him of the horror that was about to befall.

Pace—such was the settler's name—did not wait for confirmation of the tale; indeed, as he ran to the paddock to get his packhorse, he could see the smoke of burning cabins rising in the still air, and could hear, far off, the yells of the savages as they plied their work.

He sprang on the horse's back, with his musket across the withers, and set off at a gallop toward Jamestown.

Most of the colonists lived in that neighborhood; if he could get there in time many lives might be saved. As he rode, he directed his course to the cabins, on the right hand and on the left, that lay in his way, and gave the alarm. Many of the savages, who had not yet begun their work, at once took to flight; they would not face white men when on their guard. In other places, the warning came too late. The missionary, who had devoted his life to teaching the heathen that men should love one another, was inhumanly butchered. Pace arrived in season to avert the danger from the bulk of the little population; but, of the four thousand scattered over the country-side, three hundred and forty-seven died that morning, with the circumstances of hideous atrocity which were the invariable accompaniments of Indian massacre. The colonists were appalled; and for a time it seemed as if the purpose of Opechankano would be realized. Two thousand settlers came in from the outlying districts, panic-stricken, and after living for a while crowded together in unwholesome quarters in the vicinity of Jamestown, took ship and returned to England. Hardly one in ten of the plantations was not deserted. The bolder spirits, who remained, organized a war of extermination, in which they were supported and re-enforced by the company, who sent over men and weapons as soon as the news was known in England. But the campaign resolved itself into long and harassing attacks, ambuscades and reprisals, extending over many years. There could be no pitched battles with Indians; they gave way, but only to circumvent and surprise. The whites were resolved to make no peace, and to give no quarter to man, woman or child. The formerly peaceful settlement became inured to blood and cruelty. But the red men could not be wholly driven away. Just twenty years after the first massacre the same implacable chief, now a decrepit old man, planned a second one; some hundreds were murdered; but the colonists were readier and stronger now, and they gathered themselves up at once, and inflicted a crushing vengeance. The ancient chief was finally taken, and either died of wounds received in fight, or was slain by a soldier after capture. After 1646, the borders of Virginia were safe. There is no redeeming feature in this Indian warfare, which fitfully survives, in remote parts of our country, even now. It aided, perhaps, to train the race of pioneers and frontiersmen who later became one of the most remarkable features of our early population. Contact with the savage races inoculated us, perhaps, with a touch of their stoicism and grimness. But in our conflicts with them there was nothing noble or inspiring; and there could be no object in view on either side but extermination. Our Indian fighters became as savage and merciless as the creatures they pursued. The Indian must be fought by the same tactics he adopts—cunning, stealth, surprise, and then unrelenting slaughter, with the sequel of the scalping knife. They compel us to descend to their level in war, and we have utterly failed to raise them to our own in peace. Some of them have possessed certain harshly masculine traits which we can admire; some of them have showed broad and virile intelligence, the qualities of a general, a diplomatist, or even of a statesman. There have been, and are, so-called tame Indians; but such were not worth taming. As a whole, the red tribes have resisted all attempts to lift them to the civilized level and keep them there. Roger Williams, and the "apostle," John Eliot, were their friends, and won their regard; but neither Williams' influence nor Eliot's Bible left any lasting trace upon them. The Indian is irreclaimable; disappointment is the very mildest result that awaits the effort to reclaim him. He is wild to the marrow; no bird or beast is so wild as he. He is a human embodiment of the untrodden woods, the undiscovered rivers, the austere mountains, the pathless prairies—of all those parts and aspects of nature which are never brought within the smooth sway of civilization, because, as soon as civilization appears, they are, so far as their essential quality is concerned, gone.

To hear the yelp of the coyote, you must lie alone in the sage brush near the pool in the hollow of the low hills by moonlight; it will never reach your ears through the bars of the menagerie cage. To know the mountain, you must confront the avalanche and the precipice uncompanioned, and stand at last on the breathless and awful peak, which lifts itself and you into a voiceless solitude remote from man and yet no nearer to God; but if you journey with guides and jolly fellowship to some Mountain House, never so airily perched, you would as well visit a panorama. To comprehend the ocean, you must meet it in its own inviolable domain, where it tosses heavenward its careless nakedness, and laughs with death; from the deck of a steamboat you will never find it, though you sail as far as the Flying Dutchman. But the solitude which nature reveals, and which alone reveals her, does but prepare you for the inapproachableness that shines out at you from the Indian's eyes. Seas are shallow and continents but a span compared with the breadths and depths which separate him from you. The sphinx will yield her mystery, but he will not unveil his; you may touch the poles of the planet, but you can never lay your hand on him. The same God that made you, made him also in His image; but if you try to bridge the gulf between you, you will learn something of God's infinitude.

Sir George Yeardley and Sir Francis Wyatt both held the office of governor twice, and with good repute; in 1630, Sir John Harvey succeeded the former. He was the champion of monopolists; he would divide the land among a few, and keep the rest in subjection. He fought with the legislature from the first; he could not wring their rights from them, but he distressed and irritated the colony, levying arbitrary fines, and browbeating all and sundry with the brutality of an ungoverned temper. His chief patron was Lord Baltimore, a Roman Catholic, and therefore disfavored by the Protestant colony, who would not suffer him to plant in their domain. He bought a patent authorizing him to establish a colony in the northern part of Virginia, which was afterward called Maryland, being cut off from the older colony; and this diminution of their territory much displeased the Virginians. But Harvey supported him throughout; and permitted mass to be said in Virginia. He likewise prevented the settlers from carrying on the border warfare with the Indians, lest it should disturb his perquisites from the fur trade. Violent scenes took place in the hall of assembly, and hard words were given and exchanged; the planters were men of hot passions, and the conduct of the governor became intolerable to them. Matters came to a head during the last week in April of 1635. An unauthorized gathering in York complained of an unjust tax and of other malfeasances; whereupon Harvey cried mutiny, and had the leaders arrested. But the boot was on the other leg. Several members of council, with a company of musketeers at their back, came to his house; Matthews, with whom the governor had lately had a fierce quarrel, and the other planters, tramped into the broad hall of the dwelling, with swords in their hands and threatening looks, and confronted him. John Utie brought down his hand with staggering force on his shoulder, exclaiming, "I arrest you for treason!" "How, for treason?" queried the frightened governor. "You have betrayed our forts to our enemies of Maryland," replied several stern voices. Harvey glanced from one to another; in the background were the musketeers; plainly this was no time for trifling. He offered to do whatever they demanded. They required the release of prisoners, which was immediately done, and bade him prepare to answer before the assembly. They would listen to no arguments and no excuses; he was told by Matthews, with a menacing look, that the people would have none of him. "You intend no less than the subversion of Maryland," protested Harvey; but he promised to return to England, and John West, who had already acted as ad-interim governor while Harvey was on his way to Virginia, was at once elected in his place.

This incident showed of what stuff the Virginians were made. It was an early breaking-out of the American spirit, which would never brook tyranny. In offering violence to the king's governor they imperiled their own lives; but their blood was up, and they heeded no danger. When Harvey presented himself before Charles at the privy council, his majesty remarked that he must be sent back at all hazards, because the sending him to England had been an assumption on the colonists' part of regal power; and, tobacco or no tobacco, the line must be drawn there. If the charges against him were sustained, he might stay but a day; if not, his term should be extended beyond the original commission. A new commission was given him, and back he went; but this shuttlecock experience seems to have quelled his spirit, and we hear no more of quarrels with the Virginia council. Wyatt relieved him in 1639; and in 1642 came Sir William Berkeley. This man, who was born about the beginning of the century, was twice governor; his present term, lasting ten years, was followed by a nine years' interval; reappointed again in 1660, he was in power when the rebellion broke out which was led by Nathaniel Bacon. Little is known of him outside of his American record; in his first term, under Charles I., he acted simply as the creature of that monarch, and aroused no special animosities on his own account: during the reign of Cromwell, he disappeared; but when Charles II. ascended the throne, Berkeley, though then an old man, was thought to be fitted by his previous experience for the Virginia post, and was returned thither. But years seemed to have soured his disposition, and lessened his prudence, and, as we shall see, his bloodthirsty conduct after Bacon's death was the occasion of his recall in disgrace; and he died, like Andros more than half a century later, with the curse of a people on his grave.

But his first appearance was auspicious; he brought instructions designed to increase the reign of law and order in the colony, without infringing upon its existing liberties. Allegiance to God and the king were enjoined, additional courts were provided for, traffic with the Indians was regulated, annual assemblies, with a negative voice upon their acts by the governor, were commanded. The only discordant note in the instructions referred to the conditions of maritime trade, afterward known in history as the Navigation Acts. The colony desired free trade, which, as it had no manufactures, was obviously to its benefit. But it was as obviously to the interest of the king that he alone should enjoy the right of controlling all imports into the colony, and absorbing all its exports; and his rulings were framed to secure that end. But for the present the Acts were not carried into effect; and, on the other hand, the prospect was held out that there should be no taxation except what was voted by the people themselves; and their contention that they, who knew the conditions and needs of their colonial existence, were better able to regulate it than those at home, was allowed. By way of evincing their recognition of this courtesy, the assembly passed among other laws, one against toleration of any other than the episcopalian form of worship; and when Charles was beheaded, in 1649, it voted to retain Berkeley in office. But when, in the next year, the fugitive son of the dead king undertook to issue a commission confirming him in his place, Parliament intervened. Virginia was brought to her bearings; and the Navigation Acts were brought up again. Cromwell, no less than Charles, appreciated the advantages of a monopoly.

Restrictions on commerce, first imposed by Spain, were first resisted by the Dutch, with the result of rendering them the leading maritime power. Cromwell wished to appropriate or share this advantage; but instead of adopting the means employed for that purpose by the Dutch, he decreed that none but English ships should trade with the English colonies, and that foreign ships should bring to England only the products of their own countries. The restriction did little harm to Virginia, so long as England was able to take all her products, and to supply all her needs; but it brought on war with Holland, in which both the moral and the naval advantage was on the side of the Dutch. But England acquired a foothold in the West Indies, and her policy was maintained. Virginia asked that she should have representatives to act for her in England, and when a body of commissioners was appointed to examine colonial questions, among them were Richard Bennett and William Clairborne, both of them colonists, and men of force and ability. In the sequel, the liberties of the colony were enlarged, and Bennett was made governor by vote of the assembly itself, which continued to elect governors during the ascendency of Parliament in England. When Richard Cromwell, who had succeeded the great Protector, resigned his office, the Virginia burgesses chose Sir William Berkeley to rule over them, and he acknowledged their authority. Meanwhile the Navigation Acts were so little enforced that smuggling was hardly illegal; and, in 1658, the colonists actually invited foreign nations to deal with them. This was the period of Virginia's greatest freedom before the Revolution. The suffrage was in the hands of all taxpayers; in religious matters, all restrictions except those against the Quakers were removed; loyalists and roundheads mingled amicably in planting and legislation, and the differences which had arrayed them against one another in England were forgotten. The population increased to thirty thousand, and the inhabitants developed among themselves an ardent patriotism. It is not surprising. Their country was one of the richest and loveliest in the world; everything which impairs the enjoyment of life was eliminated or minimized; hucksters, pettifoggers and bigots were scarce as June snowflakes; indentured servants, on their emancipation, were speedily given the suffrage: it might almost be said that a man might do whatever he pleased, within the limits of criminal law. Assuredly, personal liberty was far greater at this epoch, in Virginia, than it is to-day in New York City or Chicago. The instinct of the Virginians, in matters of governing, was so far as possible to let themselves alone; the planters, in the seclusion of their estates, were practically subject to no law but their own pleasure. There was probably no place in the civilized world where so much intelligent happiness was to be had as in Virginia during the years immediately preceding the Restoration.

What would have been the political result had the absence of all artificial pressure indefinitely continued? Two tendencies were observable, working, apparently, in opposite directions. On one side were the planters, many of them aristocratic by origin as well as by circumstance; who lived in affluence, were friendly to the established church, enjoyed a liberal education, and naturally assumed the reins of power. The law which gave fifty acres of land to the settler who imported an emigrant, while it made for the enlargement of estates, created also a large number of tenants and dependents, who would be likely to support their patrons and proprietors, who exercised so much control over their welfare. These dependents found the conditions of existence comfortable, and even after they had become their own masters, they would be likely to consult the wishes of the men who had been the occasion of their good fortune. Neither education nor religious instruction were so readily obtainable as to threaten to render such a class discontented with their condition by opening to them hitherto unknown gates of advantage; and the suffrage, when by ownership of private property they had qualified themselves to exercise it, would at once appease their independent instincts, and at the same time make them willing, in using it, to follow the lead or suggestion of men so superior to them in intelligence and in political sagacity. From this standpoint, then, it seemed probable that a self-governing community of the special kind existing in Virginia would drift toward an aristocratic form of rule.

But the matter could be regarded in another way. Free suffrage is a power having a principle of life within itself; it creates in the mind that which did not before exist, and educates its possessor first by prompting him to ask himself of what improvement his condition is susceptible, and then by forcing him to review his desire by the light of its realization—by practical experience of its effects, in other words: a method whose teachings are more thorough and convincing than any school or college is able to supply. The use of the ballot, in short, as a means of instruction in the problems of government, takes the place of anything else; it will of itself build up a people both capable of conducting their own affairs, and resolved to do so. The plebeians of Virginia, therefore, who began by being poor and ignorant emigrants, or indentured servants, to whom the planters accorded such privileges because it had never occurred to them that a plebeian can ever become anything else—these men, unconsciously to themselves, perhaps, were on the road which leads to democracy. The time would come when they would cease to follow the lead of the planters; when their interests and the planters' would clash. In that collision, their numbers would give them the victory. With a similar community planted in the old world, such might not be the issue; the strong influence of tradition would combat it, and the surrounding pressure of settled countries, which offered no escape or asylum for the man of radical ideas. But the boundaries of Virginia were the untrammeled wilderness; any man who could not have his will in the colony had this limitless expanse at his disposal; there could be no finality for him in the decrees of assemblies, if he possessed the courage of his convictions in sufficient measure to make him match himself against the red man, and be independent not only of any special form of society, but of society itself. The consciousness of this would hearten him to entertain free thoughts, and to strive for their embodiment. It was partly this, no doubt, which, in the Seventeenth Century, drove hundreds of Ishmaels into the interior, where they became the Daniel Boones and the Davy Crocketts of legend and romance. So, although Virginia was as little likely as any of the colonies to breed a democracy, yet even there it was a more than possible outcome of the situation, even with no outside stimulus. But the old world, because it desired the oppression of America, was to become the immediate agent of its emancipation.

There was rejoicing in Virginia when Charles II. acceded to power; on the part of the planters, because they saw opportunity for political distinction; on the part of the plebeians, as the expression of a loyalty to kingship which centuries had made instinctive in them. Berkeley, putting himself in line with the predominant feeling, summoned the assembly in the name of the king, thus announcing without rebuke the termination of the era of self-government. The members who were elected were mostly royalists. They met in 1661. It was found that the Navigation Acts, which had been a dead letter ever since their passage, were to be revived in full force; and the increase of the colony in the meanwhile made them more than ever unwelcome. The exports were much larger than before, and unless the colony could have a free market for them the profits must be materially lessened. And again, since England was the only country from which the Virginian could purchase supplies, her merchants could charge him what they pleased. This was galling alike to royalists and roundheads in Virginia, and quickly healed the breach, such as it was, between the parties. Charles's true policy would have been to widen the gulf between them; instead of that, he forced them into each other's arms. It was determined to send Berkeley to England to ask relief; he accepted the commission, but his sympathies were not with the colonists, and he obtained nothing. Evidently, there could be no relief but in independence, and it was still a hundred years too early for that. The exasperation which this state of things produced in the great land owners did more for the cause of democracy than could decades of peaceful evolution. But the colonists could no longer have things their own way. Liberal laws were repealed, and intolerance and oppression took their place. Heretics were persecuted; the power of the church in civil affairs was increased;. and fines and taxes on the industry of the colony were wanton and excessive. The king of England directly ruled Virginia. The people were forced to pay Berkeley a thousand pounds sterling as his salary, and he declared he ought to get three times as much even as that. His true character was beginning to appear. The judges were appointed by the king, and the license thus given them resulted in a petty despotism; when an official wanted money, he caused a tax to be levied for the amount. Appeals were vain, and ere long were prohibited. The assembly, partisans of the king, declared themselves permanent, so that all chance for the people to be better represented was gone, and as the members fixed their own pay, and fixed it at a preposterous figure, the colony began to groan in earnest. But worse was to come. The suffrage was restricted to freeholders and householders, and at a stroke, all but a fraction of the colonists were deprived of any voice in their own government. The spread of education, never adequate, was stopped altogether. "I thank God there are no free schools nor printing," Sir William Berkeley was able to say, "and I hope we shall not have, these hundred years; for learning has brought disobedience and heresy and sects into the world, and printing has divulged them, and libels against the best government. God keep us from both!" This was a succinct and full formulation of the spirit which has ever tended to make the earth a hell for its inhabitants. "The ministers," added the governor, "should pray oftener, and preach less." But he spake in all solemnity; there was not the ghost of a sense of humor in his whole insufferable carcass.

The downward course was not to stop here. Charles, with the freehandedness of a highwayman, presented two of his favorites, in 1673, for a term of one and thirty years, with the entire colony! This act stirred even the soddenness of the legislature. At the time of their election, a dozen years before, they had been royalists indeed, but men of honor, intending the good of the colony; and had tried, as we saw, to stop the enforcement of the Navigation Acts. But when they discovered that they could continue themselves in office indefinitely, with such salary as they chose to demand, they soon became indifferent about the Navigation Acts, or anything else which respected the welfare and happiness of their fellows. Let the common folk do the work, and the better sort enjoy the proceeds: that was the true and only respectable arrangement. We may say that it sounds like a return to the dark ages; but perhaps if we enter into our closets and question ourselves closely, we shall find that precisely the same principles for which Berkeley and his assembly stood in 1673, are both avowed and carried into effect in this same country, in the very year of grace which is now passing over us. A nation, even in America, takes a great deal of teaching.

But the generosity of Charles startled the assembly out of their porcine indifference, for it threatened to bring to bear upon them the same practices by which they had destroyed the happiness of the colony. If the king had given over to these two men all sovereignty in Virginia, what was to prevent these gentlemen from dissolving the assembly, who had become, as it were, incorporate with their seats, and had hoped to die in them—and ruling the country and them without any legislative medium whatever? Accordingly, with gruntings of dismay, they chose three agents to sail forthwith to England, and expostulate with the merry monarch. The expostulation was couched in the most servile terms, as of men who love to be kicked, but hope to live, if only to be kicked again. Might the colony, they concluded, be permitted to buy itself out of the hands of its new owners, at their own price? And might the people of Virginia be free from any tax not approved by their assembly? That was the sum of their petition.

The king let his lawyers talk over the matter, and, when they reported favorably, good-naturedly said, "So let it be, then!" and permitted a charter to be drawn up. But before the broad seal could be affixed to it he altered his mind, for causes satisfactory to him, and the envoys were sent home, poorer than they came. But before relating what awaited them there, we must advert briefly to the doings of George Calvert, Lord Baltimore in the Irish peerage, in his new country of Maryland.

CHAPTER SIXTH

CATHOLIC, PHILOSOPHER, AND REBEL

THE first Lord Baltimore, whose family name was Calvert, was a Yorkshireman, born at the town of Kipling in 1580. He entered Parliament in his thirtieth year, and was James's Secretary of State ten years later. He was a man of large, tranquil nature, philosophic, charitable, loving peace; but these qualities were fused by a concrete tendency of thought, which made him a man of action, and determined that action in the direction of practical schemes of benevolence. The contemporary interest in America as a possible arena of enterprise and Mecca of religious and political dissenters, attracted his sympathetic attention; and when, in 1625, being then five-and-forty years of age, he found in the Roman Catholic communion a refuge from the clamor of warring sects, and as an immediate consequence tendered his resignation as secretary to the head of the Church of England, he found himself with leisure to put his designs in execution. He had, upon his conversion, been raised to the rank of Baron Baltimore in the peerage of Ireland; and his change of faith in no degree forfeited him the favor of the king. When therefore he asked for a charter to found a colony in Avalon, in Newfoundland, it was at once granted, and the colony was sent out; but his visits to it in 1627 and 1629 convinced him that the climate was too inclement for his purposes, and he requested that it might be transferred to the northern parts of Virginia, which he had visited on his way to England. This too was permitted; but before the new charter had been sealed Lord Baltimore died. The patent thereupon passed to his son Cecil, who was also a Catholic. He devoted his life to carrying out his father's designs. The characters of the two men were, in their larger elements, not dissimilar; and the sequel showed that colonial enterprise could be better achieved by one man of kindly and liberal disposition, and persistent resolve, than by a corporation, some of whose members were sure to thwart the wishes of others. Conditions of wider scope than the settlement of Maryland obstructed and delayed its proprietor's plans; conflicts and changes of government in England, and jealousy and violence on the part of Virginia, had their influence; but this quiet, benign, resolute young man (he was but seven-and-twenty when the grant made him sovereign of a kingdom) never lost his temper or swerved from his aim: overcame, apparently without an effort, the disabilities which might have been expected to hamper the professor of a faith as little consonant with the creed of the two Charleses as of Cromwell; was as well regarded, politically, by cavaliers as by roundheads; and finally established his ownership and control of his heritage, and, after a beneficent rule of over forty years, died in peace and honor with his people and the world. The story of colonial Maryland has a flavor of its own, and throws still further light on the subject of popular self-government—the source and solution of American history.

The idea of the Baltimores, as outlined in their charter, and followed in their practice, was to try the experiment of a democratic monarchy. They would found a state the people of which should enjoy all the freedom of action and thought that sane and well-disposed persons can desire, within the boundaries of their personal concerns; they should not be meddled with; each man's home should be his castle; they should say what taxes should be collected, and what civil officers should attend to their collective affairs. They should be like passengers on a ship, free to sleep or wake, sit or walk, speak or be mute, eat or fast, as they pleased: do anything in fact except scuttle the ship or cut the rigging—or ordain to what port she should steer, or what course the helmsman should lay. Matters of high policy, in other words, should be the care of the proprietor; everything less than that, broadly speaking, should be left to the colonists themselves. The proprietor could not get as close to their personal needs as they could: and they, preoccupied with private interests, could not see so far and wide as he could. If then it were arranged that they should be afforded every facility and encouragement to make their wants known: and if it were guaranteed that he would adopt every means that experience, wisdom and good-will suggested to gratify those wants: what more could mortal man ask? There was nothing abnormal in the idea. The principle is the same as that on which the Creator has placed man in nature: man is perfectly at liberty to do as he pleases; only, he must adapt himself to the law of gravitation, to the resistance of matter, to hot and cold, wet and dry, and to the other impersonal necessities by which the material universe is conditioned. The control of these natural laws, as they are called, could not advantageously be given in charge to man; even had he the brains to manage them, he could not spare the time from his immediate concerns. He is well content, accordingly, to leave them to the Power that put him where he is; and he does not feel his independence infringed upon in so doing. When his little business goes wrong, however, he can petition his Creator to help him out: or, what amounts to the same thing, he can find out in what respect he has failed to conform to the laws of nature, and, by returning into harmony with them, insure himself success. What the Creator was to mankind at large, Lord Baltimore proposed to be to his colony; and, following this supreme example, and binding himself to place the welfare of his people before all other considerations, how could he make a mistake?

In arguments about the best ways of managing nations or communities, it has been generally conceded that this scheme of an executive head on one side, and a people freely communicating their wants to him on the other, is sound, provided, first, that he is as solicitous about their welfare as they themselves are; and secondly, that means exist for continuous and unchecked intercommunication between them and him:—it being premised, of course, that the ability of the head is commensurate with his willingness. And leaving basic principles for the moment aside, it is notorious that one-man power is far prompter, weightier, and cleaner-cut than the confused and incomplete compromises of a body of representatives are apt to be.

All this may be conceded. And yet experience shows that the one-man system, even when the man is a Lord Baltimore, is unsatisfactory. Lord Baltimore, indeed, finally achieved a technical success; his people loved and honored him, his wishes were measurably realized, and, so far as he was concerned, Maryland was the victim of fewer mistakes than were the other colonies. But the fact that Lord Baltimore's career closed in peace and credit was due less to what he did and desired, than to the necessity his career was under of sooner or later coming to a close. Had he possessed a hundred times the ability and benevolence that were his, and had been immortal into the bargain, the people would have cast him out; they were willing to tolerate him for a few years, more or less, but as a fixture—No! "Tolerate" is too harsh a word; but another might be too weak. The truth is, men do not care half so much what they get, as how they get it. The wolf in Æsop's fable keenly wanted a share of the bones which made his friend the mastiff so sleek; but the hint that the bones and the collar went together drove him hungry but free back to his desert. It is of no avail to give a man all he asks for; he resents having to ask you for it, and wants to know by what right you have it to give. A man can be grateful for friendship, for a sympathetic look, for a brave word spoken in his behalf against odds—he can be your debtor for such things, and keep his manhood uncompromised. But if you give him food, and ease, or preferment, and condescension therewith, look for no thanks from him; esteem yourself fortunate if he do not hold you his enemy. The gifts of the soul are free; but material benefits are captivity. So the Maryland colonists, recognizing that their proprietor meant well, forgave him his generosity, and his activities in their behalf—but only because they knew that his day would presently be past. Man is infinite as well as finite: infinite in his claims, finite in his power of giving. And for Baltimore to presume to give the people all they claimed, was as much as to say that his fullness could equal their want, or that his rights and capacities were more than theirs. He gave them all that a democracy can possess—except the one thing that constitutes democracy; that is, absolute self-direction. It may well be that their little ship of state, steered by themselves, would have encountered many mishaps from which his sagacious guidance preserved it. But rather rocks with their pilotage than port with his: and beyond forgiving him their magnanimity could not go.

There is little more than this to be derived from study of the Maryland experiment. Let a man manage himself, in big as well as in little things, and he will be happy on raw clams and plain water, with a snow-drift for a pillow —as we saw him happy in Plymouth Bay: but give him roast ortolans and silken raiment, and manage him never so little, and you cannot relieve his discontent. And is it not well that it should be so? Verily it is—if America be not a dream, and immortality a delusion.

Lord Baltimore would perhaps have liked to see all his colonists Catholics; but his experience of religious intolerance had not inflamed him against other creeds than his own, as would have been the case with a Spaniard; it seemed to awaken a desire to set tolerance an example. Any one might join his community except felons and atheists; and as a matter of fact, his assortment of colonists soon became as motley as that of Williams in Providence. The landing of the first expedition on an island in the Potomac was attended by the making and erecting by the Jesuit priests of a rude cross, and the celebration of mass; but there were even then more Protestants than Catholics in the party; and though the leadership was Catholic for many years, it was not on account of the numerical majority of persons of that faith. Episcopalians ejected from New England, Puritans fleeing from the old country, Quakers and Anabaptists who were unwelcome everywhere else, met with hospitality in Maryland. Let them but believe in Jesus Christ, and all else was forgiven them. Nevertheless, Catholicism was the religion of the country. Its inhabitants might be likened to promiscuous guests at an inn whose landlord made no criticisms on their beliefs, further than to inscribe the Papal insignia on the signboard over his door. Thus liberty was discriminated from license, and in the midst of tolerance there was order.

The first settlement was made on a small creek entering the north side of the Potomac. Here an Indian village already existed; but its occupants were on the point of deserting it, and were glad to accept payment from the colonists for the site which they had no further use for. On the other hand, the colonists could avail themselves of the wigwams just as they stood, and had their maize fields ready cleared. Baltimore, meanwhile, through his agent (and brother) Leonard Calvert, furnished them with all the equipment they needed; and so well was the way smoothed before them, that the colony made progress ten times as rapidly as Virginia had done. They called their new home St. Mary's; and the date of its occupation was 1634. Their first popular assembly met for legislation in the second month of the ensuing year. In that and subsequent meetings they asserted their right of jurisdiction, their right to enact laws, the freedom of "holy church": his lordship gently giving them their head. In 1642, perhaps to disburden themselves of some of their obligation to him, they voted him a subsidy. Almost the only definite privilege which he seems to have retained was that of pre-emption of lands. At this period (1643) all England was by the ears, and Baltimore's hold upon his colony was relaxed. In Virginia and the other colonies, which had governors of their own, the neglect of the mother country gave them opportunity for progress; but the people of Maryland, no longer feeling the sway of their non-resident proprietor, and having no one else to look after them, became disorderly; which would not have happened, had they been empowered to elect a ruler from among themselves. Baltimore's enemies took advantage of these disturbances to petition for his removal from the proprietorship; but he was equal to the occasion; and by confirming his colonists in all just liberties, with freedom of conscience in the foreground, he composed their dissensions, and took away his enemies' ground of complaint. In 1649, the legislature sat for the first time in two branches, so that one might be a check upon the other. Upon this principle all American legislatures are still formed.

But the reign of Cromwell in England gave occasion for sophistries in Maryland. All other Englishmen, in the colonies or at home, were members of a commonwealth; but Baltimore still claimed the Marylanders' allegiance. On what grounds?—for since the king from whom he derived his power was done away with, so must be the derivitive power. Baltimore stood between them and republicanism. To give edge to the predicament, the colony was menaced by covetous Virginia on one hand, and by fugitive Charles II., with a governor of his own manufacture, on the other. Calamity seemed at hand.

In 1650, the year after Charles I.'s execution, the Parliament appointed commissioners to bring royalist colonies into line; Maryland was to be reannexed to Virginia; Bennett, then governor of Virginia, and Clairborne, unseated Stone, Baltimore's lieutenant, appointed an executive council, and ordered that burgesses were to be elected by supporters of Cromwell only. The question of reannexation was referred to Parliament. Baltimore protested that Maryland had been less royalist than Virginia; and before the Parliament could decide what to do, it was dissolved, carrying with it the authority of Bennett and Clairborne. Stone now reappeared defiant; but the Virginians attacked him, and he surrendered on compulsion. The Virginian government decreed that no Roman Catholics could hereafter vote or be elected.

Baltimore, taking his stand on his charter, declared these doings mutinous; and Cromwell supported him. Stone once more asserted himself; but in the skirmish with the Virginians that followed, he was defeated, yielded (he seems to have had no granite in his composition), and, with his supporters, was ordered to be shot. His life was spared, however; but Cromwell, again appealed to, refused to act. The ownership of Maryland was therefore still undetermined. It was not until 1657 that Baltimore and Bennett agreed to compromise their dispute. The boundary between the two domains was maintained, but settlers from Virginia were not to be disturbed in their holdings. The second year after Cromwell's death, the representatives of Maryland met and voted themselves an independent assembly, making Fendall, Baltimore's appointee, subject to their will. Finally, being weary of turmoil, they made it felony to alter what they had done. The colony was then abreast of Virginia in political privileges, and had a population of about ten thousand, in spite of its vicissitudes.

But the quiet, invincible Lord Baltimore was still to be reckoned with. At the Restoration, he sent his deputy to the colony, which submitted to his authority, and Fendall was convicted of treason for having allowed the assembly to overrule him. A general amnesty was proclaimed, however, and the kindliness of the government during the remainder of the proprietor's undisputed sway attracted thousands of settlers from all the nations of Europe. Between Baltimore and the people, a give-and-take policy was established, one privilege being set against another, so that their liberties were maintained, and his rights recognized. Though he stood in his own person for all that was opposed to democracy, he presided over a community which was essentially democratic; and he had the breadth of mind to acknowledge that because he owned allegiance to kings and popes, was no reason why others should do so. Suum cuique. Could he but have gone a step further, and denied himself the gratification of retaining his hard-earned proprietorship, he would have been one of the really great men of history.

The ripple of events which we have recorded may seem too insignificant; of still less import is the story of the efforts of Clairborne, from 1634 to 1647, to gain, or retain possession of Kent Island, in the Chesapeake, on which he had "squatted" before Baltimore got his charter. Yet, from another point of view, even slight matters may weigh when they are related to the stirring of the elements which are to crystallize into a nation. Maryland, like a bird half tamed, was ready to fly away when the cage door was left open, and yet was not averse to its easy confinement when the door was shut again. But, unlike the bird, time made it fonder of liberty, instead of leading it to forget it; and when the cage fell apart, it was at home in the free air.

The settlement of the Carolinas, during the twenty years or so from 1660 to 1680, presented features of singular grotesqueness. There was, on one side, a vast wilderness covering the region now occupied by North and South Carolina, and westward to the Pacific. It had been nibbled at, for a hundred years, by Spaniards, French and English, but no permanent hold had been got upon it. Here were thousands upon thousands of square miles in which nature rioted unrestrained, with semi-tropic fervor; the topography of which was unknown, and whose character in any respect was a matter of pure conjecture. This wilderness was on one side; on the other were a worthless king, a handful of courtiers, and a couple of highly gifted doctrinaires, Lord Shaftesbury and John Locke, the philosopher. We can picture Charles II. lolling in his chair, with a map of the Americas spread out on his knees, while the other gentlemen in big wigs and silk attire, and long rapiers dangling at their sides, are grouped about him. "I'll give you all south of Virginia," says he, indicating the territory with a sweep of his long fingers. "Ashley, you and your friend Locke can draw up a constitution, and stuff it full of your fine ideas; they sound well: we'll see how they work. You shall be kings every man of you; and may you like it no worse than I do! You'll have no France or Holland to thwart you—only bogs and briers and a few naked blacks. Your charter shall pass the seals to-morrow: and much good may it do you!"

So the theorists and the courtiers set out to subdue the untutored savageness of nature with a paper preamble and diagrams and rules and inhibitions, and orders of nobility and a college of heralds, and institutions of slavery and serfdom, and definitions of freeholders and landgraves, caciques and palatines; and specifications of fifths for proprietors, fifths for the nobility, and the rest for the common herd, who were never to be permitted to be anything but the common herd, with no suffrage, no privileges, and no souls. All contingencies were provided against, except the one contingency, not wholly unimportant, that none of the proposals of the Model Constitution could be carried into effect. Strange, that Ashley Cooper—as Lord Shaftesbury was then—one of the most brilliant men in Europe, and John Locke, should get together and draw squares over a sheet of paper, each representing four hundred and eighty thousand acres, with a cacique and landgraves and their appurtenances in each—and that they should fail to perceive that corresponding areas would never be marked out in the pathless forests, and that noblemen could not be found nor created to take up their stand, like chessmen, each in his lonely and inaccessible morass or mountain or thicket, and exercise the prerogatives of the paper preamble over trees and panthers and birds of the air! How could men of such radiant intelligence as Locke and Shaftesbury unquestionably were, show themselves so radically ignorant of the nature of their fellowmen, and of the elementary principles of colonization? The whole thing reads, to-day, like some stupendous jest; yet it was planned in grave earnest, and persons were found to go across the Atlantic and try to make it work.

Lord Shaftesbury was one of the Hampshire Coopers, and the first earl. He was a sort of English Voltaire: small and thin, nervous and fractious, with a great cold brain, no affections and no illusions; he had faith in organizations, but none in man; was destitute of compunctions, careless of conventions and appearances, cynical, penetrating, and frivolous. He was a skeptic in religion, but a devotee of astrology; easily worried in safety, but cool and audacious in danger. He despised if he did not hate the people, and regarded kings as an unavoidable nuisance; the state, he thought, was the aristocracy, whose business it was to keep the people down and hold the king in check. His career

—now supporting the royalists, now the roundheads, now neither—seems incoherent and unprincipled; but in truth he was one of the least variable men of his time; he held to his course, and king and parliament did the tacking. He was an incorruptible judge, though he took bribes; and an unerring one, though he disregarded forms of law. He was tried for treason, and acquitted; joined the Monmouth conspiracy, and escaped to Holland, where he died at the age of sixty-two. What he lacked was human sympathies, which are the beginning of wisdom; and this deficiency it was, no doubt, that led him into the otherwise incomprehensible folly of the Carolina scheme.

Locke could plead the excuse of being totally unfamiliar with practical life; he was a philosopher of abstractions, who made an ideal world to fit his theories about it. He could write an essay on the Understanding, but was unversed in Common-sense. His nature was more calm and normal than Shaftesbury's, but in their intellectual conclusions they were not dissimilar. The views about the common people which Sir William Berkeley expressed with stupid brutality, they stated with punctual elegance. They were well mated for the purpose in hand, and they performed it with due deliberation and sobriety. It was not until five years after the grant was made that the constitution was written and sealed. It achieved an instantaneous success in England, much as a brilliant novel might, in our time; and the authors were enthusiastically belauded. The proprietors—Albemarle, Craven, Clarendon, Berkeley, Sir William Berkeley, Sir John Colleton and Sir George Carteret, and Shaftesbury himself—began to look about for their serfs and caciques, and to think of their revenues. Meanwhile the primeval forest across three thousand miles of ocean laughed with its innumerable leaves, and waved its boughs in the breath of the spirit of liberty. The laws of the study went forth to battle with the laws of nature.

Ignorant of these courtly and scholarly proceedings, a

small knot of bona-fide settlers had built their huts on Albemarle Sound, and had for some years been living there in the homeliest and most uneducated peace and simplicity. Some had come from Virginia, some from New England, and others from the island of Bermuda. They had their little assembly and their governor Stevens, their humble plantations, their modest trade, their beloved solitudes, and the plainest and least obtrusive laws imaginable. They paddled up and down their placid bayous and rivers in birch-bark canoes; they shot deer and 'possums for food and panthers for safety, they loved their wives and begat their children, they wore shirts and leggins of deerskin like the Indians, and they breathed the pure wholesomeness of the warm southern air. When to these backwoods innocents was borne from afar the marvelous rumors of the silk-stockinged and lace-ruffled glories, originated during an idle morning in the king's dressing-room, which were to transfigure their forest into trim gardens and smug plantations, surrounding royal palaces and sumptuous hunting pavilions, perambulated by uniformed officials, cultivated by meek armies of serfs, looking up from their labors only to doff their caps to lordly palatines and lily-fingered ladies with high heels and low corsages: when they tried to picture to themselves their solemn glades and shadow-haunted streams and inviolate hills, their eyries of eagles and lairs of stag and puma, the savage beauty of their perilous swamps, all the wild magnificence of this pure home of theirs—metamorphosed by royal edict into a magnified Versailles, in which lutes and mandolins should take the place of the wolf's howl and the panther's scream, the keen scent of the pine balsam be replaced by the reek of musk and patchouli, the honest sanctity of their couches of fern give way to the embroidered corruption of a fine lady's bedchamber, the simple vigor of their pioneer parliament bewitch itself into a glittering senate chamber, where languid chancellors fingered their golden chains and exchanged witty epigrams with bigwigged, snuff-taking cavaliers:—when they attempted to house these strange ideas in their unsophisticated brains, they must have stared at one another with a naive perplexity which slowly broadened their tanned and bearded visages into contagious grins. They looked at their hearty, clear-eyed wives, and watched the gambols of their sturdy children, and shook their heads, and turned to their work once more.

The first movements of the new dispensation took the form of trying to draw the colonists together into towns, of reviving the Navigation Acts, of levying taxes on their infant commerce, and in general of tying fetters of official red tape on the brawny limbs of a primitive and natural civilization. The colony was accused of being the refuge of outlaws and traitors, rogues and heretics; and Sir William Berkeley, governor of Virginia, one of the proprietors under the Model Constitution, was deputed to make as much mischief in the virgin settlement as he could.

The colonists numbered about four thousand, spread over a large territory; they did not want to desert their palmetto-thatched cabins and strenuously-cleared acres; they disliked crowding into towns; they saw no justice in paying to intangible and alien proprietors a penny tax on their tobacco exports to New England—though they paid it nevertheless. They particularly objected to the interference of Governor Berkeley, for they knew him well. And when the free election of their assembly was attacked, they sent emissaries to England to remonstrate, and meanwhile, John Culpepper leading, and without waiting for the return of their emissaries, they arose and wiped out the things and persons that were objectionable, and then returned serenely to their business. They did not fly into a passion, and froth at the mouth, and massacre and torture; but quietly and inflexibly, with hardly a keener flash from their fearless eyes, they put things to rights, and thought no more about it.

Such treasonable proceedings, however, fluttered the

council chambers in London sorely, and stout John Culpepper, who believed in popular liberty and was not afraid to say so, went to England to justify what had been done. He was arrested and put on trial, though he demanded to be tried, if at all, in the place where the offense was committed. The intent of his adversaries was not to give him justice, but simply to hang him; and why go to the trouble and expense of carrying him to Carolina to do that? He went near to becoming a martyr, did stout John; but, unexpectedly, Shaftesbury, who might believe in despotism, but who fretted to behold injustice, undertook his defense and brought him out clear. The rest of the "rebels" were amnestied the following year, 1681. But one Seth Sothel, who had bought out Lord Clarendon's proprietary rights, was sent out as governor; and after escaping from the Algerine pirates, who captured and kept him for a couple of years, he arrived at Albemarle, commissioned, as Bancroft admirably puts it, to "Transform a log cabin into a baronial castle, a negro slave into a herd of leet-men." Sothel was not long in perceiving that this was beyond his powers, but he could steal: and so he did for a few years, when the colonists, thinking he had enough, unseated him, tried him, and sentenced him to a year's exile and to nevermore be officer of theirs.

These planters of North Carolina were good Americans from the beginning, endowed with a courage and love of liberty which foretold the spirit of Washington's army, and a religious tolerance which did not prevent them from listening with sympathy and approval to the spiritual harangues of Fox, the Quaker, who sojourned among them with gratifying results. Their prejudice against towns continued, and one must walk far to visit them, with only marks on the forest trees to guide. They were inveterately contented, and having emancipated themselves from the blight of the Model Constitution, rapidly became prosperous. The only effect of Messrs. Locke and Shaftesbury's scheme of an aristocratic Utopia was to make the settlers conscious of their strength and devoted to their freedom. Indeed, the North Carolinians were in great part men who had not only fled from the oppressions of England, but had found even the mild restraints of the other colonies irksome.

The fate of the Model in South Carolina was similar, though the preliminary experiences were different. When Joseph West, agent for the proprietors, and William Sayle, experienced in colonizing, took three shiploads of emigrants to the junction of the Ashley and Cooper rivers, about twenty miles south of latitude 33°, they had a copy of the Model with them. But the first thing they did after getting ashore was to vote that its provisions were impracticable, and to revise it to such a degree that, when it was sent over to England for approval, its authors did not recognize their work, and disowned it. But the settlers constituted their assembly on the general lines which might now be called American, and put up their huts, in 1672, on the ground where now stands Charleston. The climate was too hot for white labor, and the timely arrival of negro slaves was welcome; in a few years they doubled the number of the whites. The staple crops of the southern plantations needed much more work than those of New England and the north, and this, as well as the preference of the negroes themselves for the warmer climates, determined the distribution of black slavery on the Atlantic coast.

Dutch settlers presently joined the English; a Scotch-Irish colony at Port Royal was set upon by the Spaniards, who, in accordance with the characteristic Spanish policy, massacred the inhabitants and burned the houses. But later the revocation by Louis XIV. of the amnesty to Huguenots caused the latter to fly their country and disperse themselves over Europe and America; no higher or finer class of men and women ever joined the ranks of exile, and they were everywhere welcomed. Colonies of them settled all along the Atlantic seaboard; and around Charleston many from Languedoc found a congenial home, and became a valuable and distinguished part of the population. America could not have been complete without the leaven of the heroic French Protestants.

Meanwhile the proprietors were gradually submitting, with no good grace, however, to the inevitable. Their Model remained a model—something never to be put to practical use. On paper was it born, and on paper should it remain forever. The proprietors were kings, by grace of Charles II., but they had neither army nor navy, and their subjects declined to be serfs. They declined into the status of land speculators; the governors whom they sent out did nothing but fill their pockets and let the people have the rest. At last, it was enough for the proprietors to suggest anything for the people to negative it, whether it were good or bad. They not only avowed their natural right to do as they pleased, but deemed it due to their self-respect not to do what was pleasing to their tinsel sovereigns in London. And finally, when Colleton, one of the sovereigns in question, tried to declare martial law in the colony, on the plea of danger from Indians or Spanish, the indomitable freemen treated him as their brethren at Albemarle had treated Sothel. The next year saw William and Mary on the English throne; Shaftesbury had died seven years before; and the Great Model subsided without a bubble into the vacuum of historical absurdities.

We left Virginia awaiting the return of the envoys who had gone to ask Charles for justice and protection against the tyranny of Berkeley. Charles, as we know, first promised the reforms, and then broke his promise, as all Stuarts must. But before the envoys could return with their heavy news, there had been stirring things done and suffered in Virginia.

The character of Berkeley is as detestable as any known in the annals of the American colonies. Many of his acts, and all the closing scenes of his career, seem hardly compatible with moral sanity; in our day, when science is so prone to find the explanation of crime in insanity, he would undoubtedly have been adjudged to the nearest asylum. In his early years, he had been stupid and illiberal, but nothing worse; in his old age, he seemed to seek out opportunities of wickedness and outrage, and at last he gave way to transports which could only be likened to those of a fiend from the Pit, permitted for a season to afflict the earth. He was as base as he was wicked; a thief, and perjured, as well as an insatiable murderer. The only trait that seems to ally him with manhood is itself animal and repulsive. He had wholly abandoned any pretense of self-control; and in some of the outbursts of his frenzy he seems to have become insensible even to the suggestions of physical fear. But this can hardly be accorded the name of courage; rather is it to be attributed to the suffusion of blood to the brain which drives the Malay to run amuck.

Virginia had been nurtured in liberty, and was ill prepared for despotism. On the contrary, she was almost ready to doubt the wisdom or convenience of any government whatever, except such as was spontaneously furnished by the generous and magnanimous instincts of her people. There were no towns, and none of the vice and selfishness which crowded populations engender. Roads, bridges, public works of any sort were unknown; the population seldom met except at races or to witness court proceedings. The great planters lived in comparative comfort, but they were as much in love with freedom as were the common people. This state of things was the outcome of the growth of fifty years; and most of the eight thousand inhabitants of the colony were born on the soil, and loved it as the only home they knew.

The chief injury they had suffered was from the depredations of the Indians, who, on their side, could plead that they had received less than justice at the colonists' hands.

Border raids and killings became more and more frequent and alarming; the savages had learned the use of muskets, and were good marksmen. They built a fort on the Maryland border, and for a time resisted siege operations; and when at length some of the chiefs came out to parley, they were seized and shot. The rest of the Indian garrison escaped by night, and slaughtered promiscuously all whom they could surprise along the countryside. A force was raised to check them, and avenge the murders; but before it could come in contact with them, Berkeley sent out a peremptory summons that they should return.

What was the explanation of this extraordinary step? Simply that the Governor had the monopoly of the Indian trade, which was very valuable, and would not permit the Indians who traded with him to be driven away. In order to supply his already overloaded pockets with money, he was willing to see the red men murder with impunity, and with the brutalities of torture and outrage, the men, women and children of his own race. But the Indians themselves seem admirable in contrast with the inhumanity of this gray-haired, wine-bloated, sordid cavalier of seventy.

The troops on which the safety of the colonists depended reluctantly retired. Immediately the savages renewed their attacks; three hundred settlers were killed. Still Berkeley refused to permit anything to be done; forts might be erected on the borders, but these, besides being of great expense to the people, were wholly useless for their defense, inasmuch as the savages could without difficulty slip by them under cover of the forest. The raids continued, and the plantations were abandoned, till not one in seven remained. The inhabitants were terror-stricken; no man's life was safe. At last permission was asked that the people might raise and equip a force at their own expense, in the exercise of the universal right of self-protection; but even this was violently forbidden by the Governor, who threatened punishment on any who should presume to take arms against them. All traffic with them had also been interdicted; but it was known that Berkeley himself continued his trading with those whose hands were red with the blood of the wives, fathers and children of Virginia.

Finally, in 1676, the report came that an army of Indians were approaching Jamestown. Unless resistance were at once made, there seemed nothing to prevent the extinction of the colony. Berkeley, apparently for no better reason than that he would not recede from a position once taken, adhered to his order that nothing should be done.

There was at that time in Virginia a young Englishman of about thirty, named Nathaniel Bacon. He was descended from good ancestors, and had received a thorough education, including terms in the Inns of Court. He was intellectual, thoughtful, and self-contained, with a clear mind, a generous nature, and the power of winning and controlling men. He had arrived in the colony a little more than a year before, and had been chosen to the council; he was wealthy and aristocratic, yet a known friend of the people. Born in 1642, he was familiar with revolutions, and had formed his own opinions as to the rights of man. He had a plantation on the site of the present city of Richmond; and during the late Indian troubles, had lost his overseer. Coming down on his affairs to Jamestown, he fell into talk with some friends, who suggested crossing the river to see some of the volunteers who had come together for defense. These men were in a mood of excited exasperation at the sinister conduct of the governor, and ready to follow extreme counsels had they had a leader with the boldness and ability to put himself at their head.

The tall, slender figure and grave features of Bacon were well-known. As he advanced toward the troop of stalwart young fellows, who were sullenly discussing the situation, he was recognized; and something seems to have suggested to them that he was come with a purpose. Conclusions are sudden at such times, and impulses contagious as fire. He was the leader whom they sought. "A Bacon—a Bacon!" shouted some one; and instantly the cry was taken up. They thronged around him, welcoming him, cheering him, exclaiming that they would follow him, that with them at his back he should save the country in spite of the governor! They were fiery and emotional, after the manner of the sons of the Old Dominion, and the wrongs of many kinds which had long been rankling in their hearts now demanded to be requited by some action—no matter how daring. Virginians never shrank from danger.

Bacon had been wholly unprepared for this outburst; but he had a strong, calm soul, a ready brain, and the blood of youth. He knew what the colony had endured, and that it had nothing to hope from the present government. He had come to America after making the European tour, intending only a visit; but he had grown attached to Virginia, and now that chance had put this opportunity to help her, he resolved to accept it. He would throw in his lot with these spirited and fearless young patriots—the first men in America who had the right to call the country their own. Standing before them, with his head bared, and in a voice that all could hear, he solemnly pledged himself to lead them against the Indians, and then aid them to recover the liberties which had been wrested from them. "And do you," he added, "pledge yourselves to me!" His words were heard with tumultuous enthusiasm, and a round-robin was signed, binding all to stick to their captain and to one another. That is a document which history would fain have preserved.

With an army of three hundred Virginians, Bacon set forward against the Indians. Meanwhile Berkeley, enraged at this slight on his authority, called some troops together and dispatched them to bring back "the rebels." Thus was seen the singular spectacle of a government force marching to apprehend men who were risking their lives freely to repel a danger imminent and common to all

But Berkeley was going too far. Bacon's act had the sympathy of all except such as were as corrupt as the governor, and the men of the lower counties revolted, and demanded that the long scandal of the continuous assembly should cease forthwith. Berkeley was intimidated; he had not believed that any spirit was left in the colony; he recalled his men, and consented to the assembly's dissolution. By the time Bacon and his three hundred got back from their successful campaign, the writs for a new election were out; and he was unanimously chosen burgess from Henrico. The assembly of which he thus became a member was for the most part in sympathy with him; and though, for the benefit of the record, censure was passsd upon the irregularity of his campaign, and he was required to apologize for fighting without a commission, yet he was at the same time caressed and praised on all sides, returned to the council, and dubbed the darling of Virginia's hopes. The assembly then proceeded to undo all the evil and clean out all the rottenness that had disgraced the conduct of their predecessors. Taxes, church tyranny, restriction of the franchise, illegal assessments, fees, and liquor-dealing were done away; two magistrates were proved thieves and disfranchised, and trade with Indians was for the present stopped. Bacon received a commission; but Berkeley refused to sign it; and when Bacon appealed to the country, and returned with five hundred men to demand his rights, the governor was beside himself with fury.

Private letters and other documents, made public only long after this date, are the authority for what occurred; but though certain facts are given, explanations are seldom available. Berkeley appears to have been holding court when Bacon and his followers appeared; it is said that he ran out and confronted them, tore his shirt open and declared that sooner should they shoot him than he would sign the commission of that rebel; and the next moment, changing his tactics, he offered to settle the issue between

EARLY NEW ENGLAND SCENE—A QUAKER IN THE STOCKS

Bacon and himself by a duel. All this does not sound like the acts of a man in his sober senses. It seems probable either that the old reprobate was intoxicated, or that his mind was disordered by passion. Bacon, of course, declined to match his youthful vigor against his decrepit enemy, as the latter must have known he would: and told him temperately that the commission he demanded was to enable him to repel the savages who were murdering their fellow colonists unchecked. The governor, after some further parley, again altered his behavior, and now overpowered Bacon with maudlin professions of esteem for his patriotic energy; signed his commission, and sent dispatches to England warmly commending him. A formal amnesty, obliterating all past acts of the popular champion and his supporters which could be construed as irregular, was drawn up and ratified by the governor; and the clouds which so long had lowered over Virginia seemed to have been at last in the deep bosom of the ocean buried. To those whom coincidences interest it will be significant that this victory for the people was won on the 4th of July, 1676.

Operations against the Indians were now vigorously resumed; but Berkeley had not yet completed the catalogue of his iniquities. Bacon's back was scarcely turned, before he violated the amnesty which he had just ratified, and tried to rouse public sentiment against the liberator. In this, however, he signally failed, as also in his attempt to raise a levy to arrest him; and frightened at the revelation of his weakness, he fled in a panic to Accomack, a peninsula on the eastern side of Chesapeake Bay. Word of his proceedings had in the meantime been conveyed to Bacon by Drummond, former governor of North Carolina, and Lawrence. "Shall he who commissioned us to protect the country from the heathen, betray our lives?" said Bacon. "I appeal to the king and parliament!" He established himself in Williamsburg; at Drummond's suggestion Berkeley's flight was taken to mean his withdrawal from the governorship—

which, at any rate, had now passed its appointed limit—and a summons was sent out to the gentlemen of Virginia to meet for consultation as to the future conduct of the colony. It was at this juncture that the envoys returned from England, with the dark news that Charles had refused all relief.

At the conference, after full discussion, it was voted that the colony take the law into their own hands, and maintain themselves not only against the Indians and Berkeley, but if need were against England herself. "I fear England no more than a broken straw," said Sarah Drummond, snapping a stick in her hands as she spoke: the women of Virginia were as resolved as the men. Pending these contingencies, Bacon with his little army again set out in pursuit of the Indians; hearing which, Berkeley, with a train of mercenaries which he had contrived to collect, crossed from Accomack and landed at Jamestown, where he repeated his refrain of "rebels!" He promised freedom to whatever slaves of the colony would enlist on his side, and fortified the little town. The crews of some English ships in the harbor assisted him; and in the sequel these tars were the only ones of his rabble that stayed by him. The neighborhood was alarmed, fearing any kind of enormity, and messengers rode through the woods post haste, and swam the rivers, in the sultry September weather, to find and recall their defenders, and summon them to resist a worse foe than the red man. Before they could reach the young leader, the Indians had been routed, the army disbanded, and Bacon, with a handful of followers, was on his way to his plantation. They were weary with the fatigues of the campaign, but on learning that the prime source of the troubles was intrenched in Jamestown, and that "man, woman and child" were in peril of slavery, they turned their horses' heads southeastward, and galloped to the rescue. They gathered recruits on their way—no one could resist the eloquence of Bacon—and halting at such of the plantations as were owned by royalist sympathizers, they compelled their wives to mount and accompany them as hostages. This indicates to what extremes the violence of Berkeley was expected to go. It was evening when they came in sight of the enemy. But the moon was already aloft, and as the western light faded, her mellow radiance flooded the scene, giving it the semblance of peace. But the impatient Virginians wished to attack at once; and a lesser man than Bacon might have yielded to their urging. Knowing, however, that the country was with him, and feeling that the enemy must sooner or later succumb, he would not win by a dashing, bloody exploit what time was sure to give him. He ordered an intrenchment to be dug, and prepared for a siege. But there was no lust for battle in the disorderly and incoherent force which the frantic appeals and reckless promises of the governor had assembled; they were beaten already, and could not be induced to make a sortie. Desertions began, and all the objurgations, supplications and melodramatic extravaganzas of Berkeley were impotent to stop them; the more shrilly he shrieked, the faster did his sorry aggregation melt away. When it became evident that there would soon be none left save himself and the sailors, he ceased his blustering, and scuttled off toward Gloucester and the Rappahannock.

Bacon, Drummond, Lawrence and their men occupied the abandoned town, in which some of them owned houses, and burned it to the ground. The act was deliberate; the town records were first removed; and the men who had most to lose by the conflagration were the first to set the torch. Jamestown at that time contained hardly twenty buildings all told; but it was the first settlement of the Dominion, and sentiment would fain have preserved it. A mossy ruin, draped in vines, is all that remains of it now. The ascertainable causes of its destruction seem inadequate; yet the circumstances show that it could not have been done in mere wantonness. Civilized warfare permits the destruction of the enemy's property; but the enemy had retreated, and the expectation was that he would never return. That Bacon had reasons, his previous record justifies us in believing; but what they were is matter of conjecture. As it is, the burning of Jamestown is the only passage in his brief and gallant career which can be construed as a blemish upon it. Unfortunately, it was, also, all but the final one.

He pursued Berkeley, and the army of the latter, instead of fighting, marched over to him with a unanimity which left the governor almost without a companion in his chagrin. The whole of Virginia was now in Bacon's hand; he had no foes; he was called Deliverer; he had never met reverse; he was a man of intellect, judgment and honor, and he was in the prime of his youth; in such a country, beloved, and supported by such a people, what might he not have hoped to achieve? Men like him are rare; in a country just emerging into political consciousness, he was doubly precious. There was no one to take his place; the return of Berkeley meant all that was imaginable of evil; and yet Bacon was to die, and Berkeley was to return.

In the trenches before Jamestown Bacon had contracted the seeds of a fever which now, in the hour of his triumph, overcame him. After a short struggle he succumbed; and his men, fearing, apparently, that the ghoulish revenge of the old governor might subject his remains to insult, sunk his body in the river; and none know where lie the bones of the first American patriot who died in arms against oppression. His worth is proved by the confusion and disorganization which ensued upon his death. Cheeseman, Hansford, Wilford and Drummond could not make head against disaster. On the governor's side, Robert Beverly developed the qualities of a leader, and a series of small engagements left the patriots at his mercy. Berkeley was re-established in his place; and then began the season of his revenge.

His victims were the gentlemen of Virginia: the flower

of the province. He had no mercy; his sole thought was to add insult to the bitterness of death. He would not spare their lives; he would not shoot them; they must perish on the gallows, not as soldiers, but as rebels. When a young wife pleaded for her gallant husband, declaring that it was she who persuaded him to join the patriotic movement, Berkeley denied her prayer with coarse brutality. When Drummond was brought before him, he assured him of his pleasure in their meeting: "You shall be hanged in half an hour." One can see that mean, flushed countenance, ravaged by time and intemperance, with bloodshot eyes, gloating over the despair of his foes, and searching for means to torture their minds while destroying their bodies. Trial by jury was not quick or sure enough for Berkeley; he condemned them by court-martial, and the noose was round their necks at once. Their families were stripped of their property and sent adrift to subsist on charity. In his bloodthirstiness, he never forgot his pecuniary advantage, and his thievish fingers grasped all the valuables that his murderous instincts brought within his power. But the spectacle is too revolting for contemplation.

"He would have hanged half the country if we had let him alone," was the remark of a member of the assembly. It was voted that the execution should cease; more than two-score men had already been strangled for defending their homes and resisting oppression. Even Charles in London was annoyed when he heard of the wasteful malignity of "the old fool," and sent word of his disapproval and displeasure. A successor was sent over to supersede him; but he at first refused to go at the king's command, though he had ever used the king's name as the warrant for his crimes. He had sold powder and shot to the Indians to kill his own people with; he had appropriated the substance of widows and orphans whom he had made such; he had punished by public whipping all who were reported to have spoken against him; he forbade the printing-press; but all had been done "for the King." And now he resisted the authority of the king himself. But Charles, for once, was determined, and Berkeley, under the disgrace of severe reprimand, was forced to go. The joy bells clashed out the people's delight as the ship which carried him dropped down the harbor, and the firing of guns was like an anticipation of our celebration of Independence Day. He stood on the poop, in the beauty of the morning, shaking out curses from his trembling hands, in helpless hatred of the fair land and gallant people that he had done his utmost to make miserable. In England, the king would have none of him, and he met with nothing but rebuffs and condemnation on all sides. The power which he had misused was forever gone; he was old, and shattered in constitution; he was disgraced, flouted, friendless and alone. He died soon after his arrival, of mortification; he had lived only to do evil; and to withhold him from it was to take his life away.

It is not the function of the historian to condemn. Berkeley was by birth and training an aristocrat and a cavalier, and he was a creature of his age and station. He had been taught to believe that the patrician is of another flesh and blood than the plebeian; that authority can be enforced only by tyranny; that the only right is that of birth, and of the strongest. He was early placed in a position where every personal indulgence was made easy to him, where there was none to call in question his authority, and where there was temptation to assert authority by oppression, and by arrogating absolute license to act as the whim prompted, and to lay hands on whatever he coveted. Add to these conditions a nature congenitally without generous instincts, a narrow brain, and a sensual temperament, and we have gone far to account for the phenomenon which Berkeley finally, in his approaching senility, presented. He was the type of the worst traits that caused England ultimately to forfeit America; the concentration of whatever is opposite to popular liberties. His deeds must be execrated; but we cannot put him beyond the pale of human nature, or deny that under different circumstances he would have been a better man. We may admit, too, that, in the wisdom of Providence, he was placed where, by doing so much mischief, he was involuntarily the cause of more good than he could ever willingly have accomplished. He taught the people how to hate despotism, and how to struggle against it. He wrought a mutual understanding and sympathy between the upper and lower orders; he led them to define to their own minds what things are indispensable to the existence of true democracy. These are some of the uses which he, and such as he, in their own despite subserved. He and the young Bacon were mortal foes; but he, by opposing Bacon, and murdering his friends, aided the cause for which they laid down their lives.

After his departure there ensued a period of ten years or more, during which the pressure upon Virginia seemed rather to grow heavier than to lighten. The acts of Bacon's assembly were repealed; all the former abuses were restored; the public purse was shamelessly robbed; the suffrage was restricted; the church was restored to power. In 1677 the Dominion became the property of one Culpepper, who had the title of governor for life; and the restraints, such as they were, of its existence as a royal colony were removed. But Culpepper's course was so corrupt as to necessitate his removal, and in 1684 the king resumed his sway. James II. reached the English throne the following year, and his persecutions of his enemies in England gave good citizens to America. But the Virginians, who could be wronged and oppressed, but never crushed, protested against the arbitrary use of the king's prerogative; they were punished for their temerity, but rose more determined from the struggle. No man could be sent to Virginia who was strong enough to destroy its resolve for liberty.

And now the English Revolution was at hand; and we are to inquire what influence the new dispensation was to have on the awakening national spirit of the American colonies.

CHAPTER SEVENTH

QUAKER, YANKEE, AND KING

THE American principle, simple in that its perfection is human liberty, is of complex make. It is the sum of the ways in which a man may legitimately be free. But neither Pilgrims, Puritans, New Amsterdamers, Virginians, Carolinians nor Marylanders were free in all ways. Even the Providence people had their limitations. It is not meant, merely, that the old world still kept a grip on them: their several systems were intrinsically incomplete. Some of them put religious liberty in the first place; others, political; but each had its inconsistency, or its shortcoming. None had gone quite to the root of the matter. What was that root?—or, let us say, the mother lode, of which these were efferent veins?

The Pilgrims and Puritans, heretics in Episcopalian England, had escaped from their persecution, but had banished heretics in their turn. Tranquil Lord Baltimore having laid the burden of his doubts at the foot of God's vicegerent on earth, had sought no further, and was indifferent as to what other poor mortals might choose to think they thought about the unknown things. Roger Williams' charity, based on the dogma of free conscience, drew the line only at atheists. The other colonists, since their salient contention was on the lower ground of civil emancipation and self-direction, are not presently considered.

But, to the assembly of religious radicals, there enters a plain Man in Leather Breeches, and sees fetters on the limbs of all of them. "Does thee call it freedom, Friend Winthrop," says he, "to fear contact with such as believe otherwise than thee does? Can truth fear aught? And fear, is it not bondage? As for thee, George Calvert, thee has delivered up thine immortal soul into the keeping of a man no different from what thee thyself is, so to escape the anxious seat; but the dead also are free of anxiety, and thy bondage is most like unto death. Thee calls thy colony folk free, because thee lets them believe what they list; but they do but follow what their fathers taught them, who got it from theirs; which is to be in bondage to the past. And here is friend Roger, who makes private conscience free; but what is private conscience but the private reasonings whereby a man convinceth himself? and how shall he call his conviction the truth, since all truth is one, but the testimony of no man's private conscience is the same as another's? Nay, how does thee know that the atheist, whom thee excludes, is further from the truth than thee thyself is? Truly, I hear the clanking of the chains on ye all; but if ye will accept the Inner Light, then indeed shall ye know what freedom is!"

This Man in Leather Breeches, who also wears his hat in the king's presence, is otherwise known as George Fox, the Leicestershire weaver's son, the Quaker. In his youth he was much troubled in spirit concerning mankind, their nature and destiny, and the purpose of God concerning them. He wandered in lonely places, and fasted, and was afflicted; he sought help and light from all, but there was none could enlighten him. But at last light came to him, even out of the bosom of his own darkness; and he saw that human learning is but vanity, since within a man's self, will he but look for it, abides a great Inner Light, which changeth not, and is the same in all; being, indeed, the presence of the Spirit of God in His creature, a constant guide and revelation, withheld from none, uniting and equalizing all; for what, in comparison with God, are the distinctions of rank and wealth, or of learning?—Seek ye first the Kingdom of God and His righteousness, and these things shall be added unto you. In the lowest of men, not less than in such as are called greatest, burns this lamp of Divine Truth, and it shall shine for the hind as brightly as for the prince. In its rays, the trappings of royalty are rags, jewels are dust and ashes, the lore of science, folly; the disputes of philosophers, the crackling of thorns under the pot. By the Inner Light alone can men be free and equal, true sons of God, heirs of a liberty which can never be taken away, since bars confine not the spirit, nor do tortures or death of the body afflict it. So said George Fox and his followers; and their lives bore witness to their words.

The Society of Friends took its rise not from a discovery —for Fox himself held the Demon of Socrates, and similar traditional phenomena, to be identical with the Inner Light, or voice of the Spirit—but rather in the recognition of the universality of something which had heretofore been regarded as exceptional and extraordinary. In the Seventeenth Century there was a general revolt of the oppressed against oppression, declaring itself in all phases of the outer and inner life; of these, there must needs be one interior to all the rest, and Quakerism seems to have been it. It was a revolution within revolutions; it saw in the man's own self the only tyrant who could really enslave him; and by bringing him into the direct presence of God, it showed him the way to the only real emancipation. Historically, it was the vital element in all other emancipating movements; it was their logical antecedent: the hidden spring feeding all their rivers with the water of life. It enables us to analyze them and gauge their values; it is their measure and plummet. And this, not because it is the final or the highest word justifying the ways of God to man—for it has not proved to be so: but because it indicated, once for all, in

WILLIAM PENN MAKING A TREATY WITH THE INDIANS

what direction the real solution of the riddle of man was to be sought: a riddle never to be fully solved, but forever approximately guessed. Quakerism has not maintained its relative position in religious thought; but it was the finest perception of its day, and in the turmoil of the time it fulfilled its purpose. Probably its best effect was the development it gave to the humbler element of society—to the yeomen and laborers; affording them the needed justification for the various demands for recognition that they were urging. Puritanism banished Quakers, and even hanged them; but the Quaker was the Puritan's spiritual father, although he knew it not. And therefore the Quaker, who was among the last to appear in America as a settler in virgin soil, had a right thereto prior to any one of the others. There must be a soul before there can be a body.

On the other hand, a soul without a body is not adapted to life in this world; and an America peopled exclusively by Quakers would have been unsatisfactory. It is a prevailing tendency of man, having hit upon a truth, to begin to theorize upon it, and, as the phrase is, run it into the ground. Quakers would not fight, would not take an oath, would not baptize, or wear mourning, or flatter the senses with pictures and statues. A Quaker would resist evil and violence only by enlightening them. He would not be taxed for measures or objects which he did not approve. He could see but one way of reforming the world, and thought that God was equally circumscribed in His methods. But though the leaven may make bread wholesome, we cannot subsist on leaven alone. The essence of Americanism may be in a Quaker, but he is far from being a complete American, and therefore he was fain to take his place only as a noble ingredient in that wonderful mixture. By degrees, the singularities which distinguished him were softened; his thee and thy yielded to the common forms of speech; his drab suit altered its cut and hue; his hat came off occasionally; his women abated the rigor of their poke bonnets; he was able to say to the enemy of his country, "Friend, thee is standing just where I am going to shoot." The disintegration of his individuality set free the good that was in him to permeate surrounding society; his fellow flowers in the garden were more beautiful and fragrant for his sake.

When persecution of Quakers was at its worst, they became almost dehumanized, attaching more value to their willingness to endure ill-usage than to the spiritual principle for avouching which they were ill-used. Many persons—such is the oddity of human nature—were drawn to the sect for love of the persecution; and gave way to extravagances such as Fox would have been the first to denounce. But when toleration began, these excesses ceased, and they bethought themselves to make a home in the wilderness of their own. There was room enough. George Fox returned from his pilgrimage to the Atlantic colonies in 1674, with good accounts of the resources of the new country; and the owner of New Jersey sold half of it to John Fenwick for a thousand pounds; and the next year the latter went there with many Friends, and picked out a pleasant spot on the east bank of the Delaware for the first settlement, to which he gave the name of Salem. It was at this juncture that William Penn became, with two others, assigns of the proprietor of the colony, and thus took the first step toward assuming full responsibility for it. He did not, however, personally visit America till seven years later.

Penn was the son of an English admiral: not the kind of timber, therefore, out of which one would have supposed a great apostle of non-resistance could be made. He was brought up to the use of ample wealth, and his training and education were aristocratic. After leaving Oxford, he made the grand tour, and came home a finished young man of the world, with the pleasures and rewards of life before him. He had good brains and solid qualities, and the old admiral had high hopes of him. No doubt he would have made a very good figure in the English world of fashion; but destiny had another career marked out for him.

The plain Man with the Leather Breeches got hold of him; and all the objurgations, threats, and even the act of disinheritance of the admiral were powerless to extricate him from that grasp. Penn had found something which seemed to him more precious than rubies, and he was quite as resolute as the old hero of the Navy. Penn could endure the beating and the being turned into the streets, but he could not stop his ears and eyes to the voice and light of God in his soul. He did not care to conquer another Jamaica, but he passionately desired to minister to the spiritual good of his fellow creatures. He was of a sociable and cheerful disposition; he could disarm his adversary in a duel; he could take charge of the family estates, and qualify himself for the law; the king was ready to smile upon him; but all worldly ambitions died away in him when he heard Thomas Lee testify of the faith that overcomes the world. Nothing less than that would satisfy Penn. In 1666, when he was two and twenty, he made acquaintance with the inside of a jail on account of his conscientious perversities; but the only effect of the experience was to make him perceive that he had thereby become "his own freeman." When he got out, his friends cut him and society made game of him; finally, he was lodged in the Tower, which, he informed Charles II., seemed to him "the worst argument in the world." They let him out in less than a year, but in less than a year more he was again arrested and put on trial. The jury, after having been starved for two days and heartily cursed by the judge, brought him in not guilty; upon which the judge, with a fine sense of humor, fined them all heavily and sent him back to prison. But this was too much for the admiral, who paid his fines and got him out; and, being then on his death-bed, surrendered at discretion, restoring to him the inheritance, and observing, not without a pensive satisfaction, that he and his friends would end by "making an end of the priests."

A six months' term in Newgate was still in store for Penn; but after that they gave up this method of reforming him. He spent the next years in exhorting Parliament and reproving princes all over Europe; and in the midst of these labors he met one of the best and most beautiful women in England; she had suitors by the score, but she loved William Penn, and they were married. She was the wife of his mind and soul as well as of his bed and board. He was now doubly fortified against the world, and doubly bound to his career of human benevolence. His studies and meditations had made him a profound philosopher and an able statesman; and in all ways he was prepared to begin the great work of his life.

Meanwhile, the Quakers in the new world were building up the framework of their state. They decreed to put the power in the people, and all the articles of their constitution embody the utmost degree of freedom, with constant opportunities for the electors to revise or renew their judgments. When the agent of the Duke of York levied customs on ships going to New Jersey, the act drew from the colonists a remarkable protest, which was supported by the courts. They had planted in the wilderness, they said, in order, among other things, to escape arbitrary taxation; if they could not make their own laws in a land which they had bought, not from the Duke, but from the natives, they had lost instead of gaining liberty by leaving England. Taxes levied upon planting left them nothing to call their own, and foreshadowed a despotic government in England, when the Duke should come to the throne. The future James II. gave up his claim, and in 1680 signed an indenture to that effect. Later, at the advice of Penn, they so amended their constitution as to give them power to elect their own governor. A charter was drawn up by Penn and confirmed in 1681, and he became proprietor. No man ever assumed such a trust with less of personal ambition or desire for gain than he. "You shall be governed by laws of your own making," said he; "I shall not usurp the right of any, or oppress his person." He had already made inroads on his estate by fighting the cause of his brethren in England in the courts; but when a speculator offered him six thousand pounds down and an annual income for the monopoly of Indian trade, he declined it; the trade belonged to his people. He was ardently desirous to benefit his colony by putting in operation among them the schemes which his wisdom had evolved; but he would not override their own wishes; they should be secured even from his power to do them good; for, as liberty without obedience is confusion, so is obedience without liberty slavery. Instead therefore of imposing his designs upon them, he submitted them for their free consideration. Pennsylvania now occupied its present boundaries, with the addition of Delaware; and western New Jersey ceased to be the nominal home of the Friends in America. In 1682, Penn embarked for the Delaware. He had founded a free colony for all mankind, believing that God is in every conscience; and he was now going to witness and superintend the working of his "holy experiment."

On October 29th he was received at Newcastle by a crowd of mixed nationality, and the Duke of York's agent formally delivered up the province to him. The journey up the Delaware was continued in an open boat, and the site of Philadelphia was reached in the first week of November. There a meeting of delegates from the inhabitants was held and the rules which were to govern them were reviewed and ratified. Among these it was stipulated that every Christian sect was eligible to office, that murder only was a capital crime, that marriage was a civil contract, that convict prisons should be workhouses, that all who paid duties should be electors, and that there should be no poor rates or tithes. Then Penn proceeded to lay out the city of Philadelphia, where they "might improve an innocent course of life on a virgin Elysian shore." It was here that the Declaration of Independence was signed ninety-three years afterward.

In March, before the leaves had budded on the tall trees whose colonnades were as yet the only habitation for the emigrants, the latter set to work to settle their constitution. "Amend, alter or add as you please," was the recommendation with which Penn submitted it to them—the work of his ripest wisdom and loving good-will. To the governor and council it assigned the suggestion of all laws; these suggestions were then to be submitted by the assembly to the body of the people, who thus became the direct law-makers. To Penn was given the power to negative the doings of the council, he being responsible for all legislation; but he could originate and enforce nothing. He would accept no revenues; and, indeed, except in the way of helpfulness and counsel, never in any way imposed himself upon his people. He was the proprietor; but in all practical respects, Pennsylvania was a representative democracy. That they should be free and happy was his sole desire.

In its relations with the Indians, the colony was singularly fortunate; the doctrine of non-resistance succeeded best where least might have been expected from it. All lands were purchased, conferences being held and deeds signed; and the red men were given thoroughly to understand that nothing but mutual good was intended. They took to the new idea kindly; the law of retaliation had been the principle of their lives hitherto; but if a man did good to them, and dealt honestly by them, should not they retaliate by manifesting the same integrity and good-will? At one time it was reported that a band of Indians had assembled on the border with the design of avenging some grievance with a massacre. Six unarmed Quakers started at once for the scene of trouble, and the Indians subsided.

It has long been admitted that it takes two sides to make a fight; but this was an indication that it needs resistance to make a massacre. Penn, who was fond of visiting the Indians in their wigwams, and sharing their hospitality, formed an excellent opinion of them. He discoursed to them of their rights as men, and of their privileges as immortal souls; and they conceded to him his claim to peaceful possession of his province. Not less remarkable was the fate of witchcraft in Pennsylvania. The Swedes and Finns believed in witches, upon the authority of their native traditions; and a woman of their race having acted in a violent and unaccountable manner, they put her on her trial for witchcraft. Both Swedes and Quakers composed the jury; there were no hysterics; the matter was dispassionately canvassed; impressions and prejudices were not accepted as evidence; and in the end the verdict was that though she was guilty of being called a witch, a witch she nevertheless was not. The distinction was so well taken that no more witch trials or panics occurred. This was in 1684, eight years before the disasters in New England. But newspapers did not exist in those days, and public opinion was undeveloped.

The colony, receiving a world-wide advertisement by dint of the excellence of its institutions and the singularity of its principles, became a magnet to draw to itself the "good and oppressed" of all Europe. There were a good many of them; and within a couple of years from the time when Philadelphia meant blaze-marks on trees and three or four cottages, it had grown to be a real town of six hundred houses. The colony altogether mustered eight thousand people. With justifiable confidence, therefore, that all was well, and would stay so, Penn, with many loving words for his people, returned to England to continue the defense of the afflicted there. A dispute as to the right boundaries of Delaware and Maryland was also to be determined; but it proved to be a lingering negotiation, chiefly noteworthy on account of its leading to the fixing of the line by Charles Mason and Jeremiah Dixon, which afterward became the recognized boundary between the States where slaves might be owned and those where they might not. The line was surveyed, finally, in 1767.

Penn being gone, the people applied themselves to experimenting with their constitution. A constitution which is devised to secure liberty to the subject, including liberty to modify or change it, is as nearly unchangeable as any mortal structure can be. The inhabitants of Pennsylvania had never known before what it was to be free, and they naturally wished to test the new gift or quality in every way open to them. Not having the trained brain and unselfish wisdom that belonged to Penn, of which the constitution was the offspring, they thought that they could improve its provisions. But the more earnestly they labored to this end, the more surely were they brought to the confession that he had known how to make them free better than they themselves did. When they resolved against taxes, they found themselves without revenue; when they refused to discipline a debtor, they found that credit was no longer to be had. They fussed and fretted to their hearts' content, and no great harm came of it, because the constitution was always awaiting them with forgiveness when they had tired themselves with abusing it. The only important matter that came to judgment was the slavery question; Penn himself had slaves, though he came to doubt the righteousness of the practice, and liberated them in his will—or would have done so, had the injunction been carried out by his heirs. Slaves in Pennsylvania were to serve as such for fourteen years, and then become adscripts of the soil—that is to say, they were permitted to become the same thing under another name. Penn ultimately conceived the ambition to vindicate the presence of the Inner Light in the negroes' souls; but he met with small success—even less than with the Indians. The problem of the negro was not to be solved in that way, or at that time. No doubt, if a negro slave could be made to feel that the mere circumstance of external bondage was nothing, so long as his inner man was untrammeled, it would add greatly to the convenience both of himself and his master. But the theory did not seem to carry weight so long as the practice accompanied it; and the world, even of Pennsylvania, was not quite ready to abolish negro slavery in 1687.

Of the thirteen colonies, twelve had now had their beginning, and Georgia, the home of poor debtors, shed little or no fresh light upon the formation of the American principle. The Revolution of 1688, which put William of Orange on the English throne, was now at hand; but before examining its effect upon the American settlements we must cast a glance at the transactions of the previous dozen years in the New England division.

The theory of the English government regarding the American colonies had always been, that they were her property. The people who emigrated had been English subjects, and—to adapt the Latin proverb—Cœlum, non Regem, mutant, qui trans mare currunt. Moreover, the English, as was the custom of the age, asserted jurisdiction over all land first seen and claimed by mariners flying their flag; and though Spain and France might claim America with quite as much right as England, yet the latter would not acknowledge their pretensions. A country, then, occupied by English subjects, and owned by England, could not reasonably assert its private independence.

Such was England's position, from which she never fully receded until compelled to do so by force of arms. But the colonists looked at the matter from a different point of view. They held the right of ownership by discovery to be unsubstantial; it was a mere sentiment—a matter of national pride and prestige—not to be valued when it came in conflict with the natural right conveyed by actual emigration and settlement. The man who transferred himself, with his family and property, to a virgin country, intending to make his permanent home there, should not be subject to arbitrary interference from any one; his vital interests and welfare were involved; he should be ruled by authority appointed by himself; should pay only such taxes as he himself levied for the expenses of his establishment; and should enjoy the profits of whatever products he raised and whatever commerce he carried on. He had withdrawn himself from participation in the advantages of home civilization, and had voluntarily faced a life of struggle and peril in the wilderness, precisely because he had counted these things as nothing in comparison with the gain of controlling his own affairs; but if, nevertheless, the mother country insisted on managing them, or in any way controlling him, then all enterprise became vain, all his sacrifices had been fruitless, and he was in all ways worse off than before he took steps to better himself. An Englishman living in England might rightly be taxed for the protection to life and property and the enjoyment of privileges which she afforded him, and which he, through a representative parliament, created; but England gave no protection to her colonies, and the colonists were not represented in her parliament; neither had the English government been put to any expense or trouble in bringing those colonies into existence; to tax them, therefore, was an act of despotism; it deprived them of the right which all Englishmen possessed to the fruits of their own labor; it robbed them of values for which no equivalent had been yielded; and thus, from freemen, made them slaves. Not less unjustifiable, for the same reasons, was interference with colonial governments, and with religious liberties of all kinds.

England could not categorically refute these arguments; but she could reply that her granting of a charter to the colonies had implied some hold upon them, including a first lien upon commercial products; while so far as governmental jurisdiction was concerned, it might be considered an open question whether the colonies were capable of adequately governing themselves, and she was therefore warranted, in the interests of order, in exercising that function herself. But the reply was a weak one; and when the colonists rejoined that the charter, if it had any practical significance at all, merely gave expression to a friendly interest in the adventure, as a parent might give a son a letter hoping that he would do well; and that the question of government was not an open one, inasmuch as the orderliness and efficiency of their institutions were visible and undeniable:—it was left to England only to say that, once an English subject, always an English subject, and that when she commanded the colonies must comply.

As a matter of fact, she avoided as much as possible putting this ultimatum in precise words; and the colonies were at least as reluctant to oppose a definite defiance. Diplomacy labors long before acknowledging a finality. There was on both sides a deeply-rooted determination to prevail; but an open rupture was shunned. Furthermore, a strong sentiment of loyalty existed in the colonies, which sentimentally and sometimes practically injured the logic of their attitude. They acknowledged the English king to be theirs; they addressed him in deferential and submissive terms; they wished, in some sense, to keep hold of their mother's hand, and yet they protested against the maternal prerogative. Their status was anomalous; and it is easy to say that they should have declared their purpose, from the first, to be an independent nation in the full sense of the word. But the logical and the natural are often at variance. Liberty is not necessarily attainable only through political independence. The colonists, if they wished to be another England in miniature, had not contemplated becoming a people foreign to England, in the sense that France or Spain was. They loved the English flag, in spite of the cross which Endicott disowned; they were proud of the English history which was also theirs. Why should they sever themselves from these? It was not until English injustice and selfishness, long endured, became at last unendurable, that the resolve to live truly independent, or to die, fired the muskets of Lexington and Concord.

The most galling of the measures which weighed upon New England was that called the Navigation Acts. These were passed in the interests of the English trading class, and by their influence. In their original form, in 1651, they had involved no serious injury to the colonies, and had, moreover, been so slackly enforced that they were almost a dead letter. But after Charles II. came to the throne, they assumed a more virulent aspect. They forbade the importation into the colonies of any merchandise, except in English bottoms, captained by Englishmen, thus excluding from American ports every cargo not owned by British merchants. On the other hand, they decreed that no American produce should find its way into other than English hands, except such things as the English did not want, or could buy to better advantage elsewhere; and even these could be disposed of at no ports nearer England than the Mediterranean. Next, by an extension of the Acts, the inhabitants of one colony were forbidden to deal with those of another except on payment of duties intended to be prohibitory. And finally, the colonists were enjoined not to manufacture even for their private consumption, much less for export, any goods which English manufacturers produced. They could do nothing but grow crops, and the only reason that anything whatever was permitted to go from the colonies to foreign ports, was in order that the former might thus get money with which to pay for the forced importations from England. The result of such a policy was, of course, that money was put into the pockets of English shopkeepers, but all other Englishmen gained nothing, and the colonist lost the amount of the shopkeepers' profit, as well as the incidental and incalculable advantages of free enterprise.

These laws pressed most severely on Massachusetts, because her shipping exceeded that of all the other colonies, and the smuggling which their geographical peculiarities made easy to them was impossible for her. Besides, manufacturing was never followed by the southern colonies, and their chief products, tobacco and cotton, not being grown elsewhere, could be sold at almost as good a profit in England as anywhere else.

But if Massachusetts was the chief object of these oppressive measures, she was also more inflexible than the other colonies in insisting upon her rights. The motto of the Rattlesnake flag carried at the beginning of the Revolution—"Don't tread on Me"—expressed the temper of her people from an early period in her history. We shall shortly see how resolutely and courageously she fought her battle against hopeless odds. Meanwhile, we may inquire how and why the other colonies of the New England confederation fared better at the hands of the mother country.

One of the most agreeable figures in our colonial history is the son of that John Winthrop who brought the first colonists to Massachusetts Bay, on June 22, 1630. He had been born at Groton, in England, in 1606, and was therefore fifty-six years old when he returned to that country as agent for Connecticut, and obtained its charter from Charles. He had been educated at Dublin, and before emigrating to the colonies had been a soldier in the French wars, and had traveled on the Continent. After landing at Boston, he had helped his father in his duties, and had then founded the town of Ipswich in Massachusetts. None was more ardent than he in the work of preparing a home for the exiles in the wilderness; he added his own fortune to that of his father, and thought no effort too great. In him the elements were so kindly mixed that his heart was as warm and his mind as liberal as his energy was tireless; it was as if a Roger Williams had been mingled with an elder Winthrop; enthusiasm and charity were tempered with judgment and discretion. The love of creating means of happiness for others was his ruling motive, and he was gifted with the ability to carry it out; he felt that New England was his true home, because there he had fullest opportunity for his self-appointed work. It is almost an effort for men of this age to conceive of a nature so pure as this, and a character so blameless; we search the records for some weakness or deformity. But all witnesses testify of him with one voice; and it may be borne in mind that the spirit of Puritanism at that epoch was mighty in the individual as in the community, purging the soul of many self-indulgent vices which the laxity and skepticism of our time encourage; and when, in addition, there is a nation to be made on principles so lofty as those which Puritanism contemplated, one can imagine that there would be little space for the development of the lower instincts, or the unworthier ambitions. When all is said, however, Winthrop the Younger still remains a surprising and rare type; and it is an added pleasure to know that in all that he undertook he was successful (he never undertook anything for himself), and that he was most happy in a loving wife and in his children. It was a rounded life, such as a romancer hardly dares to draw; yet there may be many not less lovely, only less conspicuously placed.

When there was need for a man to go to England and plead before the king for Connecticut—of which, for fourteen consecutive years thereafter, he was annually elected governor—who but Winthrop could be selected? He went with all the prayers of the colony for his good fortune; and it was of good omen that he met there, in the council for the colonies appointed by the king, Edward Hyde, first Earl of Clarendon and Lord Chancellor, then in the prime of his career, and two years younger than Winthrop; and William Fiennes, Viscount Saye and Sele, who was in the eightieth and final year of his useful and honorable career, and who, in 1632, had obtained a patent for land on the Connecticut river. Through his influence the interest of the Lord Chamberlain was secured, and Clarendon himself was cordial for the charter. With such support, the way was easy, and the document was executed in April of 1662. It gave the colonists all the powers of an independent government. There was no reservation whatever; their acts were not subject even to royal inspection. Nevertheless, Charles, by effecting the amalgamation of New Haven with Hartford, not altogether with the consent of the former, arbitrarily set aside the provision of the federation compact which forbade union between any of its members except with the consent of all; and thereby he asserted his jurisdiction (if he chose to exercise it) over all the colonies. He could give gracious gifts, but on the understanding that they were of grace, not obligation. In the oppression of Massachusetts, this served as an unfortunate precedent.

Nor must it be forgotten that the happiness of Connecticut was in part due to the fact that, as a matter of high policy, it was desired to conciliate her at Massachusetts's expense. Massachusetts was much the strongest of the colonies; her tendency to disaffection was known in England; and it seemed expedient to place her in a position isolated from her sisters. Were all of them equally wronged, their union against the oppressor was inevitable. Connecticut and Rhode Island could be of small present value to England from the commercial standpoint, and their heartfelt loyalty seemed cheaply purchased by suffering that value to accumulate. Charles could be lavish and reckless, and he was constitutionally "good-humored"—that is, he liked to have things go smoothly, and if anybody suffered, wished the fact to be kept out of his sight. But he was incapable of generosity, in the sense of voluntarily sacrificing any selfish interest for a noble end; and if he patted Connecticut on the back, it was only in order that she might view with toleration his highway robbery of her sister.

All this, however, need not dash our satisfaction at the

advantages which Connecticut enjoyed, and the good they did her. The climate and physical nature of the country required an active and wholesome life in the inhabitants, while yet the conditions were not so severe as to discourage them. They were of a rustic, hardy, industrious temper, of virtuous and godly life, and animated by the consciousness of being well treated. They lived and labored on their farms, and there were not so many of them that the farms crowded upon one another, though the population increased rapidly. Each of them delighted in the cultivation of his private "conscience"; and, in the absence of wars and oppressions, they argued one with another on points of theology, fate, freewill, foreknowledge absolute. They were far from indifferent to learning, but they liked nothing quite so well as manhood and integrity. The Connecticut Yankee impressed his character on American history, and wherever in our country there has been evidence of pluck, enterprise and native intelligence, it has generally been found that a son of Connecticut was not far off. They were not averse from journeying over the earth, and many of them had the pioneer spirit, and left their place of birth to establish a miniature Connecticut elsewhere; their descendants will be found as far west as Oregon, and their whalers knew the paths of the Pacific as well as they did the channels of Long Island Sound. Tolerant, sturdy, pious, shrewd, prudent and brave, they formed the best known type of the characteristic New Englander, as represented by the national figure of Uncle Sam. They were sociable and inquisitive, yet they knew how to keep their own counsel; and the latch-string hung out all over the colony, in testimony at once of their honesty and their hospitality. Few things came to them from the outer world, and few went out from them; they were industrially as well as politically independent. They were economical in both their private and their public habits; no money was to be made in politics, partly because every one was from his youth up trained in political procedure; every town was a republic in little. The town meeting was open to all citizens, and each could have his say in it, and many an acute suggestion and shrewd criticism came from humble lips. It is in such town meetings that the legislators were trained who then, and ever since, have become leading figures in the statesmanship of the country. In England, a hereditary aristocracy were educated to govern the nation; in the colonies, a nation was educated to govern itself. Our system was the sounder and the safer of the two. But the professional politician was then unthought of; he came as the result of several conditions incident to our national development; he has perhaps already touched his apogee, and is beginning to disappear. The nation has awakened to a realization that its interests are not safe in his hands.

Calvinism prevailed in the colony, as in Massachusetts; but there were many of the colonists who did not attend at the meeting-house on the Sabbath, not because they were irreligious or vicious, but either because they lived far from the rendezvous, or because they did not find it a matter of private conscience with them to sit in a pew and listen to a sermon. Moreover, it was the rule among Calvinists that no one could join in the Communion service who had not "experienced religion"; and many excellent persons might entertain conscientious doubts whether this mysterious subjective phenomenon had taken place in them. Pending enlightenment on that point, they would naturally prefer not to sit beside their more favored brethren during the long period of prayer and discourse, only to be obliged to walk out when the vital stage of the proceedings was reached. But it was also the law that only children of communicants should receive baptism; and since not to be baptized was in the religious opinion of the day to court eternal destruction, it will easily be understood that non-communicating parents were rendered very uneasy. What could they do? One cannot get religion by an act of will; but not to get it was to imperil not only their own spiritual welfare, but that of their innocent offspring as well; they were damned to all posterity. The matter came up before the general court of Connecticut, and in 1657 a synod composed of ministers of that colony and of Massachusetts— New Haven and Plymouth declining to participate—sat upon the question, and softened the hard fate of the petitioners so far as to permit the baptism of the children of unbaptized persons who engaged to rear them in the fear of the Lord. This "half-way covenant," as it came to be termed, did not suit the scruples of Calvinists of the stricter sort; but it gave comfort to a great many deserving folk, and probably did harm to no human soul, here or hereafter.

Short are the annals of a happy people; until the Revolutionary days began, there is little to tell of Connecticut. The collegiate school which half a generation later grew into the college taking its name from its chief benefactor, Elihu Yale, had its early days in the village at the mouth of the Connecticut river, named, after Lord Saye and Sele, Saybrook. The institution of learning called after the pious and erudite son of the English butcher of Southwark, founded on the banks of the river Charles near Boston, had come into existence more than sixty years before; but Yale followed less than forty years after the granting of the Connecticut charter. New England people never lost any time about securing the means of education.

The boundaries of Rhode Island were the occasion of some trouble; though one might have supposed that since the area which they inclosed was so small, no one would have been at the pains to dispute them. But in the end, Roger Williams obtained the little he had asked for in this regard, while as to liberties, his charter made his community at least as well off as was Connecticut. Their aspiration to be allowed to prove that the best civil results may be coincident with complete religious freedom, was realized. Charles gave them everything; liberty for a people who thought more of God than of their breakfasts, and whose habitation was too small for its representation on the map to be seen without a magnifying glass, could not be a dangerous gift. The charter was delivered in 1663 to John Clarke, agent in England for the colony, and was taken to Rhode Island by the admirable Baxter in November of that year. All the two thousand or more inhabitants of the colony met together to receive the precious gift; Baxter, placed on high, read it out to them with his best voice and delivery, and then held it up so that all might behold the handsomely engrossed parchment, and the sacred seal of his dread majesty King Charles. What a picture of democratic and childlike simplicity! With how devout and earnest an exultation did the people murmur their thanks and applause! The crowd in their conical hats and dark cloaks, the chill November sky, the gray ripples of Narragansett Bay, the background of forest trees, of which only the oaks and walnuts still retained the red and yellow remnants of their autumn splendor; the quaint little ship at anchor, with its bearded crew agape along the rail; and Baxter the center of all eyes, holding up the charter with a sort of holy enthusiasm! Such a scene could be but once; and time has brought about his revenges. With what demeanor would the throng at the fashionable watering place greet a messenger from the English sovereign to-day! John Clarke, the Bedfordshire doctor, to whose fidelity and persistent care the colony owed much, fully participated in the contagion of goodness which marked the New England emigrants of the period. He served his fellow colonists all his life, and at his death left them all he had; and it seems strange that he should have been one of the founders of aristocratic Newport, and its earliest pastor. But it is not the only instance of the unexpected use to which we sometimes put the bequests of our ancestors.

The early vicissitudes of Maine, New Hampshire and Vermont are hardly of importance enough to warrant a detailed examination. Vermont was not settled till well into the Eighteenth Century. Maine had been fingered by the French, and used as a base of operations by fishermen, long before its connection with Massachusetts; the persistency of Gorges complicated its position for more than forty years. After his death, and in the irresponsiveness of his heirs, the few inhabitants of the region were constrained to shift for themselves; in 1652 the jurisdiction was found to extend three miles north of the source of the Merrimack, and Massachusetts offering its protection in enabling a government to be formed, and acting upon the priority of its grant, annexed the whole specified region. But more than twenty years afterward, in 1677, the English committee of the privy council examined the charter, and found that Massachusetts had no jurisdiction over Maine and New Hampshire (the separate existence of which last had scarcely been defined). The direct object of this decision of the committee was to provide the bastard son of Charles, Monmouth, with a kingdom of his own; no one knew anything about the resources or possibilities of the domain, and, omne ignotum pro magnifico, it was surmised that it would yield abundant revenues. But Massachusetts did not want the Duke for a neighbor; and while Charles was considering terms of purchase, she bought up the Gorges claim for some twelve hundred pounds. The Maine of that epoch was not, of course, the same as that of to-day; the French claimed down to the Kennebec, and the Duke of York, not content with New York, asserted his ownership from the Kennebec to the Penobscot; so that for Massachusetts was left only what intervened between the Kennebec and the Piscataqua. Being proprietor of this, she made it a province with a governor and council whom she appointed, and a legislature derived from the people; the province not relishing its subordination, but being forced to submit. Two years later, in 1679, New Hampshire was cut off from Massachusetts and made the first royal province of New England. The people of the province were ill-disposed to surrender any of the liberties which they saw their neighbors in the enjoyment of; and disregarding the feelings of the king's appointee, its representatives declared that only laws made by the assembly and approved by the people should be valid. Robert Mason, who had a patent to part of the region, finding himself opposed by the colonists, got permission from England to appoint an adventurer, Edward Cranfield, governor; Cranfield went forth with hopes of much plunder; but they would not admit his legitimacy, and he took the unprecedented step of dissolving the assembly; the farmers revolted, and their ringleader, Gove, was condemned for treason, and spent four years in the Tower of London. It was another attempt to convince the spirit of liberty by "the worst argument in the world"; but it was ridiculous as well as bad in Gove's case; he was but a hard-fisted uneducated countryman, whose belief that the patch of land he had cleared and planted among the New England mountains was his and not another's, was not to be dissipated by dungeons. The disputed land-titles got into the law courts, where judges and juries were fixed; but no matter which way the decisions went, the people kept their own. Cranfield sent an alarmist report of affairs to London, declaring that "factions" would bring about a separation of the colony unless a frigate were sent to Boston to enforce loyalty. Nothing was done. Cranfield tried to raise money through the assembly by a tale about an invasion, which existed nowhere save in his own imagination; the assembly refused to be stampeded. The clergy were against him, and he attempted to overcome them by restrictive orders; but they defied him; he imprisoned one of them, Moody; and succeeded in disturbing church service; but the people would rather not go to meeting than obey Cranfield. His last effort was to try to levy taxes under pretense of an Indian war; but the people thwacked the tax collectors with staves, and the women threatened them with hot water. A call for troops to quell the disturbances was utterly disregarded. How was a governor to govern people who refused to be governed?

Cranfield gave it up. He had been struggling three years, and had accomplished nothing. He wrote home that he "should esteem it the greatest happiness to be allowed to remove from these unreasonable people"; and this happiness was accorded to him; it was the only happiness which his appointment had afforded. New Hampshire was in bad odor with the English government; but the farmers could endure that with equanimity. They had demonstrated that the granite of their mountains had somehow got into their own composition; and they were let alone for the present, the rather since Massachusetts was enough to occupy the king's council at that time.

The fight between Massachusetts and Charles began with the latter's accession in 1660, and continued till his death, when it was continued by James II. The charter of the colony was adjudged to be forfeited in 1684, twenty-four years after the struggle opened. While it was at its height, the Indian war broke out to which the name of the Pokanoket chief, King Philip, has been attached. Thus both the diplomacy and the arms of the colony were tested to the utmost, at one and the same time; the American soldiers were victorious, though at a serious cost of life and treasure; the diplomatists were defeated; but Massachusetts had learned her strength in both directions, and suffered less, in the end, by her defeat than by her victory. The issue between England and her colony had become clearly defined; the people learned by practice what they already knew in theory—the hatefulness of despotism; and their resolve to throw it off when the opportunity should arrive was not discouraged, but confirmed. From the Indian war they gained less than a wise peace would have given them, and they lost women and children as well as men. Such conflicts, once begun, must be pushed to the extremity; but it cannot but be wished that the people of Massachusetts might have found a means of living with the red men, as their brethren in Pennsylvania did, in peace and amity. The conduct of Indians in war can never be approved by the white race, but, on the other hand, the provocations which set them on the warpath always can be traced to some act of injustice, real or fancied, wanton or accidental, on our part. King Philip was fighting for precisely the same object that was actuating the colonists in their battle with King Charles. Doubtless the rights of a few thousand savages are insignificant compared with the higher principles of human liberty for which we contended; but Philip could not be expected to acknowledge this, and we should extend to him precisely the same sympathy that we feel for ourselves.

A great deal of pains had been taken to convert and civilize these New England tribes. John Eliot translated the Bible for them; and it was he who made the first attempt to determine the grammar of their speech. But though many Indians professed the Christian faith, and some evinced a certain aptitude in letters, no new life was awakened in any of them, and no permanent good results were attained. Meanwhile, the Pokanokets, with Philip at their head, refused to accept the white man's God, or his learning; and they watched with anxiety his growing numbers and power. They had sold mile after mile of land to the English, not realizing that the aggregate of these transactions was literally taking the ground from under their feet; but the purchasers had the future as well as the present in view, and contrived so to distribute their holdings as gradually to push the Indians into the necks of land whence the only outlet was the sea. It was the old story of encroachment, with always a deed to justify it, signed with the mark of the savage, good in law, but to his mind a device to ensnare him to his hurt. In 1674, Philip was compelled to appear before a court and be examined, whereat his indignation was aroused, and, either with or without his privity, the informer who had procured his arrest was murdered. The murderers were apprehended and sentenced to be hanged by a jury, half white and half Indian. The tribe retaliated and war was begun.

Philip, or Metaconet, the son of Massasoit, may at this time have been about forty years old; he had been "King" for twelve years. The portraits of him show a face and head that one can hardly accept as veracious; an enormous forehead impending over a small face, with an almost delicate mouth. But he was obviously a man of ability, and his courage was hardened by desperation. His aim was to unite all the tribes in an effort to exterminate the entire English population, though this has been estimated to number in New England, at that time, more than fifty thousand persons. The odds were all upon the colonists' side; but they had not yet learned the Indian method of warfare, and the woods, hills and swamps, and the unprotected state of many of the settlements, gave the Indians opportunities to prolong the struggle which they amply improved. Had they been united, and adequately armed, the issue might have been different.

Captain Benjamin Church, a hardy pioneer of six and thirty, who had watched the ways of the Indians, and learned their strategy, soon became prominent in the war, and ended as its most conspicuous and triumphant figure. At first the colonists were successful, and Philip was driven off; but this did but enable him to spread the outbreak among other tribes. From July of 1675 till August of the next year, the life of no one on the borders was safe. The settlers went to the meeting-house armed, and turned out at the first alarm. They were killed at their plowing; they were ambuscaded and cut off, tortured, slain, and their dissevered bodies hung upon the trees. At the brook there-

AN INCIDENT OF KING PHILIP'S WAR

after called Bloody Run, near Deerfield, over seventy young men were surprised and killed. Women and children were not spared; it was hardly sparing them to carry them into captivity, as was often done. The villages which were attacked were set on fire after the tomahawking and scalping were done. Horrible struggles would take place in the confined rooms of the little cabins; blood and mangled corpses desecrated the familiar hearths, and throughout sounded the wild yell of the savages, and the flames crackled and licked through the crevices of the logs.

In December, Church commanded, or accompanied, the little army which plowed through night and snow to attack the palisaded fort and village, strongly situated on an island of high ground in the midst of a swamp, in the township of New Kingston. The Narragansetts were surprised; the soldiers burst their way through the palisades, and the red and the white men met hand to hand in a desperate conflict. Then the tomahawk measured itself against the sword, and before it faltered more than two hundred of the New Englanders had been killed or wounded, and the village was on fire. The pools of blood which the frost had congealed, bubbled in the heat of the flames. None could escape; infants, old women, all must die. It was as ghastly a fight as was ever fought. The victors remained in the charred shambles till evening, resting and caring for their wounded; and then, as the snow began to fall, went back to Wickford, carrying the wounded with them. It is said that a thousand Indian warriors fell on that day.

At Hadfield had occurred the striking episode of the congregation, surprised at their little church, and about to be overcome, being rescued by a mysterious gray champion, who appeared none knew whence, rallied them, and led them to victory. It was believed to be Goffe, one of the men who sentenced Charles I. to be beheaded, who had escaped to New England at the time of the Restoration, and had dwelt in retirement there till the peril of his fellow exiles called him forth. The war was full of harrowing scenes and strange deliverances. Anne Brackett, a prisoner in an Indian party, crossed Casco Bay in a birch-bark canoe, with her husband and infant, and was rescued by a vessel which happened to enter the harbor at the critical moment.

Church hunted the Indians with more than their own cunning and persistency; and at last it was he who led the party which effected Philip's death. The royal Indian was hemmed in in a swamp, and finally killed by a traitor from his own side. The savages could fight no more; they had caused the death of six hundred men, had burned a dozen towns, and compelled the expenditure of half a million dollars. Scattered alarms and tragedies still occurred in the East, and along the borders; but the war was over. In 1678 peace was signed. And then Massachusetts turned once more to her deadlier enemy, King Charles.

CHAPTER EIGHTH

THE STUARTS AND THE CHARTER

THE cutting off of Charles I.'s head was a deed which few persons in Massachusetts would have advocated; Cromwell himself had remarked that it was a choice between the king's head and his own. History has upon the whole accepted the choice he made as salutary. Achilles, forgetting his heel, deemed himself invulnerable, and his conduct became in consequence intolerable; Charles, convinced that his anointed royalty was sacred, was led on to commit such fantastic tricks before high heaven as made the godly weep. Achilles was disillusioned by the arrow of Paris, and Charles by the ax of Cromwell. Death is a wholesome argument at times.

But though a later age could recognize the high expediency of Charles's taking off, it was too bold and novel to meet with general approbation at the time, even from men who hated kingly rule. Prejudice has a longer root than it itself believes. And the Puritans of New England, having been removed from the immediate pressure of the king's eccentricities, were the less likely to exult over his end. Many of them were shocked at it; more regretted it; perhaps the majority accepted it with a sober equanimity. They were not bloodthirsty, but they were stern.

Neither were they demonstrative; so that they took the Parliament and the Protector calmly, if cordially, and did not use the opportunity of their predominance to cast gibes upon their predecessor. So that, when the Restoration was an established fact, they had little to retract. They addressed Charles II. gravely, as one who by experience knew the hearts of exiles, and told him that, as true men, they feared God and the king. They entreated him to consider their sacrifices and worthy purposes, and to confirm them in the enjoyment of their liberties. Of the execution, and of the ensuing "confusions," they prudently forbore to speak. It was better to say nothing than either to offend their consciences, or to utter what Charles would dislike to hear. Their case, as they well knew, was critical enough at best. Every foe of New England and of liberty would not fail to whisper malice in the king's ear. They sent over an envoy to make the best terms he could, and in particular to ask for the suspension of the Navigation Acts. But the committee had small faith in the loyalty of the colony, and even believed, or professed to do so, that it might invite the aid of Catholic and barbarous Spain against its own blood: they judged of others' profligacy by their own. The king, to gain time, sent over a polite message, which meant nothing, or rather less; for the next news was that the Acts were to be enforced.

Massachusetts thereupon proceeded to define her position. A committee composed of her ablest men caused a paper to be published by the general court affirming their right to do certain things which England, they knew, would be indisposed to permit. In brief, they claimed religious and civil independence, the latter in all but name, and left the king to be a figurehead without perquisites or power. They followed this intrepid statement by solemnly proclaiming Charles in Boston, and threw a sop to Cerberus in the shape of a letter couched in conciliating terms, feigning to believe that their attitude would win his approbation. Altogether, it was a thrust under the fifth rib, with a bow and a smile on the recover. Probably the thrust represented the will of the majority; the bow and smile, the prudence of the timid sort. Simon Bradstreet and John Norton were dispatched to London to receive the king's answer. They went in January of 1662, and after waiting through the spring and summer, not without courteous treatment, returned in the fall with Charles's reply, which, after confirming the charter and pardoning political infidelities under the Protectorate, went on to refuse all the special points which the colony had urged.

Already at this stage of the contest it had become evident that the question was less of conforming with any particular demand or command on the king's part, than of admitting his right to exercise his will at all in the premises. If the colony conceded his sovereignty, they could not afterward draw the line at which its power was to cease. And yet they could not venture to declare absolute independence, partly because, if it came to a struggle in arms, they could not hope to prevail; and partly because absolute independence was less desired than autonomy under the English flag. England was as far from granting autonomy to Massachusetts as independence, but was willing, if possible, to constrain her by fair means rather than by foul. Meanwhile, the tongue of rumor fomented discord. It was said in the colony that England designed the establishment of the Episcopal Church in Massachusetts; whereupon the laws against toleration of "heretics," which had been falling into disuse, were stringently revived. In London the story went that the escaped regicides had united the four chief colonies and were about to lead them in arms to revolt. Clarendon, to relieve anxiety, sent a reassuring message to Boston; but its good effect was spoiled by a report that commissioners were coming to regulate their affairs. The patent of the colony was placed in hiding, the trained bands were drilled, the defenses of the harbor were looked to, and a fast day was named with the double purpose of asking the favor of God, and of informing the colony as to what was in the wind. Assuredly there must have been stout souls in Boston in those days. A few thousand exiles were actually preparing to resist England!

The warning had not been groundless. The fleet which had been fitted out to drive the Dutch governor, Peter Stuyvesant, from Manhattan, stopped at Boston on its way; and we may imagine that its entrance into the harbor on that July day was observed with keen interest by the great-grandfathers of the men of Bunker Hill. It was not exactly known what the instructions of the English officers required; but it was surmised that they meant tyranny. The commission could not have come for nothing. They had no right on New England soil. The fleet, for the present, proceeded on its way, and Massachusetts voluntarily contributed a force of two hundred men; but they were well aware that the trouble was only postponed; and depending on their charter, which contained no provision for a royal commission, they were determined to thwart its proceedings to the utmost of their power. How far that might be, they would know when the time came. Anything was better than surrender to the prerogative. When, in reply to Willoughby, a royalist declared that prerogative is as necessary as the law, Major William Hawthorne, who was afterward to distinguish himself against the Indians, answered him, "Prerogative is not above law!" It was not, indeed.

Accordingly, while the fleet with its commissioners was overawing the New Netherlanders, the Puritans of Boston Bay wrote and put forth a document which well deserves reproduction, both for the terse dignity of the style, which often recalls the compositions of Lord Verulam, and still more for the courageous, courteous, and yet almost aggressive logic with which the life principles of the Massachusetts colonists are laid down. It is a remarkable State paper, and so vividly sincere that, as one reads, one can see the traditional Puritan standing out from the words—the steeple crowned hat, the severe brow, the steady eyes, the pointed beard, the dark cloak and sad-hued garments. The paper is also singular in that it remonstrates against a principle, without waiting for the provocation of overt deeds. This excited the astonishment of Clarendon and others in England; but their perplexity only showed that the men they criticised saw further and straighter than they did. It was for principles, and against them, that the Puritans always fought, since principles are the parents of all acts and control them. The royal commission was, potentially, the sum of all the wrongs from which New England suffered during the next hundred years, and though it had as yet done nothing, it implied everything.

Whose hand it was that penned the document we know not; it was probably the expression of the combined views of such men as Mather, Norton, Hawthorne, Endicott and Bellingham; it may have been revised by Davenport, at that time nearly threescore and ten years of age, the type of the Calvinist minister of the period, austere, inflexible, high-minded, faithful. Be that as it may, it certainly voiced the feeling of the people, as the sequel demonstrated. It is dated October the Twenty-fifth, 1664, and is addressed to the king.

"DREAD SOVEREIGN:—The first undertakers of this Plantation did obtain a Patent, wherein is granted full and absolute power of governing all the people of this place, by men chosen from among themselves, and according to such laws as they should see meet to establish. A royal donation, under the Great Seal, is the greatest security that may be had in human affars. Under the encouragement and security of the Royal Charter this People did, at their own charges, transport themselves, their wives and families, over the ocean, purchase the land of the Natives, and plant this Colony, with great labor, hazards, cost, and difficulties; for a long time wrestling with the wants of a Wilderness and the burdens of a new Plantation; having now also above thirty years enjoyed the privilege of Government within themselves, as their undoubted right in the sight of God and Man. To be governed by rulers of our own choosing and laws of our own, is the fundamental privilege of our Patent.

"A Commission under the Great Seal, wherein four persons (one of them our professed Enemy) are impowered to receive and determine all complaints and appeals according to their discretion, subjects us to the arbitrary power of Strangers, and will end in the subversion of us all.

"If these things go on, your Subjects will either be forced to seek new dwellings, or sink under intolerable burdens. The vigor of all new Endeavours will be enfeebled; the King himself will be a loser of the wonted benefit by customs, exported and imported from hence to England, and this hopeful Plantation will in the issue be ruined.

"If the aim should be to gratify some particular Gentlemen by Livings and Revenues here, that will also fail, for the poverty of the People. If all the charges of the whole

Government by the year were put together, and then doubled or trebled, it would not be counted for one of these Gentlemen a considerable Accommodation. To a coalition in this course the People will never come; and it will be hard to find another people that will stand under any considerable burden in this Country, seeing it is not a country where men can subsist without hard labor and great frugality.

"God knows our greatest Ambition is to live a quiet Life, in a corner of the World. We came not into this Wilderness to seek great things to ourselves; and if any come after us to seek them here, they will be disappointed. We keep ourselves within our Line; a just dependence upon, and subjection to, your Majesty, according to our Charter, it is far from our Hearts to disacknowledge. We would gladly do anything in our power to purchase the continuance of your favorable Aspect. But it is a great Unhappiness to have no testimony of our loyalty offered but this, to yield up our Liberties, which are far dearer to us than our Lives, and which we have willingly ventured our Lives and passed through many Deaths, to obtain.

"It was Job's excellency, when he sat as King among his People, that he was a Father to the Poor. A poor People, destitute of outward Favor, Wealth, and Power, now cry unto their lord the King. May your Majesty regard their Cause, and maintain their Right; it will stand among the marks of lasting Honor to after Generations."

Throughout these sentences sounds the masculine earnestness of men who see that for which they have striven valiantly and holily in danger of being treacherously ravished from them, and who are resolute to withstand the ravisher to the last. It is no wonder that documents of this tone and caliber amazed and alarmed the council in London, and made them ask one another what manner of men these might be. It would have been well for England had they given more attentive ear to their misgivings; but their hearts, like Pharaoh's, were hardened, and they would not let the people go—until the time was ripe, and the people went, and carried the spoils with them.

The secret purpose of the commission was to pave the way for the gradual subjection of the colony, and to begin by inducing them to let the governor become a royal nominee, and to put the militia under the king's orders. Of the four commissioners, Nicolls remained in New York, as we have seen; the three others landed in Boston early in 1665. Their first order was that every male inhabitant of Boston should assemble and listen to the reading of the message from King Charles. These three gentlemen—Maverick, Carr and Cartwright—were courtiers and men of fashion and blood, and were accustomed to regard the king's wish as law, no matter what might be on the other side; but it was now just thirty years since the Puritans left England; they had endured much during that time, and had tasted how sweet liberty was; and half of them were young Americans, born on the soil, who knew what kings were by report only. Young and old, speaking through the assembly, which was in complete accord with them, informed the commissioners that they would not comply with their demand. What were the commissioners, that they should venture to call a public meeting in the town of a free people? The free people went about their affairs, and left the three gentlemen from the Court to stare in one another's scandalized faces.

They were the more scandalized, because their reception in Connecticut and Rhode Island had been different. But different, also, had been the errand on which they went there. Those two colonies were the king's pets, and were to have liberty and all else they wanted; Connecticut they had protected from the rapacity of Lord Hamilton, and Rhode Island had never been other than loving and loyal to the king. They had, to be sure, been politely bowed out by little Plymouth, the yeomen Independents, who still preferred, if his majesty pleased, to conduct their own household affairs in their own way. But to be positively and explicitly rebuffed to their faces, yet glowing with the sunshine of the royal favor, was a new experience; and Cartwright, when he caught his breath, exclaimed, "He that will not attend to the request is a traitor!"

The Massachusetts assembly declined to accept the characterization. Since the king's own patent expressly relieved them from his jurisdiction, it was impossible that their refusal to meet three of his gentlemen-in-waiting could rightly be construed as treason. The commissioners finally wanted to know, yes or no, whether the colonists meant to question the validity of the royal commission? But the assembly would not thus be dislodged from the coign of vantage; they stuck to their patent, and pointed out that nothing was therein said about a commission. So far as they were concerned, the commission, as a commission, could have no existence. They recognized nothing but three somewhat arrogant persons, in huge wigs, long embroidered waistcoats under their velvet coats, and plumes waving from their hats. They presented a glittering and haughty aspect, to be sure, but they had no rights in Boston.

At length, on the twenty-third of May, matters came to a crisis. The commissioners had given out that on that day they were going to hold a court to try a case in which the colony was to defend an action against a plaintiff. This, of course, would serve to indicate that the commissioners had power—whether the assembly conceded it or not—to control the internal economy of the settlement. Betimes in the morning, the rather that it was a very pleasant one—the trees on the Common being dressed in their first green leaves since last year, while a pleasant westerly breeze sent the white clouds drifting seaward over the blue sky—a great crowd began to make its way toward the court house, whose portals frowned upon the narrow street, as if the stern spirit of justice that presided within had cast a shadow beneath them. The doors were closed, and the massive lock which secured them gleamed in the single ray of spring sunshine that slanted along the facade of the edifice.

It was a somber looking throng, as was ever the case in Puritan Boston, where the hats, cloaks and doublets of the people were made of dark, coarse materials, not designed to flatter the lust of the eye. The visages suited the garments, wearing a sedate or severe expression, whether the cast of the features above the broad white collars were broad and ruddy, or pale and hollow-cheeked. There was a touch of the fanatic in many of these countenances, as of men to whom God was a living presence in all their affairs and thoughts, who feared His displeasure more than the king's, who believed that they were His chosen ones, and who knew that His arm was mighty to defend. They were of kin to the men who stood so stubbornly and smote so sore at Marston Moor and Naseby, and afterward had not feared to drag the father of the present Charles to the block. Fiber more unbending than theirs was never wrought into the substance of our human nature; and oppression seemed but to harden it.

They conversed one with another in subdued tones, among which sounded occasionally the lighter accents of women's voices; but they were not a voluble race, and the forms of their speech still followed in great measure the semi-scriptural idioms which had been so prevalent among Cromwell's soldiers years before. They were undemonstrative; but this very immobility conveyed an impression of power in reserve which was more effective than noisy vehemence.

At length, from the extremity of the street, was heard the tramp of horses' hoofs, and the commissioners, bravely attired, with cavalier boots, and swords dangling at their sides, were seen riding forward, followed by a little knot of officers. The crowd parted before them as they came, not sullenly, perhaps, but certainly with no alacrity or suppleness of deference. There was no love lost on either side; but Cartwright, who wore the most arrogant front of the three, really feared the Puritans more than either of his colleagues; and when, seven years afterward, he was called before his majesty's council to tell what manner of men they were, his account of them was so formidable that the council gave up the consideration of the menacing message they had been about to send, and instead agreed upon a letter of amnesty, as likely to succeed better with a people of so "peevish and touchy" a humor.

The cavalcade drew up before the door, and the officials, dismounting, ascended the steps. Finding it locked, Cartwright lifted the hilt of his sword and dealt a blow upon the massive panel.

"Who shuts the door against his majesty's commissioners?" cried he angrily. "Where is the rascal with the keys, I say!"

"I marvel what his majesty's commissioners should seek in the house of Justice," said a voice in the crowd; "since it is known that, when they go in by one door, she must needs go out by the other."

At this sally, the crowd smiled grimly, and the commissioners frowned and bit their lips. Just then there was a movement in the throng, and a tall, dignified man with a white beard and an aspect of grave authority was seen pressing his way toward the court house door.

"Here is the worshipful governor Bellingham himself," said one man to his neighbor. "Now shall we see the upshot of this matter."

"And God save Massachusetts!" added the other, devoutly.

The chief magistrate of the colony advanced into the little open space at the foot of the steps, and saluted the commissioners with formal courtesy.

"I am sorry ye should be disappointed, sirs," said he;

"but I must tell you that it is the decision of the worshipful council that ye do not pass these doors, or order any business of the court, in this commonwealth. Provision is made by our laws for the proper conduct of all matters of justice within our borders, and it is not permitted that any stranger should interfere therewith."

"Truly, Mr. Bellingham," said Maverick, resting one hand on his sword, and settling his plumed hat on his wig with the other, "you take a high tone; but the king is the king, here as in England, and we bear his commission. Massachusetts can frame no laws to override his pleasure; and so we mean to teach you. I call upon all persons here present, under penalty of indictment for treason, to aid us, his majesty's commissioners, to open this court, or to break it open." His voice rang out angrily over the crowd, but no one stirred in answer.

"You forget yourself, sir," said the governor, composedly. "We here are loyal to the king, and too much his friends to believe that he would wrong himself by controverting the charter which bears the broad seal affixed by his own royal father. Your claim doth abuse him more than our refusal. But since you will not hear comfortable words, I must summon one who will speak more bluntly."

He turned, and made a signal with his hand. "Let the herald stand forth," said he; and at the word, a broad-shouldered, deep-chested personage, with a trumpet in one hand and a pike in the other, stepped into the circle and stood in the military attitude of attention.

"Hast thou the proclamation there in thy doublet, Simon?" demanded his worship.

"Aye, verily, that have I," answered Simon, in a voice like a fog horn, "and in my head and my heart, too!"

"Send it forth, then, and God's blessing go with it!" rejoined the chief magistrate, forcibly, but with something like a smile stirring under his beard.

Upon this Simon the herald filled his vast lungs with a

mighty volume of New England air, set the long brazen trumpet to his lips, and blew such a blast that the led horses of the commissioners started and threw up their heads, and the windows of the court house shook with the strident vibration. Then, taking the paper on which the proclamation was written, and holding it up before him, he proceeded to bellow forth its contents in such stentorian wise that the commissioners might have heard it, had they been on Boston wharf preparing to embark for England, instead of being within three or four paces. That proclamation, indeed, was heard over the length and breadth of New England, and even across the Atlantic in the gilded chamber of the king of Britain. "These fellows," muttered his majesty, with a vexed air, "have the hardihood to affirm that we have no jurisdiction over them. What shall be done, Clarendon?" "I have ever thought well of them," the chancellor said, rubbing his brow; "they are a sturdy race, and it were not well to wantonly provoke them; yet it is amazing that they should show themselves so froward, without so much as charging the commissioners with the least matter of crimes or exorbitances." Clarendon, indeed, was too lenient to suit the royal party, and this was one of the causes leading up to his impeachment a year or two later.

But the herald was not troubled, nor was his voice subdued, by thoughts of either royalty or royal commissioners; though, as a matter of form, he began with "In the name of King Charles," he coupled with it "by authority of the Charter"; and went on to declare that the general court of Massachusetts, in observance of their duty to God, to the king, and to their constituents, could not suffer any one to abet his majesty's honorable commissioners in their designs. There was no mistaking the defiance, and neither the people nor the commissioners affected to do so. The latter petulantly declared that "since you will misconceive our endeavors, we shall not lose more of our labors upon you";

and they departed to Maine, where they met with a less mortifying reception. The people were much pleased, and made sport of the king's gentlemen, and at their public meetings they were addressed in the same "seditious" vein by magistrates and ministers. "The commission is but a trial of our courage: the Lord will be with His people while they are with Him," said old Mr. Davenport. Endicott, on the edge of the grave, was stanch as ever for the popular liberties. Besides, "There hath been one revolution against the king in England," it was remarked; "perchance there will be another ere long; and this new war with the Netherlands may bring more changes than some think for." On the other hand, resistance was stimulated by tales of what the gold-laced freebooters of the court would do, if they were let loose upon New England. Diplomacy, however, was combined with the bolder counsels; there was hope in delays, and correspondence was carried on with England to that end. Charles's expressed displeasure with their conduct was met with such replies as "A just dependence upon and allegiance unto your majesty, according to the charter, we have, and do profess and practice, and have by our oaths of allegiance to your majesty confirmed; but to be placed upon the sandy foundations of a blind obedience unto that arbitrary, absolute, and unlimited power which these gentlemen would impose upon us—who in their actings have carried it not as indifferent persons toward us —this, as it is contrary to your majesty's gracious expressions and the liberties of Englishmen, so we can see no reason to submit thereto."

The commissioners were recalled; but Charles commanded Bellingham, Hawthorne, and a few others to appear before him in London and answer for the conduct of the colony. The general court met for prayer and debate; Bradstreet thought they ought to comply; but Willoughby and others said, No. A decision was finally handed down declining to obey the king's mandate.

"We have already furnished our views in writing," the court held, "so that the ablest persons among us could not declare our case more fully."

Under other circumstances this fresh defiance might have borne prompt and serious consequences; but Louis XIV. conveniently selected the moment to declare war on England; and Boston commended herself to the home government by arming privateers to prey upon the Canadian commerce, and by a timely gift of a cargo of masts for the English navy. Charles became so much interested in the ladies of his court that he had less leisure for the affairs of empire. Yet he still kept New England in mind; he believed Massachusetts to be rich and powerful, and from time to time revolved schemes for her reduction; and finally, when the colonists were exhausted by the Indian war, the privy council came to the conclusion that, if they were not to lose their hold upon the colony altogether, "this was the conjuncture to do something effectual for the better regulation of that government." They selected, as their agent, the best hated man who ever set foot on Massachusetts soil—Edward Randolph. His mission was to prepare the way for the revocation of its charter, and to undo all the works of liberty and happiness which the labor and heroism of near fifty years had achieved. He was also intrusted by Robert Mason with the management of his New Hampshire claims. The second round in the battle between king and people had begun.

Randolph was a remorseless, subtle, superserviceable villain, who lied to the king and robbed the colonists, and was active and indefatigable in every form of rascality. During nine years he went to and fro between London and Massachusetts, weaving a web of mischief that grew constantly stronger and more restrictive, until at length the iniquitous object was achieved. His first visit to Boston was in 1676; he stayed but a few weeks, and accomplished nothing, but his stories about the wealth and population of the colonies stimulated the greed of his employers. Envoys were ordered to come to London, and this time they were sent, but with powers so limited as to prevent any further result than the cession of the jurisdiction of Massachusetts over Maine and New Hampshire—which, as we have seen, was bought back the next year. The enforcement of the Navigation Acts was for the moment postponed. The colonists would pay duties to the king within the plantation if he would let them import directly from the other countries of Europe. But Charles wished to strengthen his grasp of colonial power, although, if possible, with the assembly's consent. In 1678, the crown lawyers gave an opinion that the colony's disregard of the Navigation Acts invalidated their charter. Randolph was appointed customs collector in New England, and it was determined to replace the laws of Massachusetts by such as were not "repugnant to the laws of England." And the view was expressed that the settlement should be made a royal colony. Manifestly, the precious liberties of the Puritans were in deadly peril.

A synod of the churches and a meeting of the general court were held to devise defense. To obviate a repeal of their laws, these were in a measure remodeled so as to bring them nearer to what it was supposed the king would require. Almost anything would be preferable to giving up the right to legislate for themselves. It was first affirmed that English laws did not operate in America, and that the Navigation Acts were despotic because there was no colonial representation in the English parliament. And then, to prove once more how far above all else they prized principle, they passed a Navigation Act of their own, which met all the king's stipulations. They would submit to the drain on their resources and the hampering of their enterprise, but only if they themselves might inflict them. Meanwhile, they cultivated to the utmost the policy of delay. Randolph came over with his patent as collector in 1679, but though the patent was acknowledged, he was able to make no arrangements for conducting the business. Orders were sent for the dispatch of agents to London with unlimited powers; but Massachusetts would not do it. Parliament would not abet the king in his despotic plans beyond a certain point; but he was at length able to dissolve it, and follow what counsels he pleased. His first act was to renew the demand for plenipotentiary envoys, or else he would immediately take steps legally to evict and avoid their charter.

Two agents, Dudley and Richards, were finally appointed to go to the king and make the best terms possible. If he were willing to compound on a pecuniary basis, which should spare the charter, let it be done, provided the colony had the means for it; but, whatever happened, the charter privileges of the commonwealth were not to be surrendered. The agents had not, therefore, unlimited powers; and when Charles discovered this, he directed them to obtain such powers, or a judicial process would be adopted. This alternative was presented to Massachusetts in the winter of 1682, and the question whether or not to yield was made the subject of general prayer, as well as of discussion. There seemed no possible hope in resistance. Might it not then be wiser to yield? They might thus secure more lenient treatment. If they held out to the bitter end, the penalty would surely be heavier. The question ultimately came up before the general court for decision.

It is probable that no other representative body in the world would have adopted the course taken by that of Massachusetts. Certainly since old Roman times, we might seek in vain for a verdict which so disregarded expediency —everything in the shape of what would now be termed "practical politics"—and based itself firmly and unequivocally on the sternest grounds of conscience and right. It was passed after thorough debate, and with clear prevision of what the result must be; but the magistrates had determined that to suffer murder was better than to commit suicide; and this is the manner in which they set forth their belief.

"Ought the government of Massachusetts to submit to the pleasure of the court as to alteration of their charter? Submission would be an offense against the majesty of heaven; the religion of the people of New England and the court's pleasure cannot consist together. By submission Massachusetts will gain nothing. The court design an essential alteration, destructive to the vitals of the charter. The corporations in England that have made an entire resignation have no advantage over those that have stood a suit in law; but, if we maintain a suit, though we should be condemned, we may bring the matter to chancery or to parliament, and in time recover all again. We ought not to act contrary to that way in which God hath owned our worthy predecessors, who in 1638, when there was a quo warranto against the charter, durst not submit. In 1664, they did not submit to the commissioners. We, their successors, should walk in their steps, and so trust in the God of our fathers that we shall see His salvation. Submission would gratify our adversaries and grieve our friends. Our enemies know it will sound ill in the world for them to take away the liberties of a poor people of God in the wilderness. A resignation will bring slavery upon us sooner than otherwise it would be; and it will grieve our friends in other colonies, whose eyes are now upon New England, expecting that the people there will not, through fear, give a pernicious example unto others.

"Blind obedience to the pleasure of the court cannot be without great sin, and incurring the high displeasure of the King of kings. Submission would be contrary unto that which hath been the unanimous advice of the ministers, given after a solemn day of prayer. The ministers of God in New England have more of the spirit of John the Baptist in them, than now, when a storm hath overtaken them, to be reeds shaken with the wind. The priests were to be the first that set their foot in the waters, and there to stand till all danger be past. Of all men, they should be an example to the Lord's people of faith, courage, and constancy. Unquestionably, if the blessed Cotton, Hooker, Davenport, Mather, Shepherd, Mitchell, were now living, they would, as is evident from their printed books, say, Do not sin in giving away the inheritance of your fathers.

"Nor ought we to submit without the consent of the body of the people. But the freemen and church members throughout New England will never consent hereunto. Therefore, the government may not do it.

"The civil liberties of New England are part of the inheritance of their fathers; and shall we give that inheritance away? Is it objected that we shall be exposed to great sufferings? Better suffer than sin. It is better to trust the God of our fathers than to put confidence in princes. If we suffer because we dare not comply with the wills of men against the will of God, we suffer in a good cause, and shall be accounted martyrs in the next generation, and at the Great Day."

The promulgation of this paper was the prelude to much calamity in New England for many years; but how well it has justified itself! Such words are a living power, surviving the lapse of many generations, and flaming up fresh and vigorous above the decay of centuries. The patriotism which they express is of more avail than the victories of armies and of navies, for these may be won in an ill cause; but the dauntless utterances of men who would rather perish than fail to keep faith with God and with their forefathers is a victory for mankind, and is everlasting. How poor and vain in comparison with this stern and sincere eloquence seem the supple time-service and euphemism of vulgar politicians of whose cunning and fruitless spiderwebs the latter years have been so prolific. It is worth while to do right from high motives, and to care for no gain that is not gained worthily. The men of Massachusetts who lived a hundred years before Jefferson were Americans of a type as lofty as any that have lived since; the work that was given them to do was so done that time can take away nothing from it, nor add anything. The soul of liberty is in it. It is easy to "believe in" our country now, when it extends from ocean to ocean, and is the home of seventy-five million human beings who lead the world in intelligence, wealth, and the sources of power. But our country two hundred years ago was a strip of seacoast with Indians on one side and tyrants on the other, inhabited by a handful of exiles, who owned little but their faith in God and their love for the freedom of man. No lesser men than they could have believed in their country then; and they vindicated their belief by resisting to the last the mighty and despotic power of England.

On November 30, 1683, the decision was made known: "The deputies consent not, but adhere to their former bills." A year afterward the English court, obstinate in the face of all remonstrances, adjudged the royal charter of Massachusetts to be forfeited. It had been in existence all but half a century. It was no more; but it had done its work. It had made Massachusetts. The people were there—the men, the women and the children—who would hand on the tradition of faith and honor through the hundred years of darkness and tribulation till the evil spell was broken by the guns of Bunker Hill. Royal governors might come and go; but the people were growing day by day, and though governors and governments are things of an hour, the people are immortal, and the time of their emancipation will come. By means of the charter, the seed of liberty was sown in favorable soil; it must lie hid awhile; but it would gather in obscurity and seeming death the elements of new and more ample life, and the genius of endless expansion. Great men and nations come to their strength through great trials, so that they may remember, and not lightly surrender what was so hardly won.

The king's privy council, now that Massachusetts lay naked and helpless before them, debated whether she should be ruled by English laws, or whether the king should appoint governors and councils over her, who should have license to work their wills upon her irresponsibly, except in so far as the king's private instructions might direct them. A minority, represented by Lord Halifax, who carried a wise head on young shoulders, advised the former plan; but the majority preferred to flatter Charles's manifest predilection, and said—not to seem embarrassingly explicit—that in their opinion the best way to govern a colony on the other side of an ocean three thousand miles broad, was to govern it—as the king thought best!

So now, after so prolonged and annoying a delay, the royal libertine had his Puritan victim gagged and bound, and could proceed to enjoy her at his leisure. But it so fell out that the judgment against the charter was received in Boston on the second of July, 1685, whereas Charles II. died in London on February 6th of the same year; so that he did not get his reward after all: not, at least, the kind of reward he was looking for. But, so far as Massachusetts was concerned, it made little difference; since James II. was as much the foe of liberty as was his predecessor, and had none of his animal amiability. The last act of the Massachusetts assembly under the old order was the appointing of a day of fasting and prayer, to beseech the Lord to have mercy upon his people.

The reign of James II. was a black season for the northern American colonies; we can say no better of it than that it did not equal the bloody horrors which were perpetrated in Scotland between 1680 and 1687. Massacres did not take place in Massachusetts; but otherwise, tyranny did its perfect work. The most conspicuous and infamous figures of the time are Sir Edmund Andros and Edward Randolph.

Andros, born in 1637, was thirty-seven years of age when he came to the colonies as governor of New York on behalf of the Duke of York. He was a lawyer, and a man of energy and ability; and his career was on the whole successful, from the point of view of his employers and himself; his tenure of office in New York was eight years; he was governor of New England from 1686 to 1689, when he was seized and thrown in jail by the people, on the outbreak of the Revolution in England; and he afterward governed Virginia for seven years (1692–1698), which finished his colonial career. But from 1704 to 1706 the island of Jersey, in the English Channel, was intrusted to his rule; and he died in London, where he was born, in 1714, being then seventy-seven years old, not one day of which long life, so far as records inform us, was marked by any act or thought on his part which was reconcilable with generosity, humanity or honor. He was a tyrant and the instrument of tyranny, hating human freedom for its own sake, greedy to handle unrighteous spoils, mocking the sufferings he wrought, triumphing in the injustice he perpetrated; foul in his private life as he was wicked in his public career. A far more intelligent man than Berkeley, of Virginia, he can, therefore, plead less excuse than he for the evil and misery of which he was the immediate cause. But no earthly punishment overtook him; for kings find such men useful, and God gives power to kings in this world, that mankind may learn the evil which is in itself, and gain courage and nobility at last to cast it out, and trample it under foot.

James II. was that most dangerous kind of despot—a stupid, cold man; even his libertinism, as it was without shame, so was it without passion. In his public acts he plodded sluggishly from detail to detail, with eyes turned downward, never comprehending the larger scope and relations of things. He was incapable of perceiving the vileness, cruelty, or folly of what he did; the almost incredible murders in Scotland never for a moment disturbed his clammy self-complacency. Perhaps no baser or more squalid soul ever wore a crown; yet no doubt ever crept into his mind that he was God's chosen and anointed. His pale eyes, staring dully from his pale face, saw in the royal prerogative the only visible witness of God's will in the domain of England; the atmosphere of him was corruption and death. But from 1685 to 1688 this man was absolute master of England and her colonies; and the disease which he bred in English vitals was hardly cured even by the sharp medicine of the Boyne.

By the time Andros came to New England, he had learned his business. The year after his appointment to New York, he attempted to assert his sovereignty up to the Connecticut River; but he was opposed by deputy governor Leet, a chip of the old roundhead block, who disowned the patent of Andros and practically kicked him out of the colony. Connecticut paid for her temerity when the owner of Andros became king. In the meanwhile he returned to New York, where he was not wanted, but was tolerated; the settlers there were a comfortable people, and prosperous in the homely and simple style natural to them: they demanded civil rights in good, clear terms, and cannot be said to have been unduly oppressed at this time. New York for a while included the Delaware settlements, and Andros claimed both east and west Jersey. The claim was contested by Carteret and by the Quakers. When the Jersey commerce began to be valuable, Andros demanded tribute from the ships, and shook the Duke's patent in the people's faces. They replied, rather feebly, with talk of Magna Charta. In 1682, the western part came by purchase into Quaker ownership, and, three years afterward, the eastern part followed by patent from the Duke. To trace the vicissitudes of this region to their end, it was surrendered to England in 1702, and united to New York; and in 1738, in compliance with the desire of the inhabitants, it became its own master. The settlers were of composite stock: Quakers, Puritans, and others; and at the time of the Scotch persecutions, large numbers of fugitive Covenanters established themselves on the eastern slopes. The principle on which land was distributed, in comparatively small parcels, made the Jerseys a favorite colony for honest and industrious persons of small means; and, upon the whole, life went well and pleasantly with them.

At the time of the return of Andros to England, in 1682, the assembly decreed free trade, and Dongan, the new Roman Catholic governor, permitted them to enact a liberal charter. In the midst of the happiness consequent upon this, the Duke became king and lost no time in breaking every contract that he had, in his unanointed state, entered into. Taxes arbitrarily levied, titles vacated in order to obtain renewal fees, and all the familiar machinery of official robbery were put in operation. But Dongan, a kindly Kildare Irishman—he was afterward Earl of Limerick—would not make oppression bitter; and the New Yorkers were not so punctilious about abstract principles as were the New England men. Favorable treaties were made with the Indians; and the despot's heel was not shod with iron, nor was it stamped down too hard. The Dongan charter, as it was called, remained in the colony's possession for over forty years. The rule of Dongan himself continued till 1688.

Andros, after an absence from the colonies of five years, during which time a native but unworthy New Englander, Joseph Dudley, had acted as president, came back to his prey with freshened appetite in 1686. He was royal governor of all New England. Randolph, an active subordinate under Dudley, had already destroyed the freedom of the press. Andros's power was practically absolute; he was to sustain his authority by force, elect his own creatures to office, make such laws as pleased him, and introduce episcopacy. He forbade any one to leave the colony without leave from himself: he seized a meeting house and made it into an Episcopal church, in spite of the protests of the Puritans, and the bell was rung for high-church service in spite of the recalcitrant Needham. Duties were increased; a tax of a penny in the pound and a poll tax of twenty pence were levied; and those who refused payment were told that they had no privilege, except "not to be sold as slaves." Magna Charta was no protection against the abolition of the right of Habeas Corpus: "Do not think the laws of England follow you to the ends of the earth!" Juries were packed, and Dudley, to avoid all mistakes, told them what verdicts to render. Randolph issued new grants for properties, and extorted grievous fees, declaring all deeds under the charter void, and those from Indians, or "from Adam," worthless. West, the secretary, increased probate duties twenty-fold. When Danforth complained that the condition of the colonists was little short of slavery, and Increase Mather added that no man could call anything his own, they got for answer that "it is not for his majesty's interest that you should thrive." In the history of Massachusetts, there is no darker day than this.

The great New England romancer, writing of this period a hundred and seventy years later, draws a vivid and memorable picture of the people and their oppressors. "The roll of the drum," he says, "had been approaching through Cornhill, louder and deeper, till with reverberations from house to house, and the regular tramp of martial footsteps, it burst into the street. A double rank of soldiers made their appearance, occupying the whole breadth of the passage, with shouldered matchlocks, and matches burning, so as to present a row of fires in the dusk. Their steady march was like the progress of a machine, that would roll irresistibly over everything in its way. Next, moving slowly, with a confused clatter of hoofs on the pavement, rode a party of mounted gentlemen, the central figure being Sir Edmund Andros, elderly, but erect and soldier-like. Those around him were his favorite councilors, and the bitterest foes of New England. At his right rode Edward Randolph, our arch-enemy, that 'blasted wretch,' as Mather calls him, who achieved the downfall of our ancient government, and was followed with a sensible curse, through life and to his grave. On the other side was Bullivant, scattering jests and mockery as he rode along. Dudley came behind, with a downcast look, dreading, as well he might, to meet the indignant gaze of the people, who beheld him, their only countryman by birth, among the oppressors of his native land. The captain of a frigate in the harbor, and two or three civil officers under the Crown, were also there. But the figure that most attracted the public eye, and stirred up the deepest feeling, was the Episcopal clergyman of King's Chapel, riding haughtily among the magistrates in his priestly vestments, the fitting representative of prelacy and persecution, the union of church and state, and all those abominations which had driven the Puritans to the wilderness. Another guard of soldiers, in double rank, brought up the rear. The whole scene was a picture of the condition of New England, and its moral, the deformity of any government that does not grow out of the nature of things and the character of the people. On one side the religious multitude, with their sad visages and dark attire, and, on the other, the group of despotic rulers, with the high churchman in the midst, and here and there a crucifix at their bosoms, all magnificently clad, flushed with wine, proud of unjust authority, and scoffing at the universal groan. And the mercenary soldiers, waiting but the word to deluge the street with blood, showed the only means by which obedience could be secured."

Education was temporarily paralyzed, and the right of

franchise was rendered nugatory by the order that oaths must be taken with the hand on the Bible—a "popish" ceremony which the Puritans would not undergo. The town meetings, which were the essence of New Englandism, were forbidden except for the election of local officers, and ballot voting was stopped: "There is no such thing as a town in the whole country," Andros declared. Verily, it was "a time when New England groaned under the actual pressure of heavier wrongs than those threatened ones which brought on the Revolution." Yet the spirit of the people was not crushed; their leaders did not desert them; in private meetings they kept their faith and hope alive; the ministers told them that "God would yet be exalted among the heathen"; and one at least among them, Willard, significantly bade them take note that they "had not yet resisted unto blood, warring against sin!"

Boston was Andros's headquarters, and in 1688 was made the capital of the whole region along the coast from the French possessions in the north to Maryland in the south. But Andros had not yet received the submission of Rhode Island and Connecticut. Walter Clarke was the governor of the former colony in 1687, when, in the dead of winter, Andros appeared there and ordered the charter to be given up. Roger Williams had died three years before. Clarke tried to temporize, and asked that the surrender be postponed till a fitter season. But Andros dissolved the government summarily, and broke its seal; and it is not on record that the Rhode Islanders offered any visible resistance to the outrage. From Rhode Island Andros, with his retinue and soldiers, proceeded to Hartford, which had lost its Winthrop longer ago than the former its Williams. Governor Dongan of New York had warned Connecticut of what was to come, and had counseled them to submit. Three writs of quo warranto were issued, one upon another, and the colony finally petitioned the king to be permitted to retain its liberties; but in any case to be merged rather in

Massachusetts than in New York. It was on the last day of October, 1687; Andros entered the assembly hall, where the assembly was then in session, with Governor Treat presiding. The scene which followed has entered into the domain of legend; but there is nothing miraculous in it; a deed which depended for its success upon the secrecy with which it was accomplished would naturally be lacking in documentary confirmation. Upon Andros's entrance, hungry for the charter, Treat opposed him, and entered upon a defense of the right of the colony to retain the ancient and honorable document, hallowed as it was by associations which endeared it to its possessors, aside from its political value. Andros, of course, would not yield; the only thing that such men ever yield to is superior force; but force being on his side, he entertained no thought of departing from his purpose. The dispute was maintained until so late in the afternoon that candles must be lighted; some were fixed in sconces round the walls, and there were others on the table, where also lay the charter, with its engrossed text, and its broad seal. The assemblymen, as the debate seemed to approach its climax, left their seats and crowded round the table, where stood on one side the royal governor, in his scarlet coat laced with gold, his heavy but sharp-featured countenance flushed with irritation, one hand on the hilt of his sword, the other stretched out toward the coveted document:—on the other, the governor chosen by the people, in plain black, with a plain white collar turned down over his doublet, his eyes dark with emotion, his voice vibrating hoarsely as he pleaded with the licensed highwayman of England. Around, is the ring of strong visages, rustic but brainy, frowning, agitated, eager, angry; and the flame of the candles flickering in their heavily-drawn breath.

Suddenly and simultaneously, by a preconcerted signal, the lights are out, and the black darkness has swallowed up the scene. In the momentary silence of astonishment,

Andros feels himself violently shoved aside; the hand with which he would draw his sword is in an iron grasp, as heavy as that which he has laid upon colonial freedom. There is a surging of unseen men about him, the shuffling of feet, vague outcries: he knows not what is to come: death, perhaps. Is Sir Edmund afraid? We have no information as to the physical courage of the man, further than that in 1675 he had been frightened into submission by the farmers and fishermen at Fort Saybrook. But he need not have been a coward to feel the blood rush to his heart during those few blind moments. Men of such lives as his are always ready to suspect assassination.

But assassination is not an American method of righting wrong. Anon the steel had struck the flint, and the spark had caught the tinder, and one after another the candles were alight once more. All stared at one another: what had happened? Andros, his face mottled with pallor, was pulling himself together, and striving to resume the arrogant insolence of his customary bearing. He opens his mouth to speak, but only a husky murmur replaces the harsh stridency of his usual utterance. "What devilish foolery is this—" But ere he can get further, some bucolic statesman brings his massive palm down on the table with a bang that makes the oaken plank crack, and thunders out —"The charter! Where's our charter?"

Where, indeed? That is one of those historic secrets which will probably never be decided one way or the other. "There is no contemporary record of this event." No: but, somehow or other, one hears of Yankee Captain Joe Wadsworth, with the imaginative audacity and promptness of resource of his race, snatching the parchment from the table in the midst of the groping panic, and slipping out through the crowd: he has passed the door and is inhaling with grateful lungs the fresh coolness of the cloudy October night. Has any one seen him go? Did any one know what he did?—None who will reveal it. He is astride his mare, and they are off toward the old farm, where his boyhood was spent, and where stands the great hollow oak which, thirty years ago, Captain Joe used to canvass for woodpeckers' nests and squirrel hordes. He had thought, in those boyish days, what a good hiding-place the old tree would make; and the thought had flashed back into his mind while he listened to that fight for the charter to-day. It did not take him long to lay his plot, and to agree with his few fellow-conspirators. Sir Edmund can snatch the government, and scrawl Finis at the foot of the Connecticut records; but that charter he shall never have, nor shall any man again behold it, until years have passed away, and Andros has vanished forever from New England.

Meanwhile, he returned to Boston, there, for a season, to make "the wicked walk on every side, and the vilest to be exalted." Then came that famous April day of 1689; and, following, event after event, one storming upon another's heels, as the people rose from their long bondage, and hurled their oppressors down. The bearer of the news that William of Orange had landed in England, was imprisoned, but it was too late. Andros ordered his soldiers under arms; but the commander of the frigate had been taken prisoner by the Boston ship-carpenters; the sheriff was arrested; hundreds of determined men surrounded the regimental headquarters; the major resisted in vain; the colors and drums were theirs; a vast throng at the town house greeted the venerable Bradstreet; the insurrection was proclaimed, and Andros and his wretched followers, flying to the frigate, were seized and cast into prison. "Down with Andros and Randolph!" was the cry; and "The old charter once more!" It was a hundred years to a day before that shot fired at Concord and heard round the world.

CHAPTER NINTH

THE NEW LEAF, AND THE BLOT ON IT

POPULAR liberty is one thing; political independence is another. The latter cannot be securely and lastingly established until the former has fitted the nation to use it intelligently. When the component individuals have thrown off the bondage of superstition and of formulas, their next step must be, as an organization, to abrogate external subordination to others, and, like a son come of age, to begin life on a basis and with an aim of their own.

But such movements are organic, and chronologically slow; so that we do not comprehend them until historical perspective shows them to us in their mass and tendency. They are thus protected against their enemies, who, if they knew the significance of the helpless seed, would destroy it before it could become the invincible and abounding tree. Great human revolutions make themselves felt, at first, as a trifling and unreasonable annoyance: a crumpling in the roseleaf bed of the orthodox and usual. They are brushed petulantly aside and the sleeper composes himself to rest once more. But inasmuch as there was vital truth as the predisposing cause of the annoyance, it cannot thus be disposed of; it spreads and multiplies. Had its opponents understood its meaning, they would have humored it into inoffensiveness; but the means they adopt to extirpate it are the sure way to develop it. Truth can no more be smothered by intolerance, than a sown field can be rendered unproductive by covering it with manure.

When Christ came, the common people had no recognized existence except as a common basis on which aristocratic institutions might rest. That they could have rights was as little conceived as that inanimate sticks and stones could have them; to enfranchise them—to surrender to them the reins of government—such an idea the veriest madness would have started from. Philosophy was blind to it; religion was abhorrent to it; the common people themselves were as far from entertaining it as cattle in the fields are to-day. Christ's sayings—Love one another—Do as ye would be done by—struck at the root of all arbitrary power, and furnished the clew to all possible emancipations; but their infinite meaning has even yet been grasped but partially. A thousand years are but as yesterday in the counsels of the Lord. The early Christians were indeed a democracy; but they were common people to begin with, and the law of love suggested to them no thought of altering their condition in that respect. The only liberty they dreamed of claiming was liberty to die for their faith; and that was accorded to them in full measure. Indeed, an apprenticeship, the years of which were centuries, must be served before they could be qualified to realize even that they could become the trustees of power.

Their simple priesthood, beginning by sheltering them from physical violence, ended by subjecting them to a yet more enslaving spiritual tyranny. Philosophers could frame imaginative theories of human liberty; but the people could be helped only from within themselves. Wiclif, giving them the Bible in a living language, and intimating that force was not necessarily right, began their education; and Luther, in his dogma of justification by faith alone, forged a tremendous weapon in their behalf. Beggars could have faith; princes and prelates might lack it; of what avail was it to gain the whole world if the soul must be lost at last?

The reasonings and discussions to which his dogma gave rise called into existence two world-covering armies to fight for and against it. Peace has not been declared between them yet; but there has long ceased to be any question as to who shall have the victory.

When the battle began, however, the other side had the stronger battalions, and there would have been little chance for liberty, but for the timely revelation of the western continent. And, inevitably, it was the people who went, and the aristocrats who stayed behind; because the new idea favored the former and menaced the latter. Inevitably, too, it was the man who had the future in him that was the exile, and the man of the past who drove him forth. And whenever we find a man of the aristocratic order emigrating to the colonies, we find in him the same love of liberty which animates his plebeian companion, graced by a motive even higher, because opposed to his inherited interests and advantages. Thus the refuge of the oppressed became by the nature of things the citadel of the purest and soundest civilization.

Luther, Calvin, and Jonathan Edwards were in the line of succession one from the other; each defined the truth more nearly than his predecessor, but left it still in the rough. The whole truth is never revealed at one time, but so much only as may forge a sword for the immediate combat. Faith alone was a good blade for the first downright strokes of the battle; predestination had a finer edge; and Edwards's dialetical subtleties on the freedom of the will sharpen logic to so fine a point that we begin to perceive that not logic but love is the true weapon of the Christian: the mystery of God is not revealed in syllogisms. But each fresh discrimination was useful in its place and time, and had to exist in order to prepare the way for its successor. The Puritans would have been less stubborn without their background of spiritual damnation. That awful conscience of theirs would have faltered without its lake of fire and brimstone to keep out of; and if it had faltered, the American nation would have been strangled in its cradle.

America, then, having no permanent attractions as a residence for any of the upper classes of European society, became the home of the common people, in whom alone the doctrine of liberty could find a safe anchorage, because in them alone did the need for it abide. The philosophy, the religion, the tolerance, the civil forms, which are broad enough to suit the common people, must be nearly as broad as truth itself, and therefore as unconquerable. But the broader they appear, the more must they be offensive to the orthodox and conventional, who by the instinct of self-preservation will be impelled to attack them. There was never a more obvious chain of cause and effect than that which is revealed in the history of the United States; and having shown the conditions which led to the planting in the wilderness of the elements which constitute our present commonwealth, we shall now proceed to trace the manner in which they came to be wrought into a united whole. They were as yet mainly unconscious of one another; the opportunity for mutual knowledge had not yet been presented, nor had the causes conducive to crystallization been introduced. Oppression had awakened the colonists to the value of their religious and civic principles; something more than oppression was requisite to mold them into independent and homogeneous form. This was afforded, during the next eighty years, by their increase in numbers, wealth, familiarity with their country, and in the facilities for intercommunication; and also, coincidently, by the French and Indian wars, which apprised them of their strength, trained them in arms, created the comradeship which arises from common dangers and aims, and developed vast tracts of land which had otherwise been unknown. A country which has been fought for, on whose soil blood has been shed, becomes dear to its inhabitants; and the heroism of the Revolution gathered heart and perseverance from the traditions and the graves of the soldiers of the Intercolonial wars.

The English Revolution benefited the colonies, though to a less extent than might have been expected. William of Orange was the logical consequence, by reaction, of James II. The latter had so corrupted and confused the kingdom, that William, whose connection with England arose from his marriage with Mary, James's daughter, was invited to usurp the throne by Tories, Whigs and Presbyterians—each party from a motive of its own. The people were not appealed to, but they acquiesced. The Roman Catholics were discriminated against, and the nonconformists were not requited for their services; but out of many minor injustices and wrongs, a condition better than anything which had preceded it was soon discernible. The principle was established that royal power was not absolute, nor self-continuing; it could be created only by the representatives of the people, who could take it away again if its trustee were guilty of breach of contract. The dynastic theory was disallowed; kings were to come by election, not succession. The nobility were recognized as the medium between the king and the people, but not before they had conceded to the commons the right to elect a king for life; and presently there came into existence a new power—that of the commercial classes, the moneyed interest, which, in return for loans to government, received political consideration. Ownership of land ceased to be the sole condition on which a candidate could appeal to the electors; and merchants were raised to a position where they could control national policies. Merchants might not be wiser or less selfish than the aristocracy; but at all events they were of the people, and the more widely power is diffused, the less likely is any class to be oppressed. It was no longer possible for freemen to be ruled otherwise than by governments of their own making, and subject to their approval. Freedom of the press, which means liberty to criticise all state and social procedure, was established,

THE NEW LEAF, AND THE BLOT ON IT

and public opinion, instead of being crushed, was consulted. The aristocracy could retain its ascendency only by permitting more weight to the middle class, whose influence was therefore bound gradually to increase. Popular legislatures were the final arbiters; and the advantages which the English had obtained would naturally be imparted to the colonies, which, in addition, were unhampered by the relics of decaying systems which still impeded the old country.

William cared little for England, nor were the English in love with him; but he was the most far-seeing statesman of his day, and his effect was liberalizing and beneficial. He kept Louis XIV. from working the mischief that he desired, and prevented the disturbance of political equilibrium which was threatened by the proposed successor to the extinct Hapsburg dynasty on the Spanish throne. William was outwardly cold and dry, but there was fire within him, if you would apply friction enough. He was under no illusions; he perfectly understood why he was wanted in England; and for his part, he accepted the throne in order to be able to check Louis in his designs upon the liberties of Holland. In defending his countrymen he defended all others in Europe, whose freedom was endangered.

But if William's designs were large, they were also, and partly for that reason, unjust in particulars. He was at war with France; France held possessions in America; and it was necessary to carry on war against her there as well as in Europe. The colonists, then, should be made to assist in the operations; they must furnish men, forts, and, to some extent at least, supplies. It was easy to reach this determination, but difficult to enforce it under the circumstances. The various colonies lacked the homogeneity which was desirable to secure co-operative action from them; some of them were royal provinces, some proprietary, some were in an anomalous state, or practically without any recognizable form of government whatever. Each had its separate interests to regard, and could not be brought to perceive that what was the concern of one must in the end be the concern of all. But the greatest difficulty was to secure obedience of orders after they had been promulgated; the colonial legislatures pleaded all manner of rights and privileges, under Magna Charta and other charters; they claimed the privileges of Englishmen, and they stood upon their "natural" rights as discoverers and inhabitants of a new country. They were spread over a vast extent of territory, so that in many cases a journey of weeks would be required, through pathless forests, across unbridged rivers, over difficult mountains, by swamps and morasses—in order to carry information of the commands of the government to no more than a score or a hundred of persons. And then these persons would look around at the miles of unconquerable nature stretching out on every side; and they would reflect upon the thousands of leagues of salt water that parted them from the king who was the source of these unwelcome orders; and, finally, they would glance at the travel-stained and weary envoy with a pitying smile, and offer him food and drink and a bed—but not obedience. The colonists had imagination, when they cared to exercise it; but not imagination of the kind to bring vividly home to them the waving of a royal scepter across the broad Atlantic.

Another cause of embarrassment to the king was the reluctance of Parliament to pass laws inhibiting the reasonable liberties of the colonies. The influence of the Lords somewhat preponderated, because they controlled many of the elections to the Commons; but neither branch was disposed to increase the power of the king, and they were, besides, split by internal factions. It was not until the mercantile interest got into the saddle that Parliament saw the expediency of restricting the productive and commercial freedom of the colonies, and the necessity, in order to secure these ends, of diminishing their legislative license. Meanwhile, William tried more than one device of his own. First, by dint of the prerogative, he ordered that each colony

ESTING A WOMAN CHARGED WITH WITCHCRAFT

north of Carolina should appoint a fixed quota of men and money for the defense of New York against the common enemy; this order it was found impossible to carry out. Next, he caused a board of trade to be appointed in 1696 to inquire into the condition of the colonies, and as to what should be done about them; and after a year, this board reported that in their opinion what was wanted was a captain-general to exercise a sort of military dictatorship over all the North American provinces. But the ministry held this plan to be imprudent, and it fell through. At the same time, William Penn worked out a scheme truly statesmanlike, proposing an annual congress of two delegates from each province to devise ways and means, which they could more intelligently do than could any council or board in England. The plan was advocated by Charles Davenant, a writer on political economy, who observed that the stronger the colonies became, the more profitable to England would they be; only despotism could drive them to rebellion; and innovations in their charters would be prejudicial to the king's power. But this also was rejected; and finally the conduct of necessary measures was given to "royal instructions," that is, to the king; but to the king subject to the usual parliamentary restraint. And none of the better class of Englishmen wished to tyrannize over their fellow Englishmen across the sea.

Under this arrangement, the appointment of judges was taken from the people; Habeas Corpus was refused, or permitted as a favor; censorship of the press was revived; license to preach except as granted by a bishop was denied; charters were withheld from dissenters; slavery was encouraged; and the colonies not as yet under royal control were told that the common weal demanded that they should be placed in the same condition of dependency as those who were. But William died in 1702, before this arrangement could be carried out. Queen Anne, however, listened to alarmist reports of the unruly and disaffected condition of the colonies, and allowed a bill for their "better regulation" to be introduced. It was now that the mercantile interest began to show its power.

The old argument, that every nation may claim the services of its own subjects, wherever they are, was revived; and that England ought to be the sole buyer and seller of American trade. All the oppressive and irritating commercial regulations were put in force, and all colonial laws opposing them were abrogated. Complaints under these regulations were taken out of the hands of colonial judges and juries, on the plea that they were often the offenders. Woolen manufactures, as interfering with English industry, were so rigorously forbidden, that a sailor in an American port could not buy himself a flannel shirt, and the Virginians were put to it to clothe themselves at all. Naturally, the people resisted so far as they could, and that was not a little; England could not spare a sufficient force to insure obedience to laws of such a kind. "We have a right to the same liberties as Englishmen," was the burden of all remonstrances, and it was supported by councilors on the bench and ministers in the pulpit. The revenues were so small as hardly to repay the cost of management. It is hard to coerce a nation and get a profit over expenses; and the colonies were a nation—they numbered nearly three hundred thousand in Anne's reign—without the advantage of being coherent; they were a baker's dozen of disputatious and recalcitrant incoherencies. The only arbitrary measure of taxation that was amiably accepted was the post-office tax, which was seen to be productive of a useful service at a reasonable cost; and an act to secure suitable trees for masts for the navy was tolerated because there were so many trees. The coinage system was no system at all, and led to much confusion and loss; and the severe laws against piracy, which had grown to be common, and in the profits of which persons high in the community were often suspected and sometimes proved to have been participants, were less effective than they certainly ought to have been; but they, and the bloody and desperate objects of them, added a picturesque page to the annals of the time.

Concerning the condition of the several colonies during the years following the Revolution of 1688, it may be said, in general, that it was much better in fact than it was in theory. There were narrow and unjust and shortsighted laws and regulations, and there were men of a corresponding stamp to execute them; but the success such persons met with was sporadic, uncertain, and partial. The people were grown too big, and too well aware of their bigness, to be ground down and kept in subjection, even had the will so to afflict them been steady and virulent—which it cannot be said to have been. The people knew that, be the law what it might, it could, on the whole, be evaded or disregarded, unless or until the mother country undertook to enforce it by landing an army and regularly making war; and England had too many troubles of her own, and also contained too many liberal-minded men, to attempt such a thing for the present. The proof that the colonies were not seriously or consistently oppressed is evident from the fact that they all increased rapidly in population and wealth, notwithstanding their "troubles"; and it was not until England had settled down under her Georges, and that Providence had inspired the third of that name with the pig-headedness that cost his adopted subjects so dear, that the Revolution became a possibility. Yet even now there was no lack of talk of such an eventuality; the remark was common that in process of time the colonies would declare their independence. But perhaps it was made rather with intent to spur England to adopt preventative measures in season, than from a real conviction that the event would actually take place.

New York, at the time of William's accession, had been under the control of Andros, who at that epoch commanded a domain two or three times as large as Britain. Nicholson was his lieutenant; and on the news of the Revolution Jacob Leisler, a German, who had come over in 1660 as a soldier of the Dutch West India Company, and had made a fortune, unseated Nicholson and proclaimed William and Mary. Supported by the mass of the Dutch inhabitants, but without other warrant, he assumed the functions of royal lieutenant-governor, pending the arrival of the new king's appointee. In the interests of order, it was the best thing to do. But he made active enemies among the other elements of the cosmopolitan population of New York, and they awaited an opportunity to be avenged on him. This came with the arrival of Henry Sloughter in 1691, with the king's commission. Sloughter can only be described as a drunken profligate. At the earliest moment, Leisler sent to know his commands, and offered to surrender the fort. Sloughter answered by arresting him and Milborne, his son-in-law, on the charge of high treason—an absurdity; but they were arraigned before a partisan court and condemned to be hanged—they refusing to plead and appealing to the king. It is said that Sloughter did not intend to carry the sentence into effect; but the local enemies of Leisler made the governor drunk that night, and secured his signature to the decree. This was on May 14, 1691; on the 15th, the house disapproved the sentence, but on the 16th it was carried out, the victims meeting their fate with dignity and courage. In 1695, the attainder was reversed by act of parliament; but it remains the most disgraceful episode of William's government of the colonies.

Meanwhile, Sloughter was recalled, and Fletcher sent out. He was not a sodden imbecile, but he was ill-chosen for his office. He described the New Yorkers of that day as "divided, contentious and impoverished," and immediately began a conflict with them. His attitude may be judged from a passage in his remarks to the assembly soon afterward: "There never was an amendment desired by the council board but what was rejected. It is a sign of a stubborn ill-temper. . . . While I stay in this government I will take care that neither heresy, schism, nor rebellion be preached among you, nor vice and profanity be encouraged. You seem to take the power into your own hands and set up for everything." This last observation was probably not devoid of truth; nor was a subsequent one, "There are none of you but what are big with the privileges of Englishmen and Magna Charta." That well describes the colonist of the period, whether in New York or elsewhere. It had been said of New Yorkers, however, that they were a conquered people, who had no rights that a king was bound to respect; and the grain of truth in the saying may have made the New Yorkers more than commonly anxious to keep out the small end of the wedge. Bellomont's incumbency was mild, and chiefly memorable by reason of his having commissioned a certain William Kidd to suppress piracy; but Kidd—if tradition is to be believed:—certainly his most unfair and prejudiced trial in London afforded no evidence of it—found more pleasure in the observance than in the breach, and became the most famous pirate of them all. There is gold enough of his getting buried along the coasts to buy a modern ironclad fleet, according to the belief of the credulous. A little later, Steed Bonnet, Richard Worley, and Edward Teach, nicknamed Blackbeard, had similar fame and fate. Their business, like others of great profit, incurred great risks.

Of Lord Cornbury, the next governor, Bancroft remarks, with unwonted energy, that "He joined the worst form of arrogance to intellectual imbecility," and that "happily for New York, he had every vice of character necessary to discipline a colony into self-reliance and resistance." He began by stealing $1,500 appropriated to fortify the Narrows; it was the last money he got from the various assemblies that he called and dissolved, and the assemblies became steadily more independent and embarrassing. In 1707, the Quaker speaker read out in meeting a paper accusing him of bribe taking. Cornbury disappears from American history the next year; and completed his career, in England, as the third Earl of Clarendon.

Under Lovelace, the assembly refused supplies and assumed executive powers; when Hunter came, he found a fertile and wealthy country, but nothing in it for him: "Sancho Panza was but a type of me." He was a man of humor and sagacity, and perceived that "the colonists are infants at their mother's breasts, but will wean themselves when they come of age." Before he got through with the New Yorkers, he had reason to suspect that the weaning time had all but arrived.

New Jersey passed through many trivial vicissitudes, changes of ownership, vexed land-titles, and royal encroachments. For several years the people had no visible government at all. They did not hold themselves so well in hand as did New York, and were less audacious and aggressive in resistance; but in one way or another, they fairly held their own, prospered and multiplied. Pennsylvania enjoyed from the first more undisturbed independence and self-direction than the others; at one time it seemed to be their ambition to discover something which Penn would not grant them, and then to ask for it. But the great Quaker was equal to the occasion; no selfishness, crankiness, or whimsicality on their part could wear out his patience and benevolence. In the intervals of his imprisonments in England he labored for their welfare. The queen contemplated making Pennsylvania a royal province, but Penn, though poor, would not let it go except on condition it might retain its democratic liberties. The people, in short, kept everything in their own hands, and their difficulties arose chiefly from their disputes as to what to do with so much freedom. It was a colony where everybody was equal, without an established church, where any one was welcome to enter and dwell, which was destitute of arms or defense or even police, which yet grew in all good things more rapidly than any of its sister colonies. The people waxed fat and kicked, but they did no

THE NEW LEAF, AND THE BLOT ON IT 249

evil in the sight of the Lord, whatever England may have thought of them; and after the contentious little appendage of Delaware had finally been cut off from its big foster sister (though they shared the same governors until the Revolution) there is little more to be said of either of them.

The Roman Catholic owners of Maryland fared ill after William came into power; he made the colony a royal province in 1691, and for thirty years or more there were no more Baltimores in the government. Under Copley, the first royal governor, the Church of England was declared to be established; but dissenters were afterward protected; only the Catholics were treated with intolerance in the garden themselves had made. The people soon settled down and became contented, and slowly their numbers augmented. But the Baltimores were persistent, and the fourth lord, in 1715, took advantage of his infancy to compass a blameless reconciliation with the Church of England, thereby securing his installation in the proprietary rights of his forefathers, from which the family was not evicted until the Revolution of the colonies in 1775 opened a new chapter in the history of the world.

Virginia recovered rapidly from Berkeley, and suffered little from Andros, who was governor in 1692, but with his fangs drawn, and an experience to remember. The people still eschewed towns, and lived each family in its own solitude, hospitable to all, but content with their own company. The love of independence grew alike in the descendants of the cavaliers and in the common people, and the wide application of the suffrage equalized power, and even enabled the lower sort to keep the gentry, when the fancy took them, out of the places of authority and trust. Democracy was in the woods and streams and the blue sky, and all breathed it in and absorbed it into their blood and bone. They early petitioned William for home rule in all its purity; he permitted land grants to be confirmed, but would not let their assembly supplant the English parliament as a governing power.

He sought, unsuccessfully, to increase the authority of the church; for though the bishop might license and the governor recommend, the parish would not present. It was a leisurely, good-natured, careless, but spirited people, indifferent to commerce, content to harvest their fields and rule their slaves, and let the world go by. A more enviable existence than theirs it would be hard to imagine. All their financial transactions were done in tobacco, even to the clergyman's stipend and the judge's fee. No enemy menaced them; politics were rather an amusement than a serious duty; yet in these fertile regions were made the brains and characters which afterward, for so many years, ruled the councils of the United States, or led her armies in war. They lay fallow for seventy-five years, and then gave the best of accounts of themselves. England did not quite know what to make of the Virginians; to judge by the reports of the governors, they were changeable as a pretty woman. But they were simply capricious humorists, full of life and intelligence, who did what they pleased and did not take themselves too seriously. They indulged themselves with the novel toy, the post-office; and founded William and Mary College in 1693. This venerable institution passed its second centennial with one hundred and sixty students on its roll; but, soon after, it "ceased upon the midnight, without pain." Anybody may have a college in these days.

The Carolinas, no longer pestered by Grand Models, became another rustic paradise. Their suns were warm, their forests vast, their people delighting in a sort of wild civilization. When James II. went down, the Carolinians needed no care-taker, and declined to avail themselves of the martial law suggested by the anxious proprietors. But in 1690 they allowed Seth Sothel to occupy the gubernatorial seat, and sent up a legislature. The southern section was subjected to some superficial annoyance by the proprietors, who wished to make an income from the country, but were unwilling to put their hands in their pockets in the first place; they insisted upon their authority, and the colonists did not say them nay, but maintained freedom of action in all their concerns nevertheless. A series of proprietary governors were sent out to them—Ludwell first, then Smith; both failed, and retired. Then came Archdale, the Quaker, who struck a popular note in his remark that dissenters could cut wood and hoe crops as well as the highest churchmen; his policy was to concede, to conciliate and to harmonize, and he was welcome and useful. The Indians, and even the Spaniards, were brought into friendly relations. Liberty of conscience was accorded to all but "papists," who were certainly hardly used in these times. An attempt to base political power on possession of land was defeated in 1702. The Church of England was accepted in 1704, and though dissenters were tolerated, it remained the official dispenser of religion until the Revolution. All these things were on the surface; the colony, inside, was free, happy and prosperous; it had adopted rice culture, with a great supply of negro slaves, and it brought furs from far in the interior. The Huguenots had been enfranchised as soon as it was known that England had turned her back on Catholicism and James. None of the colonies had before them a future more peaceful and profitable than South Carolina. The slaves were her only burden; but at that period they seemed not a burden, but the assurance of her prosperity.

North Carolina was as happy and as peaceful as her southern sister, but the conditions of life there were different. The proprietors attempted to control the people, but were worsted in almost every encounter. Laws were passed only to be disregarded. Here, as elsewhere, the Quakers became conspicuous in inculcating liberal notions, and were paid the compliment of being hated and feared by the emissaries of England. What was to be done with a population made up of fugitives of all kinds, not from Europe only, but from the other colonies; who held all creeds, or none at all;

who lived by hunting and tree-cutting; who were as averse from towns as Virginia, and many of whom could not be said to have any fixed abode at all? If restraints were proposed, they ignored them; if they were pressed, they resisted them, sometimes boisterously, but never with bloodshed. Robert Daniel, deputy governor in 1704, tried to establish the Church of England; a building was erected, but in all the province there was but one clergyman, with an absentee congregation scattered over hundreds of miles of mountain and forest. In the following year there were two governors elected by opposite factions, each with his own legislature; and in 1711 Edward Hyde, going out to restore order, confounded the confusion. He called in Spotswood from Virginia to help him; but there were too many Quakers; and the old soldier, after landing a party of marines to indicate his disapproval of anarchy, retired. Meantime, fresh emigrants kept arriving, including many Palatinates from Germany. It was not a profitable country to its reputed owners, who, in 1714, received a hundred dollars apiece from it. But it supported its inhabitants all the better; and it was eight years more before they supplied themselves with a court house, and forty, before they felt the need of a printing press.

In New England, Connecticut and Rhode Island, which had suffered comparatively little from the despotism of James, readily recovered such minor rights as they had been deprived of. There was a dispute between Fitz-John Winthrop and Fletcher as to the command of the local militia, the former, with his fellow colonists, demanding that the control be kept by the colony; Winthrop went to England and got confirmation of his plea; and from the people, on his return, the governorship. There were a score and a half of flourishing towns in Connecticut, each with its meeting house and school. Little Rhode Island recovered its charter, whether the original from the hollow oak, or a duplicate. An act was pending in England to abrogate all colonial charters, and was backed by the strong mercantile influence; but the French war caused it to go over. Lord Cornbury, and Joseph Dudley, the Massachusetts-born traitor, did their best to get a royal governor for these colonies, but they failed; though Dudley, at the instance of Cotton Mather, was afterward made governor of Massachusetts.

But no son of Massachusetts has so well deserved the condemnation of history as Cotton Mather himself. Such political sins as his advocacy of Dudley, and his opposition to the revival of the old charter, are trifling; they might have been the result of ordinary blindness or selfishness merely; but his part in the witchcraft delusion cannot be so accounted for. In his persecution of the accused persons he was actuated by a spirit of inflamed vanity and malignity truly diabolic; and if there can be a crime which Heaven cannot forgive, assuredly Cotton Mather steeped himself in it. He was a singular being; yet he represented the evil tendencies of Puritanism; they drained into him, so to say, until he became their sensible incarnation. In his person, at last, the Puritans of Massachusetts beheld united every devilish trait to which the tenets of their belief could incline them; and the hideousness of the spectacle so impressed them that, from that time forward, any further Cotton Mathers became impossible. There is no feature in Mather's case that can be held to palliate his conduct. He had the best education of the time, coming, as he did, from a line of scholars, and out-Heroding them in the variety and curiousness of his accomplishments, and in the number of his published "works"—three hundred and eighty-three. Nothing that he produced has any original value; but his erudition was enormous. Of "Magnalia," his chief and representative work, it has been said that "it is a heterogeneous and polyglot compilation of information useful and useless, of unbridled pedantry, of religious adjurations, biographical anecdotes, political maxims, and theories of education. . . .

Indeed, it contains everything except order, accuracy, sobriety, proportion, development, and upshot." This man, born in 1663, was not yet thirty years of age when his campaign against the witches began; indeed, he had given a hint of his direction some years earlier. In his multifarious reading he had become acquainted with all existing traditions and speculations concerning witchcraft, and his profession as minister in the Calvinist communion predisposed him to investigate all accessible details concerning the devil. He was passionately hungry for notoriety and conspicuousness: Tydides melior patre was the ambition he proposed to himself. A huge memory, stored with the promiscuous rubbish of libraries, and with facts which were transformed into rubbish by his treatment of them, was combined in him with a diseased imagination, and a personal vanity almost surpassing belief. His mental shallowness and consequent restlessness rendered anything like original thought impossible to him; and the faculty of intellectual digestion was not less beyond him. It is probable that curiosity was the motive which originally drew him to the study of witchcraft; a vague credence of such things was common at the time; and in France and England many executions for the supposed crime had taken place. Mather had no convictions on the subject; he was incapable of convictions of any kind; and the revelation of his private diary shows that at the very time he was wallowing in murders, and shrieking out for ever more victims, he was in secret doubting the truth of all religion, and coquetting with atheism. But men of no religious faith are prone to superstitions; the man who denies God is the first to seek for guidance from the stars. Suppose there should be a devil?—was Mather's thought. It is not to be wondered at that such a man should be fascinated by the notion; and we may perhaps concede to Mather that, if at any time in his career he approached belief in anything, the devil was the subject of his belief. Had his character been genuine and vigorous, such a belief would have led him to plunge into witchcraft, not as a persecutor, but as a performer; he would have aimed to be chief at the witches' Sabbath, and to have rioted in the terrible powers with which Satan's children were credited. But he was far from owning this bold and trenchant fiber; though he could not believe in God, he dared not defy Him; and still he could not refrain from dabbling in the forbidden mysteries. Moreover, there was an obscure and questionable faculty inherent in certain persons, unaccountable on any recognized natural grounds, which gave support to the witchcraft theory. We call this faculty hypnotism now; and physiology seeks to connect it with the nervous affections of hysteria and epilepsy At all times, and in all quarters of the earth, manifestations of it have not been wanting; and in Africa it has for centuries existed as a so-called religious cult, to which in this country the name of Hoodooism or Voodooism has been applied. It is a savage form of devil worship, including snake-charming, and the lore of fetiches and charms; and its professors are able to produce abnormal effects, within certain limits, upon the nerves and imaginations of their clients or victims. Among the negro slaves in Massachusetts in 1692, and the negro-Indian mongrels, there were persons able to exercise this power. They attracted the attention of Cotton Mather.

Gradually, we may suppose, the idea took form in his mind that if he could not be a witch himself, he might gain the notoriety he craved by becoming the denouncer of witchcraft in others. Ministers in that day still had great influence in New England, and had grasped at temporal as well as spiritual sway, maintaining that the former should rightly involve the latter. What a minister said, had weight; what so well-known a minister as Cotton Mather said, would carry conviction to many. If Mather could procure the execution of a witch or two, it could not fail to add greatly to his spiritual glory and ascendency. It is, of course, not to be imagined that he had any conception, beforehand, of the extent to which the agitation he was about to begin would be carried. But when evil is once let loose, it multiplies itself and gains impetus, and rages like a fire. The only thing for Mather to do was to keep abreast of the mischief which he had created. If he faltered or relented, he would be himself destroyed. He was whirled along with the foul storm by a mingling of terror, malice, vanity, triumph and fascination: as repulsive and dastardly a figure as has ever stained the records of our country. He was ready to sacrifice the population of Massachusetts rather than confess that the deeds for which he was responsible were based on what, in his secret soul, he unquestionably felt was a delusion. For though he may have half-believed in witchcraft while it presented itself to him as a theory, yet as soon as he had reached the stage of actual examinations and court testimony, he could not fail to perceive that the theory was utterly devoid of reasonable foundation; that convictions could not be had except by aid of open perjury, suppression and intimidation. Yet Cotton Mather scrupled not to put in operation these and other devices; to hound on the magistrates, to browbeat and sophisticate the juries, and to scream threats, warnings and self-glorifications from the pulpit. Needs must, when the devil drives. Had he paused, had he even held his peace, that noose, slimy with the death-sweat of a score of innocent victims, would have settled greedily round his own guilty neck, and strangled his life. But Cotton Mather was too nimble, too voluble, too false and too cowardly for the gallows; he lived to a good age, and died in the odor of sanctity.

Immediately after the news of William's accession was known in New England, Mather opposed the restoration of the ancient charter, because it would have interfered with the plans of his personal political ambition. He caused the presentation of an address to the king, purporting to represent the desire of the majority of reputable citizens of Boston,

THE NEW LEAF, AND THE BLOT ON IT 257

placing themselves at the royal disposal, without suggesting that the charter rights be revived. Cotton Mather's father, Increase, was the actual agent to England; but it was the views of Cotton Mather rather than his own that he submitted to his majesty. The blatant hypocrite had dominated his father. The king gave Massachusetts a new charter which was entirely satisfactory to the petitioners, for it took away the right of the people to elect their own officers and manage their own affairs, and made the king the fountain of power and honor. It was identical with all charters of royal colonies, except that the council was elected jointly by the people and by its own members. Sir William Phips, at Increase Mather's suggestion, was made governor, and William Stoughton lieutenant-governor. The members of the council were "every man of them a friend to the interests of the churches," and of Cotton Mather. He did not conceal his delight. "The time for favor is come, yea, the set time is come! Instead of my being made a sacrifice to wicked rulers, my father-in-law, with several related to me, and several brethren of my own church, are among the council. The governor is not my enemy, but one whom I baptized, and one of my own flock, and one of my dearest friends.—I obtained of the Lord that He would use me to be a herald of His kingdom now approaching." Such was the attitude of Cotton Mather regarding the political outlook. Obviously the field was prepared for him to achieve his crowning distinction as champion of God against the devil in Massachusetts. In February of the next year he found his first opportunity.

There was in Salem a certain Reverend Samuel Parris who had a daughter, a niece, and a negro-Indian servant called Tituba. The children were about twelve years of age, and much in Tituba's society. Parris was an Englishman born, and was at this time forty-one years old; he had left Harvard College without a degree, had been in trade in Boston, and had entered the ministry and obtained the pastorship of the Congregational church at Danvers, then a part of Salem, three or four years before. He had not lived at peace with his people; he had quarreled bitterly with some of them, and the scandal had been noised abroad. He was a man of brutal temper, and without moral integrity. These were the dramatis personæ employed by Cotton Mather in the first scene of his hideous farce.

The children, at the critical age between childhood and puberty, were in a condition to be readily worked upon; it is the age when the nervous system is disorganized, the moral sense unformed, and the imagination ignorant and unbridled. Many children are liars and deceivers, and self-deceivers, then, who afterward develop into sanity and goodness. But these unhappy little creatures were under the fascination of the illiterate and abnormal mongrel, and she secretly ravished and fascinated them with her inexplicable powers and obscure devices. Their antics aroused suspicions in the coarse and perhaps superstitious mind of Parris; he catechised them; the woman's husband told what he knew; and Parris beat her till she consented to say she was a witch. Such phenomena could only be due to witchcraft. The cunning and seeming malignity of the children would tax belief, were it not so familiar a fact in children; and notable also was their histrionic ability. They were excited by the sensation they aroused, and vain of it; they were willing to do what they could to prolong it. But they hardly needed to invent anything; more than was necessary was suggested to them by questions and comments. They were quick to take hints, and improve upon them. Sarah Good, Martha Cory, Rebecca Nourse, and all the rest, must be their victims; but God will forgive the children, for they know not what they do. Presently, the contagion spread; though, upon strict examination of the evidence, not nearly so far as was supposed. Hundreds were bewildered and terrified, as well they might be; the magistrates—Stoughton, Sewall, John Hathorne, poor Octogenarian Bradstreet, Sir William Phips—these and others to whom it fell to investigate and pronounce sentence—let us hope that some, if not all of them, truly believed that their sentences were just. "God will give you blood to drink!" was what Sarah Good said to Noyes, as she stood on the scaffold. But why may they not have believed they were in the right? There was Cotton Mather, the holy man, the champion against the Evil One, the saint who walked with God, and daily lifted up his voice in prayer and defiance and thanksgiving—he was ever at hand, to cross-question, to insinuate, to surmise, to bluster, to interpret, to terrify, to perplex, to vociferate: surely, this paragon of learning and virtue must know more about the devil than any mere layman could pretend to know; and they must accept his assurance and guidance. "I stake my reputation," he shouted, "upon the truth of these accusations." And he pointedly prayed that the trial might "have a good issue." When Deliverance Hobbs was under examination, she did but cast a glance toward the meeting house, "and," cries the Reverend gentleman, in an ecstasy of indignation, "immediately a demon, invisibly entering the house, tore down a part of it!" No wonder a man so gifted as he, was conscious of a certain gratification amid all the horrors of the diabolic visitation, for how could he regard it otherwise than as—in his own words—"a particular defiance unto myself!" Such was the pose which he adopted before his countrymen: that of a semi-divine, or quite Divine man, standing between his fellow creatures and the assaults of hell. And then Cotton Mather would go home to his secret chamber, and write in his diary that God and religion were perhaps, after all, but an old wives' tale.

Parris, as soon as he comprehended Mather's drift, ably seconded him. He had his own grudges against his neighbors to work off, and nothing could be easier. All that was needed was for one of the children, or any one else, to affirm that they were afflicted, and perhaps to foam at the mouth, or be contorted as in a fit, and to accuse whatever person they chose as being the cause of their trouble. Accusation was equivalent to condemnation; for to deny it, was to be subjected to torture until confession was extorted; if the accused did not confess, he or she was, according to Cotton Mather, supported by the evil one, and being a witch, must die. If they did confess, they were spared or executed according to circumstances. If any one expressed any doubt as to the justice of the sentence, or as to the existence of witchcraft, it was proof that that person was a witch. The only security was to join the ranks of the afflicted. In the course of a few months a reign of terror was established, and hundreds of people, some of them citizens of distinction, were in jail or under suspicion. Twenty were hanged on Witches' Hill, west of the town of Salem, while Cotton Mather sate comfortably by on his horse, and assured the people that all was well, and that the devil could sometimes assume the appearance of an angel of light—as, indeed, he might have good cause to believe. But the mass of the people were averse from bloodshed, and none too sure that these executions were other than murders; and when the wife of Governor Phips was accused, the frenzy had passed its height. It was perceived that the community, or a part of it, had been stampeded by a panic or infatuation. They had done and countenanced things which now seemed impossible even to themselves. How could they have condemned the Reverend George Burroughs on the ground that he had exhibited remarkable physical strength, and that the witnesses against him had pretended dumbness? "Why is the devil so loth to have testimony borne against you?" Judge Stoughton had asked; and Cotton Mather had said "Enough!" But was it enough, indeed? If a witness simply by holding his peace can hang a minister of blameless life, who may escape hanging by a witness who will talk? It was remembered that Parris had been Burroughs's rival, and instrumental in his conviction; and now that the frenzy was past it was easy to point out the relation between the two facts. There, too, was the venerable Giles Cory, who had been pressed to death, not for pleading guilty, nor yet for pleading not guilty, but for declining to plead at all. There, once more, was John Willard, to whom the duty of arresting accused witches had been assigned; he, as a person of common sense and honesty, had intimated his disbelief in the reality of witchcraft by refusing to arrest; and for this, and no other crime, had he been hanged. Had it really come to this, then—that one must die for having it inferred, from some act of his, that he held an opinion on the subject of witchcraft different from that announced by Mather and the magistrates?—It had come to precisely that, in a community who were exiles in order to secure liberty to have what opinions they liked. Then, it was time that the witchcraft persecutions came to an end: and they did, as abruptly as they had begun. Mather, indeed, and a few more, frightened lest the people, in their recovered sanity, should turn upon them for an accounting, strove their best to keep up the horror; but it was not to be. No more convictions could be obtained. In February of 1693, Parris was banished from Salem; others, except Stoughton, who remained obdurate, made public confession of error. But Cotton Mather, the soul of the whole iniquity, shrouded himself in a cuttle-fish cloud of turgid rhetoric, and escaped scot-free. So great was the power of theological prestige in New England two hundred years ago.

There is little doubt that the sincere believers in the witchcraft delusion were very scanty. The vast majority of the people were simply victims of moral and physical cowardice. They feared to exchange views with one another frankly, lest their interlocutor turn out an informer. They repeated, parrot-like, the conventional utterances—the shibboleths—of the hour, and thus hid from one another the real thoughts which would have scotched the mania at the outset. Once plant mutual suspicion and dread among a people, and, for a time, you may drive them whither you will. It was by that means that the Council of Ten ruled in Venice, the Inquisition in Spain, and the Vehmgericht in Germany; and it was by that means that Cotton Mather enslaved Salem. The episode is a stain on the fair page of our history; but Cotton Mather was the origin and agent of it; Parris may have voluntarily assisted him, and some or all of the magistrates and others concerned may have been his dupes; but beyond this handful, the support was never more than perfunctory. The instant the weight of dread was lightened everybody discovered that everybody else had believed all along that the whole thing was either a delusion or a fraud. Until then, they had none of them had the courage to say so—that was all. And let us not be scornful: the kind of courage that *would* say so is the very rarest and highest courage in the world.

But though Cotton Mather is almost or entirely chargeable with the guilt of the twenty murders on Witches' Hill, not to mention the incalculable agony of soul and domestic misery incidentally occasioned, yet it must not be forgotten that he was of Puritan stock and training, and that false and detestable though his individual nature doubtless was, his crimes, but for Puritanism, could not have taken the form they did. Puritanism was prone to brood over predestination, over the flames of hell, and him who kept them burning; it was severe in repressing natural expressions of gayety; it was intolerant of unlicensed opinions, and it crushed spontaneity and innocent frivolity. It aimed, in a word, to deform human nature, and make of it somewhat rigid and artificial. These were some of the faults of Puritanism, and it was these which made possible such a monstrosity as Cotton Mather. He was, in a measure, a creature of his time and place, and in this degree we must consider Puritanism as amenable, with him, at the bar of history. It is for this reason solely that the witchcraft episode assumes historical importance, instead of being a side-scene of ghastly picturesqueness. For the Puritans took it to heart; they never forgot it; it modified their character, and gave a favorable turn to their future. Gradually the evil of their system was purged out of it, while the good remained; they became less harsh, but not less strong; they were high-minded, still, but they abjured narrowness. They would not go so far as to deny that the devil might afflict mankind, but they declared themselves unqualified to prove it. There began in them, in short, the dawn of human sympathies, and the growth of spiritual humility. Cotton Mather, with all that he represented, sinks into the mire; but the true Puritan arises, and goes forward with lightened heart to the mighty destiny that awaits him.

As for bluff Sir William Phips, he is better remembered for his youthful exploits of hoisting treasure from the fifty-year-old wreck of a Spanish galleon, in the reign of King James, and of building with some of the proceeds his "fair brick house, in the Green Lane of Boston," than for his administration of government during his term of office. He was an uneducated, rough-handed, rough-natured man, a ship-carpenter by trade, and a mariner of experience; statesmanship and diplomacy were not his proper business. A wise head as well as a strong hand was needed at the helm of Massachusetts just at that juncture. But he did not prevent the legislature from passing some good laws, and from renewing the life of New England towns, which had been suppressed by Andros. The new charter had greatly enlarged the Massachusetts domain, which now extended over the northern and eastern regions that included Maine; but, as we shall presently see, the obligation to defend this territory against the French and Indians cost the colony much more than could be recompensed by any benefit they got from it. Phips captured Port Royal, but failed to take Quebec. The legislature, advised by the public-spirited

Elisha Cooke, kept the royal officials in hand by refusing to vote them permanent salaries or regular revenues. Bellomont succeeded Phips, and Dudley, in 1702, followed Bellomont, upon the solicitation of Cotton Mather; who long ere this, in his "Book of Memorable Providences," had shifted all blame for the late tragic occurrences from his own shoulders to those of the Almighty. Dudley retained the governorship till 1715. The weight of what authority he had was on the side of restricting charter privileges; but he could produce no measurable effect in retarding the mighty growth of liberty. We shall not meet him again.

New Hampshire fully maintained her reputation for intractability; and the general drift of colonial affairs toward freedom was so marked as to become a common subject of remark in Europe. Some of the best heads there began to suggest that such a consummation might not be inexpedient. But before England and her Colonies were to try their strength against one another, there were to occur the four colonial wars, by which the colonists were unwittingly trained to meet their most formidable and their final adversary.

CHAPTER TENTH

FIFTY YEARS OF FOOLS AND HEROES

WHEN thieves fall out, honest men come by their own. The first clause of this sentence may serve to describe the Colonial Wars in America; the second, to point the moral of the American Revolution.

Columbus, and the other great mariners of the Fifteenth and Sixteenth Centuries, might claim for their motives an admixture, at least, of thoughts higher than mere material gain: the desire to enlarge knowledge, to win glory, to solve problems. But the patrons and proprietors of the adventurers had an eye single to profit. To make money was their aim. In overland trading there was small profit and scanty business; but the opening of the sea as a path to foreign countries, and a revelation of their existence—and of the fortuitous fact that they were inhabited by savages who could not defend themselves—completely transformed the situation.

Ships could bring in months more—a hundred-fold more merchandise than caravans could transport in years; and the expenses of carriage were minimized. Goods thus placed in the market could be sold at a vast profit. This was the first obvious fact. Secondly, this profit could be made to inure exclusively to that country whose ships made the discovery, by the simple device of claiming, as integral parts of the kingdom, whatever new lands they discovered; the ships of all other nations could then be forbidden to trade there. Thirdly, colonists could be sent out, who would serve a double use:—they would develop and export the products of the new country; and they would constitute an ever-increasing market for the exports of the home country.

Such was the ideal. To realize it, three things were necessary: first, that the natives—the "heathen"—should be dominated, and either converted or exterminated; next, that the fiat of exclusion against other nations should be made good; and finally (most vital of all, though the last to be considered), that the colonists themselves should forfeit all but a fraction of their personal interests in favor of the monopolists at home.

Now, as to the heathen, some of them, like the Caribbeans, could be—and by Spanish methods, they were—exterminated. Others, such as the Mexican and Central and South American tribes, could be in part killed off, in part "converted" as it was called. Others again, like the Indians of North America, could neither be converted nor exterminated; but they could be in a measure conciliated, and they could always be fought. The general result was that the natives co-operated to a certain extent in providing articles for export (chiefly furs), and on the other hand, delayed colonization by occasionally massacring the first small groups of colonists. In the long run however most of them disappeared, so far as power either for use or for offense was concerned.

The attempt of the several colonizing powers to make their rivals keep out of their preserves was not successful. Piracy, smuggling, privateering, and open war were the answers of the nations to one another's inhibitions, though, all the while, none of them questioned the correctness of the excluding principle. Each of them practiced it themselves, though trying to defeat its practice by others. Portugal, the first of the foreign-trading and monopolizing nations, was early forced out of the business by more powerful rivals; Holland was the first to call the principle itself in question, and to fight in the cause of free commerce; though even she had her little private treasure-box in Java. Spain's commerce was, during the next centuries, seriously impaired by the growing might of England. France was the next to suffer; and finally England, after meeting with much opposition from her own colonies, was called upon to confront a European coalition; and while she was putting forth her strength to overcome that, her colonies revolted, and achieved their independence. Such was the history and fate of the colonial system; though Spain still retained much of her American possessions (owing to peculiar conditions) for years afterward.

But England might have retained her settlements too, so far as Europe was concerned; the real cause of her discomfiture lay in the fact that her colonists were mainly people of her own blood, all of them with an inextinguishable love of liberty, which was fostered and confirmed by their marriage with the wilderness; and many of whom were also actuated by considerations of religion and conscience, the value of which they placed above everything else. They wished to be "loyal," but they would not surrender what they termed innate rights; they would not be taxed without representation, nor be debarred from manufacturing; nor consent to make England their sole depot and source of supplies. They would not surrender their privliege to be governed by representatives elected by themselves. England, as we have seen, contended against this spirit by all manner of more or less successful enactments and acts of despotism; until at last, near the opening of the Eighteenth Century, it became evident to a few far-seeing persons on both sides that the matter could only be settled by open force. But this method of arbitrament was postponed for half a century by the Colonial Wars, which made of the colonists a united people, and educated them, from farmers and traders, into a military nation. Then the war came, and the United States was its consequence.

The Colonial Wars were between England on one side, and Spain and France on the other. Spain was not a serious foe, or obstacle; England had no special hankering after Florida and Mexico, and she knew nothing about the great Californian region. But France harried her on the north, and pushed her back on the west, the first collisions in this direction occurring at the Alleghanies and along the Ohio River. France had discovered, claimed, and in a certain sense occupied, a huge wedge of the present United States: an area which (apart from Canada) extended from Maine to Oregon, and down in converging lines to the Gulf of Mexico. They called it Louisiana. The story of the men who explored it is a story of heroism, devotion, energy and sublime courage perhaps unequaled in the history of the world. But France failed to follow up these men with substantial colonies. Colonies could not help the fur trade at the north, and the climate there was anything but attractive; and mishaps of various kinds prevented the colonizing of the great Mississippi valley. There was a little French settlement near the mouths of that river, the descendants of which still give character to New Orleans; but the rest of the enormous triangle was occupied chiefly by missionaries and trappers, and, during the wars, with the operating military forces. France would have made a far less effective resistance than she did, had she not observed, from the first, the policy of allying herself with the Indian tribes, and even incorporating them with herself. All converted Indians were French citizens by law; the French soldiers and settlers intermarried to a large extent with the red men, and the half-breed became almost a race of itself. The savages took much more kindly to the picturesque and emotional Church of Rome than to the gloomy severities of the Puritan Calvinists; the "praying Indians" were numerous; and the Cross became a real link between the red men and the white. This fact was of immense value in the wars with the English; and had it not been for the neutrality or active friendliness of a group of tribes whom the Jesuit missionaries had failed to win, the English colonies might have been quite obliterated. The policy of employing savages in warfare between civilized states was denounced then and afterward; it led to the perpetration of sickening barbarities; but it was France's only chance, and, speaking practically, it was hardly avoidable. Besides, the English did not hesitate to enlist Indians on their side, when they could. Had the savages fought after the manner of the white men, it would have been well enough; but on the contrary, they imposed their methods upon the whites; and most of the conflicts had more of the character of massacres than of battles. Women and children were mercilessly slain, or carried into captivity. But it must be remembered that the American continent, at that time, did not admit of such tactics as were employed in Europe—as Braddock found to his cost; operations must be chiefly by ambuscade and surprise; when the town or the fort was captured, it was not easy to restrain the wild men; and if they plied the tomahawk without regard to sex or age, the white soldiers, little less savage, readily learned to follow their example. After all, the wars were necessarily for extermination, and there is no better way to exterminate a people—as Spain has uniformly shown from the beginning to the end of her history—than by murdering their women and children. They are "innocent," no doubt, so far as active hostilities are concerned; but they breed, or become, men and thereby threaten the future. Moreover, not a few of the women did deeds of warlike valor themselves. It was a savage time, and war has its hideous side always, and in this period seemed to have hardly any other.

The pioneering on this continent of the Spanish and the French, though in itself a captivating story, cannot properly be dwelt on in a history of the growth of the American principle. Ponce de Leon traversed Florida in the first quarter of the Sixteenth Century, hunting for the Fountain of Immortality, and finding death. Hernando de Soto wandered over the area of several of our present Southern States, and discovered the lower reaches of the Mississippi; he was a man of blood, and his blood was shed. Some score of years later Spaniards massacred the Huguenot colony at St. Augustine, and built that oldest of American cities. Beyond this, on the Atlantic slope, they never proceeded, having enough to do further south. But they lay claim, even in these closing years of the Nineteenth Century, to the entire American continent—"if they had their rights."

The French began their American career with an Italian employé, Verrazano, who spied out the coast from Florida to Newfoundland in 1524. Then Cartier peered into the wide mouth of the St. Lawrence, and tried to get to India by that route, but got no further than the present Montreal. In the next century, Champlain, one of the great explorers and the first governor of Canada, laid the corner-stone of Quebec; it became at once the center of Canadian trade which it has ever since remained. This was in 1608. In respect of enterprise as explorers, the French easily surpassed the farm-loving, home-building, multiplying colonists of England. But England took advantage of French discoveries, and stayed, and prevailed. God makes men help each other in their own despite.

Richelieu said in 1627 that the name, New France, designated the whole continent of America from the North Pole down to Florida. The Jesuits, who arose as a counteracting force to Luther and the Reformation, supplanted the Franciscans as missionaries among the heathen, and performed what can only be called prodigies of self-sacrifice and intrepidity. Loyola was a worthy antagonist of Calvin, and the first achievements of his followers were the more striking. But the magnificent exploits of these men were not the preliminary of commensurate colonization. The spirit of Calvin inspired large bodies of men and women to establish themselves in the wilderness in order to cultivate his doctrines without interference; the spirit of

Loyola embodied no new religious principle; it simply kindled individuals to fresh exertions to promulgate the unchanging dogmas of the Roman Church. The Jesuits were leaders without followers; their mission was to bring the Church to the heathen, and the heathen into the Church; and the impressiveness of their activity was due to the daring and faith which pitted units against thousands, and refused to accept defeat. They were the knight-errantry of religion. The fame of their deeds inspired enthusiasm in France, so that noble women gave up their luxurious lives, for the sake of planting faith in the inhospitable immensities of the Canadian forests; but the mass of the common people were not stimulated or attracted; the profits of the fur-trade employed but a handful; and the blood of the Jesuit martyrs—none more genuine ever died—was poured out almost without practical results. Our estimate of human nature is exalted; but there are no happy communities to-day which owe their existence to the Jesuit pioneers. The priests themselves were wifeless and childless, and the family hearthstone could not be planted on the sites of their immolations and triumphs. Nor were the disciples of Loyola aided, as were the Calvinists, by persecution at home. All alike were good Catholics. But had the Jesuits advocated but a single principle of human freedom, France might have been mistress of America to-day.

So, under the One Hundred Assistants, as the French colonizing Company of the early Seventeenth Century was called, missions were dotted throughout the loneliness and terror of the wilderness; Brebœuf and Daniel did their work and met their fate; Raymbault carried the cross to Lake Superior; Gabriel Dreuilettes came down the Kennebec; Jogues was tortured by the Mohawks; Lallemand shed his blood serenely; Chaumont and Dablon built their chapel where now stands Syracuse; and after all, there stood the primeval forests, pathless as before, and the red men were but partially and transiently affected. The Hundred Assistants were dissolved, and a new colonial organization was operating in 1664; soldiers were sent over, and the Jesuits, still unweariedly in the van, pushed westward to Michigan, and Marquette and Joliet, two young men of thirty-six and twenty-seven, discovered the Mississippi, and descended it as far as Des Moines; but still, all the inhabitants of New France could easily have mustered in a ten-acre field. Then, in 1666 came Robert Cavelier La Salle, a cadet of a good family, educated in a Jesuit seminary, but destined to incur the enmity of the order, and at last to perish, not indeed at their hands, but in consequence of conditions largely due to them. The towering genius of this young man—he was but just past his majority when he came to Montreal, and he was murdered by his treacherous traveling companion, Duhaut, on a branch of Trinity River in Texas, before he had reached the age of five and forty—his indomitable courage, his tact and firmness in dealing with all kinds of men, from the Grand Monarch to the humblest savage, his great thoughts and his wonderful exploits, his brilliant fortune and his appalling calamities, both of which he met with an equal mind:—these qualities and the events which displayed them make La Salle the peer, at least, of any of his countrymen of that age. What must be the temper of a man who, after encountering and overcoming incredible opposition, after being the victim of unrelenting misfortune, including loss of means, friends, and credit, of deadly fevers, of shipwreck,—could rise to his feet amid the destruction of all that he had labored for twenty years to build up, and confidently and cheerfully undertake the enterprise of traveling on foot from Galveston in Texas to Montreal in Canada, to ask for help to re-establish his colony? It is a formidable journey to-day, with all the appliances of steam and the luxury of food and accommodation that science and ingenuity can frame; it would be a portentous trip for the most accomplished modern pedestrian, assisted though he would be by roads, friendly wayside inns and farms, maps of the route, and hobnailed walking boots. La Salle undertook it with thousands of miles of uncharted wilderness before him, through tribes assumed to be hostile till they proved themselves otherwise, with doubtful and quarreling companions, and shod with moccasins of green hide. Even of the Frenchmen whom he might meet after reaching Illinois, the majority, being under Jesuit influence, would be hostile. But he had faced and conquered difficulties as great as these, and he had no fear. At the time the scoundrel Duhaut shot him from ambush, he was making hopeful progress. But it was decreed that France was not to stay in America. La Salle discovered the Ohio and the Illinois, built Fort Crevecœur, and started a colony on the coast of Texas; he received a patent of nobility, and lost his fortune and his life. The pathos of such a death lies in the consideration that his plans died with him. It was the year before the accession of William of Orange; and the first war with France began two years later.

France, after all drawbacks, was far from being a foe to be slighted. The English colonists outnumbered hers, but hers were all soldiers; they had trained the Indians to the use of firearms, had taught them how to build forts, and by treating them as equals, had won the confidence and friendship of many of them. The English colonies, on the other hand, had as yet no idea of co-operation; each had its own ideas and ways of existence; they had never met and formed acquaintance with one another through a common congress of representatives. They were planters, farmers and merchants, with no further knowledge of war than was to be gained by repelling the attacks of savages, and retaliating in kind. They had the friendship of the Five Nations, and they received help from English regiments. But the latter had no experience of forest fighting, and made several times the fatal mistake of undervaluing their enemy, as well as clinging to impracticable formations and tactics. The English officers did not conceal their contempt for the "provincia.' troops, who were not, indeed, comely to look at from the conventional military standpoint, but who bore the brunt of the fighting, won most of the successes, and were entirely capable of resenting the slights to which they were unjustly subjected. What was quite as important, bearing in mind what was to happen in 1775, they learned to gauge the British fighting capacity, and did not fear, when the time came, to match themselves against it.

King William's War lasted from 1689 to 1697. Louis XIV. had refused to recognize William as a legitimate king of England, and undertook to champion the cause of the dethroned James. The conduct of the war in Europe does not belong to our inquiry. The proper course for the French to have adopted in America would have been to encourage the English colonies to revolt against the king; but the statesmanship of that age had not conceived the idea of colonial independence. Besides, the colonies would not at that epoch have fallen in with the scheme; they might have been influenced to rise against a Stuart, but not against a William. There was no general plan of campaign on either side. There was no question as yet about the western borders. There was but one point of contact of New France and the English colonies—the northern boundaries of New England and New York. The position of the English, strung along a thousand miles of the Atlantic coast, did not favor concentration against the enemy, and still less was it possible for the latter, with their small force, to march south and overrun the country. What could be done then? Obviously, nothing but to make incursions across the line, after the style of the English and Scottish border warfare. Nothing could be gained, except the making of each other miserable. But that was enough, since two kings, neither of whom any of the combatants had seen, were angry with each other three thousand miles away. Louis does not admit the right of William, doesn't he?—says the Massachusetts farmer to the Canadian coureur des bois; and without more ado they fly at each others' throats.

The successes, such as they were, were chiefly on the side of the French. Small parties of Indians, or of French and Indians combined, would steal down upon the New York and New England farms and villages, suddenly leap out upon the man and his sons working in their clearings, upon the woman and her children in the hut: a whoop, a popping of musket shots and whistling of arrows, then the vicious swish and crash of the murderous tomahawk, followed by the dexterous twist of the scalping-knife, and the snatching of the tuft of hair from the bleeding skull. That is all—but, no: there still remains a baby or two who must be caught up by the leg, and have its brains dashed out on the door-jamb; and if any able-bodied persons survive, they are to be loaded with their own household goods, and driven hundreds of miles over snows, or through heats, to Canada, as slaves. Should they drop by the way, as Mrs. Williams did, down comes the tomahawk again. Or perhaps a Mrs. Dustin learns how to use the weapon so as to kill at a blow, and that night puts her knowledge to the proof on the skulls of ten sleeping savages, and so escapes. Occasionally there is a more important massacre, like that at Schenectady, or Deerfield. But these Indian surprises are not only revolting, but monotonous to weariness, and, as they accomplished nothing but a given number of murders, there is nothing to be learned from them. They are meaningless; and we can hardly imagine even the Grand Monarch, or William of Orange, being elated or depressed by their details.

There were no French farms or small villages to be attacked in requital, so it was necessary for the English to proceed against Port Royal or Quebec. The aged but bloodthirsty Frontenac was governor of Canada at this time, and proved himself able (aided by the imbecility of the attack) to defend it. In March of 1690 a sort of congress had met at Albany, which sent word to the several colonial governors to dispatch commissioners to Rhode Island for a general conference for adopting measures of defense and offense. The delegates met in May or the last of April, at New York, and decided to conquer Canada by a two-headed campaign; one army to go by way of Lake Champlain to Montreal, while a fleet should proceed against Quebec. Sir William Phips of Massachusetts was off to Port Royal within four weeks, and took it without an effort, there being hardly any one to defend it. But Leisler of New York and Winthrop of Connecticut quarreled at Lake Champlain, and that part of the plan came to a disgraceful end forthwith. A month or so later, Phips was blundering pilotless into the St. Lawrence, with two thousand Massachusetts men on thirty-four vessels. Their coming had been prepared for, and when they demanded the surrender of the impregnable fortress, with a garrison more numerous than themselves, they were answered with jeers; and it is painful to add that they turned round and set out for home again without striking a blow. A storm completed their discomfiture; and when Phips at last brought what was left of his fleet into harbor, he found the treasury empty, and was forced to issue paper money to pay his bills.

No further talk of "On to Quebec" was heard for some time. Port Royal was retaken by a French vessel. Parties of Indians, encouraged by the Jesuits, again stole over the border and did the familiar work. Schuyler, on the English side, succeeded in making a successful foray in 1691; and a fort was built at Pemaquid—to be taken, five years afterward, by Iberville and Castin. In 1693 an English fleet, which had been beaten at Martinique, came to Boston with orders to conquer Canada; but as it was manned by warriors half of whom were dying of malignant yellow fever, Canada was spared once more. The only really formidable enemies that Frontenac could discover were the Five Nations, whom he tried in vain to frighten or to conciliate. He himself, at the age of seventy-four, headed the last expedition against them, in the summer of 1696. It returned without having accomplished anything except the burning of villages and the laying waste of lands. The following year peace was signed at Ryswick, a village in South Holland. France had done well in the field and by negotiations; but England had sustained no serious reverses, and having borrowed money from a group of private capitalists, whom it chartered as the Bank of England in 1694, was financially stronger than ever. Louis accepted the results of the English Revolution, but kept his American holdings; and the boundaries between these and the English colonies were not settled. The Five Nations were not pacified till 1700. The French continued their occupation of the Mississippi basin, and in 1699 Lemoine Iberville sailed for the Mississippi, and built a fort on the bay of Biloxi. Communication was now established between the Gulf of Mexico and Quebec. The English, through the agency of a New Jerseyman named Coxe, and a forged journal of exploration by Hennepin, tried to get a foothold on the great river, but the attempt was fruitless. Fruitless, likewise, were French efforts to find gold, or, indeed, to establish a substantial colony themselves in the feverish Louisiana region. Iberville caught the yellow plague and never fully recovered; and the desert-girded fort at Mobile seemed a small result for so much exertion.

In truth, on both sides of the Atlantic, peace existed nowhere except on the paper signed at Ryswick; and in 1702 William saw that he must either fight again, or submit to a union between France and Spain, Louis XIV. becoming, by the death without issue of the Spanish king, sovereign of both countries, to the upsetting of the European balance of power. Spain had become a nonentity; she had no money, no navy, no commerce, no manufactures, and a population reduced by emigration, and by the expulsion of Jews and Moors, to about seven millions: nothing remained to her but that "pride" of which she was always so solicitous, based as it was upon her achievements as a robber, a murderer, a despot and a bigot. She now had no king, which was the least of her losses, but gave her the power of disturbing Europe by lapsing to the French Bourbons.

William himself was close to death, and died before the opening year of the war was over. Louis was alive, and was to remain alive for thirteen years longer; but he was sixty-four, was becoming weary and discouraged, and had lost his ministers and generals. On the English side was Marlborough; and the battle of Blenheim, not to speak of the European combination against France, showed how the game was going. But the peace of Utrecht in 1713, though it lasted thirty years, was not based on justice, and could not stand. Spain was deprived of her possessions in the Netherlands, but was allowed to keep her colonies, and the loss of Gibraltar confirmed her hatred of England. Belgium, Antwerp and Austria were wronged, and France was insulted by the destruction of Dunkirk harbor. England embarked with her whole heart in the African slave trade, securing the monopoly of importing negroes into the West Indies for thirty years, and being the exclusive dealer in the same commodity along the Atlantic coast. Half the stock in the business was owned by the English people, and the other half was divided equally between Queen Anne and Philip of Spain. The profits were enormous. Meanwhile the treaty between Spain and England allowed and legitimatized the smuggling operations of the latter in the West Indies, a measure which was sure to involve our colonies sooner or later in the irrepressible conflict. England, again, got Hudson's Bay, Newfoundland, Nova Scotia, but not the Mississippi valley, from France. Boundary lines were not accurately determined; and could not be until the wars between 1744 and 1763 finally decided these and other matters in England's favor. The most commendable clause in the treaty was the one inserted by Bolingbroke that defined contraband, and the rights of blockade, and laid down the rule that free ships should give freedom to goods carried in them.

Anne, a daughter of James II., but a partisan of William, succeeded him in 1702 at the age of thirty-seven; she was herself governed by the Marlboroughs and Mrs. Masham—an intelligent woman of humble birth, who became keeper of her majesty's privy purse. The war which the queen inherited, and which was called by her name, lasted till the final year of her reign. Only New England on the north and Carolina on the south were participants in the fray on this side, and no great glory or advantage accrued to either. New York was sheltered by the neutrality of the Five Nations, and Pennsylvania, Virginia and the rest were beyond the reach of French operations.

The force raised by South Carolina to capture St. Augustine had expected to receive cannon for the siege from Jamaica; but the cannon failed them, and they retreated with nothing to show but a debt which they liquidated in paper. They had better luck with an expedition to sever the Spanish line of communication with Louisiana; the Spanish and Indians were beaten in December, 1705, and the neighboring inhabitants along the Gulf emigrated to South Carolina. Then the French set out to take Charleston; but the Huguenots were mindful of St. Bartholomew and of the revocation of the Edict of Nantes, and they set upon the invaders when they landed, and slew three out of every eight of them. The South Carolinians were let alone thereafter.

In the north, the French secured the neutrality of the Senecas, but the English failed to do the like with the Abenakis, and the massacring season set in with marked severity on the Maine border in the summer of 1703. It was in the ensuing winter that the Deerfield affair took place; the crusted snow was so deep that it not only gave the French and Indian war party good walking down from Canada, but enabled them to mount up the drifts against the palisades of the town and leap down inside. The sentinels were not on guard that morning, though, warned by the Mohawks, the people had been looking for the attack all winter long. What is to be said of these tragedies? When we have realized the awful pang in a mother's heart, wakened from sleep by that shrill, triumphant yell of the Indian, and knowing that in a moment she will see her children's faces covered with the blood and brains from their crushed skulls, we shall have nothing more to learn from Indian warfare. How many mothers felt that pang in the pale dawn of that frosty morning in Deerfield? After the war party had done the work, and departed exulting with their captives, how many motionless corpses, in what ghastly attitudes, lay huddled in the darksome rooms of the little houses, or were tossed upon the trodden snow without, the looks of mortal agony frozen on their features? But you will hear the howl of the wolves by-and-by; and the black bear will come shuffling and sniffing through the broken doors; and when the frightful feast is over, there will be, in place of these poses of death, only disordered heaps of gnawed bones, and shreds of garments rent asunder, and the grin of half-eaten skulls. Nothing else remains of a happy and innocent community. Why were they killed? Had they harmed their killers? Was any military advantage gained by their death?—They had harmed no one, and nothing was gained, or pretended to be gained, by their murder: nothing except to establish the principle that, since two countries in Europe were at war, those emigrants of theirs who had voyaged hither in quest of peace and happiness should lie in wait to destroy one another. Human sympathies have, sometimes, strange ways of avouching themselves.

People become accustomed even to massacre. But the children born in these years, who were themselves to be the fathers and mothers of the generation of the Revolution, must have sucked in stern and fierce qualities with the milk from their mothers' breasts. No one, even in the midst of Massachusetts, was safe during that first decade of the Eighteenth Century. A single Indian, in search of glory, would spend weeks in creeping southward from the far border; he would await his chance long and patiently; he would leap out, and strike, and vanish again, leaving that silent horror behind him. Such deeds, and the constant possibility of them, left their mark upon the whole population. They grew up familiar with violent death in its most terrible forms. The effect of Indian warfare upon the natures of those who engage in it, or are subjected to its perils, is different from that of what we must call civilized fighting. The end as well as the aim of the Indian's battle is death—a scalp. Murder for the mere pleasure of murdering has an influence upon a community far more sinister than that of death by war waged for recognizable causes. The Puritans of the Eighteenth Century were another people than those of the Seventeenth. There had been reason in the early Indian struggles, when the savages might have hoped to exterminate the settlers and leave their wilderness a wilderness once more; but there could be no such hope now. The desire for revenge was awakened and fostered as it had never been before. Many other circumstances combined to modify the character of the people of New England during this century; but perhaps this new capacity for revenge was not the least potent of the influences that made the seven years of the Revolution possible.

Peter Schuyler protested in vain against the "savage and boundless butchery" into which the conflict between "Christian princes, bound to the exactest laws of honor and generosity," was degenerating; but the only way to stop it appeared to be to extirpate the perpetrators; and to that end a fifth part of the population were constantly in arms. The musket became more familiar to their hands than the plow and spade; and their marksmanship was near perfection. They gradually developed a system of tactics of their own, foreign to the manuals. The first thing you were aware of in the provincial soldier was the puff of smoke from the muzzle of his weapon; almost simultaneously came the thud of his bullet in your breast, or crashing through your brain. He loaded his gun lying on his back beneath the ferns and shrubbery; he advanced or retreated invisibly, from tree to tree. Your only means of estimating his numbers was from your own losses. It was thus that the American troops afterward gained their reputation of being almost invincible behind an intrenchment; it gave its character to the engagements at Concord and along the Boston Road, and sent hundreds of redcoats to death on the slopes of Bunker Hill. It was not magnificent—to look at; but it was war; combined with the European tactics acquired later on, it survived reverses that would have driven other troops from the field, and, with Washington at the head, won our independence at last.

The least revolting feature of the Indian warfare was the habit they acquired, through French suggestion doubtless, of taking large numbers of persons captive, and carrying them north. If they weakened on the journey, they were of course tomahawked out of the way at once; but if they survived, they were either sold as slaves to the Canadians, or were kept by the Indians, who adopted them into their tribes, having no system of slavery. Many a woman and little girl from New England became the mother of Indian children; and when the captives were young enough at the beginning, they generally grew to love the wild life too well to leave it. Indeed, they were generally treated well by both the Canadians and the Indians after they got to their destination. On the other hand, there were the fathers and mothers and relatives of the lost planning their redemption or rescue, and raising money to buy them back. Many a thrilling tale could be told of these episodes. But we must imagine beautiful young women, who had been taken away in childhood, found after years of heart-breaking search and asked to return to their homes. What was their home?

They had forgotten New England, and those who loved them and had sorrowed for them there. The eyes of these young women, clear and bright, had a wildness in their look that is never seen in the children of civilization; their faces were tanned by sun and breeze, their figures lithe and athletic, their dress of deerskin and wampum, their light feet clad in moccasins; their tongues and ears were strange to the language of their childhood homes. No: they would not return. Sometimes, curiosity, or a vague expectation, would induce them to revisit those who yearned for them; but, having arrived, they received the embraces of their own flesh and blood shyly and coldly; they were stifled and hampered by the houses, the customs, the ordered ways of white people's existence. A night must come when they would arise silently, resume with a deep in-breathing of delight the deerskin raiment, and be gone without one last loving look at the faces of those who had given them life, but from whom their souls were forever parted. There is a harrowing mystery in these estrangements: how strong, and yet how helpless is the human heart; all the world cannot break the bonds it ties, nor can all the world tie them again, once the heart itself has dissolved them.

Thus, in more ways than one, the blood of the English colonists became wedded to the soil of the wilderness, if wilderness the settlements could now be called. And they became like the captives we have just been imagining, who cared no longer for the land and the people that had been their home. Not more because they were estranged by England's behavior than because they had formed new attachments beside which the old ones seemed pale, were they now able to contemplate with composure the idea of a final separation. America was no longer England's daughter. She had acquired a life of her own, and could look forward to a destiny which the older country could never share. The ways of the two had parted more fully than either, as yet, quite realized; and if they were ever to meet again hereafter, it must be the older, and not the younger, who must change.

Apart from the Indian episodes, little was done until 1710, when a large fleet left Boston and again captured Port Royal, to which the name of Annapolis was given as a compliment to the snuffy little woman who sat on the English throne. This success was made the basis of a proposition to put an end to the development of the French settlements west of the Alleghanies. It was represented to the English government that the entire Indian population in the west was being amalgamated with the French; the Jesuits ensnaring them on the spiritual side, and the intermarrying system on the other. The English Secretary of State was Bolingbroke—or Saint-John as he was then—a man of three and thirty, brilliant, graceful, gifted, versatile; but without principle or constancy, who never emancipated his superb intellect from his restless and sensuous nature. After hearing what the American envoys had to say, and thinking the matter over, Saint-John made up his mind that it could do no harm, as a beginning, to capture Quebec; and that being safe in English hands, the rest of the programme could be finished at leisure. Seven regiments of Marlborough's veterans, the best soldiers in the world at that time, a battalion of marines, and fifteen men-of-war, were intrusted to the utterly incompetent and preposterous Hovenden Walker, with the not less absurd Jack Hill, brother of Mrs. Masham, as second in command. In short, the expedition was what would now be called a "job" for the favorites and hangers-on of the Court; the taking of the Canadian fortress was deemed so easy a feat that even fools and Merry-Andrews could accomplish it. The Americans had meantime made their preparations to co-operate with this imposing armada; an army of colonists and Iroquois were at Albany, ready for a dash on Montreal. But week after week passed away, and the fleet, having got to Boston, seemed unable to get away from it. No doubt Hovenden, Hill and the rest of the rabble were enjoying themselves in the Puritan capital. The Boston of stern-visaged, sad-garmented, scripture-quoting men and women, of unpaved streets and mean houses, was gone; Boston in the first quarter of the Eighteenth Century was a city—a place of gayety, fashion and almost luxury. The scarlet coats of the British officers made the narrow but briskly-moving streets brilliant; but even without them, the embroidered coats, silken small clothes and clocked stockings, powdered wigs and cocked hats of the fine gentlemen, and the wide hoops and imposing headdresses of the women, made a handsome show. People of many nationalities mingled in the throng, for commerce had brought the world in all its various forms to the home of the prayers of Winthrop and Higginson; the royal governors maintained a fitting state, and traveled Americans, then as now, brought back with them from Europe the freshest ideas of modishness and style. There were folk of quality there, personages of importance and dignity, forming an inner aristocratic circle who conversed of London and the Court, and whose august society it was the dear ambition of the lesser lights to ape, if they could not join it. Democratic manners were at a discount in these little hotbeds of amateur cockneyism; the gloomy severities of the old-fashioned religion were put aside; there was an increasing gap between the higher and the lower orders of the population. This appearance was no doubt superficial; and the beaumonde is never so numerous as its conspicuousness leads one to imagine. When the rumblings of the Revolutionary earthquake began to make themselves heard in earnest, the gingerbread aristocracy came tumbling down in a hurry, and the old, invincible spirit, temporarily screened by the waving of scented handkerchiefs, the flutter of fans, and the swish of hoop skirts, made itself once more manifest and dominant. But that epoch was still far off; for the present, court was paid to Hovenden and his officers; and the British coffee-house in King Street was a noble sight.

What bottles of wine those warriors drank, what snuff they took, what long pipes they smoked, how they swore and ruffled, and what tales they told of Marlborough and the wars! The British army swore frightfully in Flanders, and in King Street, too. There, also, they read the news in the newspapers of the day, and discussed matters of high policy and strategy, while the civilians listened with respectful admiration. And see how that dapper young officer seated in the window arches his handsome eyebrows and smirks as two pretty Boston girls go by! Yes, it is no wonder that the British fleet needed a long time to refit in Boston harbor, before going up to annihilate those French jumping-jacks on the banks of the St. Lawrence. "La, Captain, I hope you won't get hurt!" says pretty Miss Betty, with her white wig and her beauty spots; and that heroic young gentleman lifts her hand to his lips, and swears deeply that, for a glance from her bright eyes, he would go forth and capture Quebec single-handed.

While these dalliances were in progress, the French jumping-jacks were putting things in order to receive their expected guests in a becoming manner. They held a great pow-wow of representatives of Indian tribes from all parts of the seat of the projected war, and bound them by compacts to their assistance. Everybody, even the women, worked on the fortifications, or on anything that might aid in the common defense. Before the end of August, at which time the outlookers reported signs of a fleet of near a hundred sail, flying the British flag, all was ready for them in the French strongholds. So now let the mighty combat begin.

But it was not to come this time: the era of William Pitt and General Wolfe was nearly half a century distant. The latter would not be born for sixteen years, and the former was a pap-eating babe of three. Meanwhile the redoubtable Hovenden was snoring in bed, while his fleet was struggling in a dense fog at night, being driven on the shoals of the

Egg Islands near the mouth of the St. Lawrence. "For the Lord's sake, come on deck!" roars Captain Goddard, thrusting his head into the cabin for the second time, "or we shall all be lost!" Thus adjured, the old imbecile huddles on his dressing gown and slippers, and finds himself, sure enough, close on a lee shore. He made shift to get his own vessel out of harm's way, but eight others went down, and near nine hundred men were drowned. "Impossible to go on," was the vote of the council of war the next morning; and "It's all for the best," added this remarkable admiral; "for had we got to Quebec, ten or twelve thousand of us must have perished of cold and hunger; Providence took eight hundred to save the rest!"

So back they went, with their tails between their legs, without having had a glimpse of the citadel which they were to have captured without an effort; and of course the army waiting at Albany for the word to advance got news of a different color, and Montreal was as safe as Quebec. In the west, the Foxes, having planned an attack on Detroit, did really lay siege to it; but Du Buisson, who defended it, summoned a swarm of Indian allies to his aid, and the Foxes found that the boot was on the other leg; they were all either slain or carried into slavery. Down in the Carolinas, a party of Tuscaroras attacked a settlement of Palatines near Pamlico Sound, and wiped them out; and some Huguenots at Bath fared little better. Disputes btweeen the governor and the burgesses prevented aid from Virginia; but Barnwell of South Carolina succeeded in making terms with the enemy. A desultory and exhausting warfare continued however, complicated with an outbreak of yellow fever, and it was not until 1713 that the Tuscaroras were driven finally out of the country, and were incorporated with the Iroquois in the north. The war in Europe had by that time come also to an end, and the treaty of Utrecht brought about an ambiguous peace for a generation.

George I. now became king of England; because he was

the son of Sophia, granddaughter of James I., and professed the Protestant religion. He was a Hanoverian German, and did not understand the English language; he was stupid and disreputable, and better fitted to administer a German bierstube than a great kingdom. But the Act of Settlement of 1701 had stipulated that if William or Anne died childless, the Protestant issue of Sophia should succeed. That such a man should prove an acceptable sovereign both to Great Britain and her American colonies, showed that the individuality on the throne had become secondary to the principles which he stood for; besides, George profited by the easy, sagacious, good-humored leadership of that unprincipled but common-sensible man-of-the-world, Sir Robert Walpole, who was prime minister from 1715 to 1741, with an interval of only a couple of years. Walpole's aim was to avoid wars and develop commerce and manufactures; and while he lived, the colonies enjoyed immunity from conflicts with the French and Spanish.

They were not to forget the use of arms, however; for the Indians were inevitably encroached upon by the expanding white population, and resented it in the usual way. In 1715 the Yemasses began a massacre on the Carolina borders; they were driven off by Charles Craven, after the colonists had lost four hundred men. The proprietors had given no help in the war, and after it was over, the colony renounced allegiance to them, and the English government supported their revolt, regarding it in the light of an act of loyalty to George. Francis Nicholson, a governor by profession, and of great experience in that calling, was appointed royal governor, and made peace with the tribes; and in 1729 the crown bought out the claims of the proprietors. North Carolina, without a revolt, enjoyed the benefits obtained by their southern brethren. The Cherokees became a buffer against the encroachments of the French from the west.

In the north, meanwhile, the Abenakis, in sympathy with the French, claimed the region between the Kennebec and the St. Croix, and applied to the French for assistance. Sebastian Rasles, a saintly Jesuit priest and Indian missionary, had made his abode at Norridgwock on the Kennebec; he was regarded by Massachusetts as an instigator of the enemy. They seized his post, he escaping for the time; the Indians burned Brunswick; but in 1723 Westbrooke with a company of hardy provincials, who knew more of Indian warfare than the Indians themselves, attacked an Indian fort near the present Bangor and destroyed it; the next year Norridgwock was surprised, and Rasles slain. He met his death with the sublime cheerfulness and courage which were the badge of his order. French influence in northeastern Massachusetts was at an end, and John Lovewell, before he lost his life by an ambush of Saco Indians at Battle Brook, had made it necessary for the Indians to sue for peace. Commerce took the place of religion as a subjugating force, and an era of prosperity began for the northeastern settlements.

There was no settled boundary between northern New York and the French regions. Each party used diplomatic devices to gain advantage. Both built trading stations on doubtful territory, which developed into forts. Burnet of New York founded Oswego in 1727, and gained a strip of land from the Iroquois; France built a fort on Lake Champlain in 1731. Six years before that, they had established, by the agency of the sagacious trader Joncaire, a not less important fort at Niagara. Upon the whole, the French gained the better of their rivals in these negotiations.

Louisiana, as the French possessions, or claims, south of Canada were called, was meanwhile bidding fair to cover most of the continent west of the Alleghanies and north of the indeterminate Spanish region which overspread the present Texas, New Mexico, Arizona, California and Mexico. No boundary lines could be run in those enormous western expanses; and it made little practical difference whether a given claim lay a thousand miles this way or that. But on the east it was another matter. The French pursued their settled policy of conciliating the Indians wherever they hoped to establish themselves; but though this was well, it was not enough. Narrow though the English strip of territory was, the inhabitants greatly outnumbered the French, and were correspondingly more wealthy. Spotswood of Virginia, in 1710, was for pushing out beyond the mountains, and Logan of Pennsylvania also called Walpole's attention to the troubles ahead; but the prime minister would take no action. On the other hand, the white population of Louisiana was ridiculously small, and their trade nothing worth mentioning; but when Anthony Crozar resigned the charter he had received for the district, it was taken up by the famous John Law, the English goldsmith's son, who had become chief financial adviser of the Regent of France; and immediately the face of things underwent a change like the magic transformations of a pantomime.

The Regent inherited from Louis XIV. a debt which there was not money enough in all France to pay. Law had a plan to pay it by the issue of paper. Louisiana offered itself as just the thing for purposes of investment, and a pretext for the issue of unlimited "shares." Not to speak of the gold and silver, there was unlimited wealth in the unknown country, and Law assumed that it could be produced at once. Companies were formed, and thousands of settlers rushed to the promised paradise. But we have to do with the Mississippi Bubble only as it affected America. The Bubble burst, but the settlers remained, and were able to prosper, in moderation, like other settlers in a fertile country. A great area of land was occupied. Local tribes of Indians joined in a massacre of the colonists in 1729. They in turn were nearly exterminated by the French forces during the next two years, but the war aroused a new hostility among the red tribes against the French, which redounded to the English advantage. In 1740, Bienville was more than willing to make a peace, which left to France no more than nominal control of the tract of country drained by the southern twelve hundred miles of the Mississippi. The population, after all the expense and efforts of half a century, numbered about five thousand white persons, with upward of two thousand slaves. The horse is his who rides it. The French had not proved themselves as good horsemen as the English. The English colonies had at the same time a population of about half a million; their import and export trade aggregated nearly four million dollars; they had a wide and profitable trade; and the only thing they could complain of was the worthless or infamous character of the majority of the officials which the shameless corruption of the Walpole administration sent out to govern—in other words, to prey upon—them. But if this was the only subject of complaint, it could not be termed a small subject. It meant the enforcement of the Navigation Acts in their worst form, and the restriction of all manner of manufactures. Manufactures would tend to make the colonies set up for themselves, and therefore they must be forbidden:—such was the undisguised argument. It was a case of the goose laying golden eggs. America had in fact become so enormously valuable that England wanted it to become profit and nothing else—and all the profit to be England's. They still failed to realize that it was inhabited by human beings, and that those human beings were of English blood. And because the northern colonies, though the more industrious, produced things which might interfere with British goods, therefore they were held down more than the southern colonies, which grew only tobacco, sugar, rice and indigo, which could in no degree interfere with the sacred shopkeepers and mill-owners of England. An insanity of blindness and perversity seized upon the English government, and upon most of the people; they actually were incapable of seeing justice, or even their own best interests. It seems strange to us now; but it was a mania, like that of witchcraft, though it lasted thrice as many years as that did months.

The will of England in respect of the colonies became as despotic as under the Stuarts; but though it delayed progress, it could not break down the resistance of the assemblies; and Walpole would consent to no suggestion looking toward enforcing it by arms. Stamp duties were spoken of, but not enacted. The governors raged and complained, but the assemblies held the purse-strings. Would-be tyrants like Shute of Boston might denounce woe, and Crosby of New York bellow treason, but they were fain to succumb. Paper money wrought huge mischief, but nothing could prevent the growing power and wealth of the colonies, fed, also, by the troubles in Europe. In 1727 the Irish, always friends of liberty, began to arrive in large numbers. But what was of better augury than all else was the birth of two men, one in Virginia, the other in Boston. The latter was named Benjamin Franklin: the former, George Washington.

CHAPTER ELEVENTH

QUEM JUPITER VULT PERDERE

HERE are times when, upon nations as upon individuals, there comes a wave of evil tendency, which seems to them not evil, but good. Under its influence they do and think things which afterward amaze them in the retrospect. But such ill seasons are always balanced by the presence and opposition of those who desire good, whether from selfish or altruistic motives. And since good alone has a root, connecting it with the eternal springs of life, therefore in the end it prevails, and the movement of the race is on the whole, and in the lapse of time, toward better conditions.

England, during the Eighteenth Century, came under the influence of a selfish spirit which could not but lead her toward disaster, though at the time it seemed as if it promoted only prosperity and power. She thought she could strengthen her own life by restricting the natural enterprise and development of her colonies: that she could subsist by sucking human blood. She believed that by compelling the produce of America to flow toward herself alone, and by making America the sole recipient of her own manufactures, she must be immeasurably and continually benefited; not perceiving that the colonies could never reach the full limit of their productiveness unless freedom were conceded to all the impulses of their energy, or that the greater the number of those nations who were allowed freely to supply colonial wants, the greater those wants would become. Moreover, selfishness is never consistent, because it does not respect the selfishness of others; and England, at the same time that she was maintaining her own trade monopolies, was illicitly undermining the similar monopolies of other nations. She promoted smuggling in the Spanish West Indies, and made might right in all her dealings with foreign peoples. The assiento—the treaty giving her exclusive right to supply the West Indian islands with African slaves—was actively carried out, and the slave-trade reached enormous proportions; it is estimated that from three to nine millions of Africans were imported into the American and Spanish colonies during the first half of the Eighteenth Century, yielding a revenue for their importation alone of at least four hundred million dollars. But the profit did not end there; for their labor on the plantations in the southern colonies (where alone they could be used in appreciable numbers) multiplied the production and diminished the cost of the articles of commerce which those colonies raised. There were individuals, almost from the beginning, who objected to slavery on grounds of abstract morality; and others who held that a converted African should cease to be a slave. But these opinions did not impress the bulk of the people; and laws were passed classing negroes with merchandise. "The trade is very beneficial to the country" was the stereotyped reply to all humanitarian arguments. The cruelties of transportation in small vessels were regarded as an unavoidable, if disagreeable, necessity; it was pointed out that the masters of slaves would be prompted by self-interest to treat them well after they were landed; and it was obvious that negroes, after a generation of captivity, were less remote from civilization than when fresh from Africa.

The good to balance this ill was supplied by the American colonies. Their resistance to English selfishness may have been in part animated by selfishness of their own; but it none the less had justice and right behind it. In any argument on fundamental principles, the colonists always had the better of it. Their rights as free men and as chartered communities were indefeasible, were always asserted, and never given up. They did not hesitate to disregard the more unjust of England's exactions and restrictions; it was only by such defiance that they maintained their life. And against the importation of slaves there was a general feeling, even among the Southern planters; because, not to speak of other considerations, they multiplied there to an alarming extent, and the fact that they cheapened production and lowered prices was manifestly as unwelcome to the planters as it was favorable to English traders.

But in order to be effective, the protest of a people—their enlightenment, their virtue and patriotism, their courage and philosophy, their firmness and self-reliance, their hatred of shams, dishonesty and tyranny—must be embodied and summed up in certain individuals among them, who may thus be recognized by the community as their representatives in the fullest sense, and therefore as their natural champions and leaders. America has never lacked such men, adapted to her need; and at this period they were coming to maturity as Franklin and Washington. They will be with us during the critical hours of our formative history, and we shall have opportunity to measure their characters. Meanwhile there is another good man deserving of passing attention; not born on our soil, but meriting to be called, in the best sense, an American. In the midst of a corrupt and self-seeking age, he was unselfish and pure; and while many uttered pretty sentiments of philanthropy, and devised fanciful Utopias for the transfiguration of the human race, he went to work with his hands and purse as well as with his heart and head, and created a home and happiness for unhappy and unfortunate people in one of the loveliest and most fertile spots in the western world. If he was not as wise as Penn, he was as kind; and if his colony did not succeed precisely as he had planned it should, at any rate it became a happy and prosperous settlement, which would not have existed but for him. He had not fully fathomed the truth that in order to bestow upon man the best chance for earthly felicity, we must, after having provided him with the environment and the means for it, let him alone to work it out in his own way. But he had such magnanimity that when he found that his carefully-arranged and detailed schemes were inefficient, he showed no resentment, and did not try to enforce what had seemed to him expedient, against the wishes of his beneficiaries; but retired amiably and with dignity, and thus merited the purest gratitude that men may properly accord to a man.

James Edward Oglethorpe was already five years old when the Eighteenth Century began. He was a Londoner by birth, and had a fortune which he did not misuse. He was a valiant soldier against the Turks; he was present with Prince Eugene at the capitulation of Belgrade; and he sat for more than thirty years in Parliament. He died at the age of ninety; though there is a portrait of him extant said to have been taken when he was one hundred and two. If long life be the reward of virtue, he deserved to survive at least a century.

The speculative fever in England had brought about much poverty; and debtors were lodged in jail in order, one might suppose, to prevent them from taking any measures to liquidate their debts. Besides these unhappy persons, there were many Protestants on the Continent who were persecuted for their faith's sake. England compassionated these persons, having learned by experience what persecution is; and did not offer any objection to a scheme for improving the lot of debtors in her own land, if any feasible one could be devised.

General Oglethorpe had devised one. He was then, according to our reckoning, a mature man of about seven-and-thirty; he had visited the prisons, and convinced himself that there was neither political economy nor humanity in this method of preserving the impecunious class. Why not take them to America? Why not found a new colony there where men might dwell in peace and comfort, with the aim not of amassing wealth, but of living sober and useful lives? On the southern side of South Carolina there was a region fitted for such an enterprise, which, owing to its proximity to the Spanish colony at St. Augustine, had been vexed by border quarrels; but Oglethorpe, with his military experience, would be able to keep the Spaniards in their place with one hand, while he was planting gardens for his proteges with the other. Thus his colony would be useful on grounds of high policy, as well as for its own ends. And in order additionally to conciliate the good will of the home government, controlled as it was by mercantile interests chiefly, the silk-worm should be cultivated there, and England thus saved the duties on the Italian fabrics. Should there be slaves in the new Eden?—On all accounts, No: first because slavery was intrinsically wrong, and secondly because it would lead to idleness, if not to wealth, among the colonists. For the same reason, land could only pass to the eldest son, or failing male issue, back to the state; if permission were given to divide it, or to sell it, there would soon be great landed properties and an aristocracy. Nor should the importation of rum be permitted, for if men have rum, they are prone to drink it, and drunkenness was incompatible with the kind of existence which the good General wished his colonists to lead. In a word, by removing temptations to vice and avarice, he thought he could make his people forget that such evils had ever belonged to human nature. But experiments founded upon the innate impeccability of man have furnished many comedies and not a few tragedies since the world began.

The Oglethorpe idea, however, appealed to the public, and became a sort of fashionable fad. It was commended, and after Parliament had voted ten thousand pounds toward it, it was everywhere accepted as the correct thing. The charter was given in June 1732, and a suitable design was not wanting for the corporation seal—silkworms, with the motto, Non Sibi, sed Aliis. This might refer either to the colonists or to the patrons, since the latter were to receive no emoluments for their services, and the former were to work for the sake, in part at least, of vindicating the nobility of labor. It is true that the silkworm is an involuntary and unconscious altruist; but we must allow some latitude in symbols; and besides, all executive and legislative power was given to the trustees, or such council as they might choose to appoint.

In November the general conducted his hundred or more human derelicts to Port Royal, and, going up the stream, chose the site for his city of Savannah, and laid it out in liberal parallelograms. While it was building he tented beneath a quartette of primeval pines, and exchanged friendly greetings and promises with the various Indian tribes who sent deputies to him. A year from that time, the German Protestant refugees began to arrive, and started a town of their own further inland. A party of Moravians followed; and the two Wesleys aided to introduce an exalted religious sentiment which might have recalled the days of the Pilgrims. For the present, all went harmoniously; the debtors were thankful to be out of prison; the religious folk were happy so long as they might wreak themselves on their religion; and the silk-culture paid a revenue so long as England paid bounties on it. But the time must come when the colonists would demand to do what they liked with their own land, and other things; when they would import rum by stealth and hardly blush to be found out; when some of the less democratically-minded decided that there were advantages in slaves after all; and when some of the more independent declared they could not endure oppression, and migrated to other colonies. After struggling a score of years against the inevitable, the trustees surrendered their trusteeship, and the colony came under the management of the Second George. Oglethorpe had long ere this retired to England, after having kept his promise of reducing the Spaniards to order; and at his home at Cranham Hall in Essex he continued to be the friend of man until after the close of the American Revolution.

The war with Spain, of which Oglethorpe's unsuccessful attack upon St. Augustine and triumphant defense of his own place was but a very minor feature, raged for a while in the West Indies with no very marked advantage to either contestant, and then drew the other nations of Europe into the fray. Nothing creditable was being fought for on either side. England, to be sure, had declared war with the object of expunging Spain from America; but it had been only in order that she herself might replace Spain there as a monopolist. France came in to prevent England from enjoying this monopoly. The death of the Austrian king and a consequent dispute as to the succession added that power to the melee. Russia received an invitation to join, and this finally led to the Peace of Aix La Chapelle in 1748, which replaced all things in dispute just where they were before innumerable lives and enormous treasure had been expended. But the Eighteenth was a fighting Century, for it was the transition period from the old to the new order of civilized life.

The part borne by the American colonies in this struggle was quite subordinate and sympathetic; but it was not the less interesting to the Americans. In 1744 the Six Nations (as the Five had been called since the accession of the Tuscaroras) made a treaty of alliance with the English whereby the Ohio valley was secured to the latter as against the French—so far, that is, as the Indians could secure it. But the Pennsylvanians understood that more than Indian treaties would be needed against France, and as their country was likely to be among the first involved, they determined to raise money and men for the campaign. There were, of course, men in Pennsylvania who were not of the Quaker way of thinking; but even the Quakers forbore to oppose the measure, and many of them gave it explicit approval. The incident gains its chief interest however from the fact that the man most active and efficient in getting both the funds and the soldiers was Benjamin Franklin, the Boston boy, in whose veins flowed the blood of both Quaker and Calvinist, but who was himself of far too original a character to be either. He was at this epoch just past forty, and had been a resident of Philadelphia for some twenty years, and a famous printer, writer, and man of mark. He hit upon the scheme—which, like so many of his, was more practical than orthodox—of persuading dollars out of men's pockets by means of a lottery. He knew that, whatever a fastidious morality might protest, lotteries are friendly to human nature; and if there be any part of human nature with which Franklin was unacquainted, it has not yet been announced. Having got the money, his next care was for the men; and his plans resulted in assembling an organized force of ten or twelve thousand militiamen. But the energy and ingenuity of this incomparable Franklin of ours could be equaled only by his modesty; he would not accept a colonelcy, but shouldered his musket along with the rank and file; and doubtless the company to which he belonged forgot the labors of war in their enjoyment of his wit, humor, anecdotes, parables, and resources of all kinds.

After so much waste and folly as had marked the conduct of the war in Europe, it is good to hear the tale of the capture of Louisburg. It was an adventure which gave the colonists merited confidence in themselves, and the character of the little army, and the management of the campaign, were an excellent and suggestive dress rehearsal of the great drama of thirty years later. The army was a combination of Yankees with arms in their hands to effect an object eminently conducive to the common welfare. For Louisburg was the key to the St. Lawrence, it commanded the fisheries, and it threatened Acadia, or rather Nova Scotia, which was inhabited chiefly by Bretons, liable to afford succor to their belligerent brethren. The fort had been built, after the close of the former war, by those who had preferred not to live under the government of the House of Hanover, on the eastern extremity of the island called Cape Breton, itself lying northeast of the Nova Scotian promontory. The site was good for defense, and the fortifications, scientifically designed, were held to be impregnable. Had Louisburg rested content with being strong, it might have been allowed to remain at peace; but at the beginning of the war, and before the frontier people in Nova Scotia had heard of it, a French party swooped down from Louisburg on the settlement at Canso (the gut between Cape Breton and Nova Scotia), destroyed all that was destructible, and carried eighty men as prisoners of war to their stronghold. After keeping them there during the summer, these men were paroled and went to Boston. This was a mistake on the Louisburgers' part; for the men had made themselves well acquainted with the fortifications and the topography of the neighborhood, and placed this useful information at the disposal of William Shirley, a lawyer of ability, who was afterward governor of the colony and a warrior of some note. It was Shirley's opinion that Louisburg must be taken, and the idea immediately became popular. It was the main topic of discussion in Boston, and all over New England, during the autumn and winter; Massachusetts decided that it could be done, and that she could do it, though the help of other colonies would be gladly accepted. Yet the feeling was not unanimous, if the vote of the legislature be a criterion; the bill passed there by a majority of one. Be that as it may, once resolved upon, the enterprise was pushed with ardor, not unmingled with prayer—the old Puritan leaven reappearing as soon as deeds of real moment were in the wind. In every village and hamlet there was excitement and preparation—the warm courage of men glad to have a chance at the hated fortress, and the pale bravery of women keeping down the heavy throbbing of their hearts so that their sons and husbands might feel no weakness for their sakes. The fishermen of Marblehead, used to face the storms and fogs of the Newfoundland Banks; the farmers and mechanics, who could hit a Bay shilling (if one could be found in that era of paper money) at fifty paces; and the hunters, who knew the craft of the Indians and were inured to every fatigue and hardship—finer material for an army was never got together before: independent, bold, cunning, handy, inventive, full of resource; but utterly ignorant of drill, and indifferent to it. Their officers were chosen by themselves, of the same rank and character as they; their only uniforms were their flintlocks and hangers. They marched and camped as nature prompted, but they had common-sense developed to the utmost by the exigencies of their daily lives, and they created, simply by being together, a discipline and tactics of their own; they even learned enough of the arts of fortification and intrenchment, during the siege, to serve all their requirements. They had the American instinct to break loose from tradition and solve problems from an original point of view; they laughed at the jargon and technicalities of conventional war, but they had their own passwords, and they understood one another in and out. The carpenters and other mechanics among them carried their skill along, and were ever ready to put it in practice for the general behoof. Most of them left wives and children at home; but "Suffer no anxious thoughts to rest in your mind about me," writes his wife to Seth Pomeroy, who had sent word to her that he was "willing to stay till God's time comes to deliver the city into our hands":— "I leave you in the hands of God," added she; and subjoined, by way of village gossip, that "the whole town is much engaged with concern for the expedition, how Providence will order the affair, for which religious meetings every week are maintained." We can imagine those meetings, held in the village meeting-house, with an infirm old veteran of King William's War to lead in prayer, and the benches occupied by the women, devout but spirited, with the little children by their sides. What hearty prayers: what sighs irrepressibly heaving those brave, tender bosoms; what secret tears, denied by smiles when the face was lifted from the clasping hands! Righteous prayers, which were fulfilled.

Over three thousand men went from Massachusetts alone; New Hampshire added five hundred, and more than that number arrived from Connecticut, after the rest had gone into camp at Canso. The three hundred from little Rhode Island came too late. Other colonies sent rations and money. But the four thousand were enough, with Pepperel of Kittery for commander, and a good cause. They set out alone while the Cape Breton ice still filled the harbors; for Commodore Warren of the English fleet at Antigua would not go except by order from England— which, however, came soon afterward, so that he and his ships joined them after all before hostilities began. The expedition first set eyes on their objective point on the day before May day, 1745.

The fortress bristled with guns of all sizes, and the walls

were of enormous thickness, so that no cannon belonging to the besiegers could hope to make a breach in them. But the hearts of the garrison were less stout than their defenses; and when four hundred cheering volunteers approached a battery on shore, the Frenchmen spiked their guns and ran away.

The siege lasted six weeks, with unusually fine weather. In the intervals of attacks upon the island battery, which resisted them, the men hunted, fished, played rough outdoor games, and kept up their spirits; and they pounded Louisburg gates with their guns; but no advantage was gained; and a night-attack, in the Indian style, was discovered prematurely, and nearly two hundred men were killed or captured. Finally, there seemed to be nothing for it but to escalade the walls, Warren—who had done nothing thus far except prevent relief from approaching by sea—bombarding the city meanwhile. It hardly seems possible the attempt could have succeeded; at best, the losses would have been enormous. But at the critical moment, depressed, perhaps, by having witnessed the taking of an incautious French frigate which had tried to run the blockade, what should the French commander do but hang out a white flag! Yes, the place had capitulated! The gates that could not be hammered in with cannon-balls were thrown open, and in crowded the Yankee army, laughing, staring, and thanking the Lord of Hosts for His mercies. Truly, it was like David overcoming Goliath, without his sling. It was a great day for New England; and on the same day thirty years later the British redcoats fell beneath the volleys on Bunker Hill.

The French tried to recapture the place next year, but storms, pestilence and other disasters prevented; and the only other notable incident of the war was the affair of Commander Knowles at Boston in 1747. He was anchored off Nantasket with a squadron, when some of his tars deserted, as was not surprising, considering the sort of commander he was, and the charms of the famous town.

Knowles, ignorant of the spirit of a Boston mob, impressed a number of wharfmen and seamen from vessels in the harbor; he had done the same thing before in England, and why not here? But the mob was on fire at once, and after the timid governor had declined to seize such of the British naval officers as were in the town, the crowd, terrible in its anger, came thundering down King Street and played the sheriff for itself. The hair of His Majesty's haughty commanders and lieutenants must have crisped under their wigs when they looked out of the windows of the coffee-house and saw them. In walks the citizens' deputation, with scant ceremony: protests are unavailing: off to jail His Majesty's officers must straightway march, leaving their bottles of wine half emptied, and their chairs upset on the sawdusted floor; and in jail must they abide, until those impressed Bostonians have been liberated. It was a wholesome lesson; and among the children who ran and shouted beside the procession to the prison were those who, when they were men grown, threw the tea into Boston Harbor.

In 1748 the Peace was made, and the Duke of Newcastle, a flighty, trivial and faithless creature, gave place to the strict, honest, and narrow Duke of Bedford as Secretary of the Colonies. The colonies had been under the charge of the Board of Commissioners, who could issue what orders they chose, but had no power to enforce them; and as the colonial assemblies slighted their commands except when it pleased them to do otherwise, much exasperation ensued on the Commissioners' part. The difficulties would have been minimized had it not been the habit of Newcastle to send out as colonial officials the offscourings of the British aristocracy: and when a British aristocrat is worthless, nothing can be more worthless than he. The upshot of the situation was that the colonists did what they pleased, regardless of orders from home; while yet the promulgation of those orders, aiming to defend injustices and iniquities, kept up a chronic and growing disaffection toward England. So it had been under Newcastle, who had uniformly avoided personal annoyance by omitting to read the constant complaints of the Commissioners; but Bedford was a man of another stamp, fond of business, granite in his decisions, and resolved to be master in his department. It was easy to surmise that his appointment would hasten the drift of things toward a crisis. England would not tamely relinquish her claim to absolute jurisdiction over her colonies. But the bulwarks of popular liberty were rising in America, and every year saw them strengthened and more ably manned. English legislative opposition only defined and solidified the colonial resistance. What was to be the result? There would be no lack of English statesmen competent to consider it; men like Pitt, Murray and Townshend were already above the horizon of history. But it was not by statesmanship that the issue was to be decided. Man is proud of his intellect; but it is generally observable that it is the armed hand that settles the political problems of the world.

There were in the colonies men of ability, and of consideration, who were traitors to the cause of freedom. Such were Thomas Hutchinson, a plausible hypocrite, not devoid of good qualities, but intent upon filling his pockets from the public purse; Oliver, a man of less ability but equal avarice; and William Shirley, the scheming lawyer from England, who had made America his home in order to squeeze a living out of it. These men went to England to promote the passage of a law insuring a regular revenue for the civil list from the colonists, independent of the latter's approval; the immediate pretext being that money was needed to protect the colonies against French encroachments. The several assemblies refused to consent to such a tax; and the question was then raised whether Parliament had not the right to override the colonists' will. Lord Halifax, the First Commissioner, was urgent in favor of the proposition; he was an ignorant, arbitrary man, who laid out a plan for the subjugation of the colonies as lightly and willfully as he might have directed the ditch-digging and fence-building on his estates. Murray, afterward Lord Mansfield, held that Parliament had the requisite power; but in the face of the united protest of the colonies, that body laid the measure aside for the present. Meanwhile the conditions of future trouble were preparing in the Ohio Valley, where French and English were making conflicting claims and planting rival stations; and in Nova Scotia, where the town of Halifax was founded in an uninviting fir forest, and the project was mooted of transporting the French Acadians to some place or places where they would cease to constitute a peril by serving as a stage for French machinations against the English rule.

Another and final war with France was already appearing inevitable; the colonists must bear a hand in it, but they also were at odds with England herself on questions vital to their prosperity and happiness. In the welter of events of the next few years we find a mingling of conditions deliberately created (with a view, on England's part, of checking the independent tendencies of the Americans and of forcing tribute from them) and of unforeseen occurrences due to fortuitous causes beyond the calculation and control of persons in power. Finally, the declaration of war against France in 1756—though it had unofficially existed at least two years before—and its able management by the great Pitt, enabled England to dictate a peace in 1763 giving her all she asked for in Europe and the East, and the whole of the French possessions in America, besides islands in the West Indies. Her triumph was great; but she did not foresee (though a few acute observers did) that this great conquest would within a few years fall into the hands of the colonists, making them potentially the greatest of nations. At the era of the Revolution, the white inhabitants in the colonies numbered about two millions, and the black about half a million.

In 1754, the French had upward of sixty posts west of

the Alleghanies, and were sending expeditions to drive out whatever Englishmen could be found. The Indian tribes who believed themselves to own the land were aroused, and appealed to the Americans to assist them; which the latter were willing to do, though not for the Indians' sake. Virginia was especially concerned, because she claimed beyond the western mountains, and had definite designs in that direction. In order to find out just what the disposition of the French might be, Robert Dinwiddie, a Scot, governor of Virginia, selected a trustworthy envoy to proceed to the French commanders in the disputed districts and ask their purposes. His choice fell upon George Washington, a young man of blameless character, steady, courageous and observant, wise in judgment and of mature mind, though he was but one and twenty years of age. He was the son of a Virginia planter, had had such schooling as his neighborhood afforded until he was sixteen, and had then begun life as a surveyor—a good calling in a country whose inhabitants were daily increasing and whose lands were practically limitless. Life in the open air, and the custom of the woods and hills, had developed a frame originally powerful into that of a tall and hardened athlete, able to run, wrestle, swim, leap, ride, as well as to use the musket and the sword. His intellect was not brilliant, but it was clear, and his habit of thought methodical; he was of great modesty, yet one of those who rise to the emergency, and are kindled into greater and greater power by responsibilities or difficulties which would overwhelm feebler or less constant natures. None would have been less likely than Washington himself to foretell his own greatness; but when others believed in him he was compelled by his religious and conscientious nature to act up to their belief. The marvelous selflessness of the man, while it concealed from him what he was, immeasurably increased his power to act; to do his duty was all that he ever proposed to himself, and therefore he was able to concentrate his every faculty on that alone. The lessons of experience were never thrown away upon him, and his faith in an overruling Providence rendered him calm at all times, except on the rare occasions when some subordinate's incompetence or negligence at a critical moment caused to burst forth in him that terrific wrath which was more appalling to its object than the guns of a battery. There was always great personal dignity in Washington, insomuch that nothing like comradeship, in the familiar sense, was ever possible to any one with him; he was totally devoid of the sense of humor, and was therefore debarred from one whole region of human sympathies which Franklin loved to dwell in. It is one of the marvels of history that a man with a mind of such moderate compass as Washington's should have gained the reputation, which he amply deserved, of being the foremost American of his age, and one of the leading figures in human annals. But, in truth, we attach far too much weight to intellect in our estimates of human worth. Washington was competent for the work that was given him to do, and that work was one of the most important that ever fell to the lot of a man. Faith, firmness, integrity, grasp, simplicity, and the exceptional physical endowment which enabled him to support the tremendous fatigues and trials of his campaigns, and of the opposition he encountered from selfish and shortsighted politicians in Congress—these qualities were almost sufficient to account for Washington. Almost, but perhaps not quite; there must have been in addition an inestimable personal equation which fused all into a harmonious individuality that isolates him in our regard: a wholeness, which can be felt, but which is hardly to be set down in phrases.

Washington's instructions required him to proceed to Venango and Waterford, a distance of more than four hundred miles, through forests and over mountains, with rivers to cross and hostile Indians to beware of; and it was the middle of November when he set out, with the most inclement season of the year before him. Kit Gist, a hunter and trapper of the Natty Bumppo order, was his guide; they laid their course through the dense but naked forests as a mariner over a sullen sea. Four or five attendants, including an interpreter, made up the party. Day after day they rode, sleeping at night round a fire, with the snow or the freezing rain falling on their blankets, and the immense silence of the winter woods around them. On the 23d of the month they came to the point of junction between two great rivers—the Monongahela and the Alleghany. A wild and solitary spot it was, hardly visited till then by white men; the land on the fork was level and broad, with mighty trees thronging upon it; opposite were steep bluffs. The Alleghany hurried downward at the rate a man would walk; the Monongahela loitered, deep and glassy. Washington had acted as adjutant of a body of Virginia troops for the past two or three years, and he examined the place with the eyes of a soldier as well as of a surveyor. It seemed to him that a fort and a town could be well placed there; but in the pure frosty air of that ancient forest, untenanted save by wild beasts, there was no foreshadowing of the grimy smoke and roar, the flaring smelting-works, the crowded and eager population of the Pittsburgh that was to be. Having fixed the scene in his memory, Washington rode his horse down the river bank, and plunging into the icy current, swam across. On the northwest shore a fire was built, where the party dried their garments, and slept the sleep of frontiersmen.

Conducted now by the Delawares, they crossed low-lying, fertile lands to Logstown, where they got news of a junction between French troops from Louisiana and from Erie. Arriving in due season at Venango, Washington found the French officer in command there very positive that the Ohio was theirs, and that they would keep it; they admitted that the English outnumbered them; but "they are too dilatory," said the Frenchman, staring up with an affectation of superciliousness at the tall, blue-eyed young

Virginian. The latter thanked the testy Gaul, with his customary grave courtesy, and continued his journey to Fort Le Bœuf. It was a structure characteristic of the place and period; a rude but effective redoubt of logs and clay, with the muzzles of cannon pouting from the embrasures, and more than two hundred boats and canoes for the trip down the river. "I shall seize every Englishman in the valley," was the polite assurance of the commander; but, being a man of pith himself, he knew another when he saw him, and offered Washington the hospitalities of the post. But the serious young soldier had no taste for hobnobbing, and returned at once to Venango, where he found his horses unavailable, and continued southward on foot, meeting bad weather and deep snow. He borrowed a deerskin shirt and leggins from the tallest of the Indians, dismissed his attendants, left the Indian trail, and struck out for the Forks by compass, with Gist as his companion. A misguided red man, hoping for glory from the white chief's scalp, prepared an ambush, and as Washington passed within a few paces, pulled the trigger on him. He did not know that the destiny of half the world hung upon his aim; but indeed the bullet was never molded that could draw blood from Washington. The red man missed; and the next moment Gist had him helpless, with a knife at his throat. But no: the man who could pour out the lives of his country's enemies, and of his own soldiers, without stint, when duty demanded it, and could hang a gallant and gently nurtured youth as a spy, was averse from bloodshed when only his insignificant self was concerned. Gist must sulkily put up his knife, and the would-be assassin was suffered to depart in peace. But in order to avoid the possible consequences of this magnanimity, the envoy and his companion traveled without pausing for more than sixty miles. And then, here was the Alleghany to cross again, and no horse to help one. Swimming was out of the question, even for the iron Washington, for the river was hurtling with jagged cakes of ice.

A day's hacking with a little hatchet cut down trees enough —not apple trees—to make a raft, on which they adventured; but in mid-stream Washington's pole upset him, and he was fain to get ashore on an island. There must they pass the night; and so cold was it, that the next morning they were able to reach the mainland dry shod, on the ice. What was crossing the Delaware (almost exactly twenty-three years afterward) compared to this? Washington was destined to do much of his work amid snow and ice; but for aught anybody could say, the poles or the equator were all one to him.

In consequence of his report a fort was begun on the site of Pittsburgh, and he was appointed lieutenant-colonel to take charge of it, with a hundred and fifty men, and orders to destroy whomsoever presumed to stay him. Two hundred square miles of fertile Ohio lands were to be their reward. An invitation to other colonies to join in the assertion of English ownership met with scanty response, or none at all. The idea of a union was in the air, but it was complicated with that old bugbear of a regular revenue to be exacted by act of Parliament, which Shirley and the others still continued to press with hungry zeal; while the assemblies were not less set upon making all grants annual, with specifications as to person and object. While the matter hung in the wind, the Virginians were exposed to superior forces; but in the spring of 1754 Washington, with forty men, surprised a party under Jumonville, defeated them, killed Jumonville, and took the survivors prisoners. Washington was exposed to the thickest showers of the bullets; they whistled to him familiarly, and "believe me," he assured a correspondent, "there is something charming in the sound." His life was to be sweetened by a great deal of that kind of charm.

But the French were gathering like hornets, and the Lieutenant-colonel must needs take refuge in a stockaded post named Fort Necessity, where his small force was besieged by seven hundred French and Indians who, in a nine hours' attack, killed thirty of his men, but used up most of their own ammunition. A parley resulted in Washington's marching out with all his survivors and their baggage and retiring from the Ohio valley. The war was begun; and it is worth noting that Washington's command to "fire!" on Jumonville's party was the word that began it. But still the other colonies held off. The Six Nations began to murmur: "The French are men," said they; "you are like women." In June, 1754, a convocation or congress of deputies from all colonies north of the Potomac came together at Albany. Franklin was among them, with the draught of a plan of union in his ample pocket, and dauntless and deep thoughts in his broad mind. He was always far in advance of his time; one of the most "modern" men of that century; but he had the final excellence of wisdom which consists in never forcing his contemporaries to bite off more than there was reasonable prospect of their being able to chew. He lifted them gently up step after step of the ascent toward the stars.

Philadelphia is a central spot (this was the gist of his proposal), so let it be the seat of our federal government. Let us have a triennial grand council to originate bills, allowing King George to appoint the governor-general who may have a negative voice, and who shall choose the military officers, as against the civil appointees of the council. All war measures, external land purchases and organization, general laws and taxes should be the province of the federal government, but each colony should keep its private constitution, and money should issue only by common consent. Once a year should the council meet, to sit not more than six weeks, under a speaker of their own choosing.—In the debate, the scheme was closely criticised, but the suave wielder of the lightning gently disarmed all opponents, and won a substantial victory—"not altogether to my mind"; but he insisted upon no counsel of perfection. England, and some of the colonies themselves, were somewhat uneasy after thinking it over; mutual sympathy is not created by reason. England doubted on other grounds; a united country might be more easy to govern than thirteen who each demanded special treatment; but then, what if the federation decline to be governed at all? Meanwhile, there was the federation; and Franklin, looking westward, foresaw the Nineteenth Century.

Doubtless, however, outside pressure would be necessary to re-enforce the somewhat lukewarm sentiment among the colonies in favor of union. A review of their several conditions at this time would show general prosperity and enjoyment of liberty, but great unlikenesses in manners and customs and private prejudices. Virginia, most important of the southern group, showed the apparent contradiction of a people with republican ideas living after the style of aristocrats; breeding great gentlemen like Washington, Jefferson, Madison and Patrick Henry, who were to be leaders in the work of founding and defending the first great democracy of the world. Maryland was a picturesque principality under the rule of a dissolute young prince, who enjoyed a great private revenue from his possessions, and yet interfered but little with the individual freedom of his subjects. Pennsylvania was administering itself on a basis of sheer civic equality, and was absorbing from Franklin the principles of liberal thought and education. New York was so largely tinged with Dutchmanship that it resented more than the others the authority of alien England, and fought its royal governors to the finish. New England was an aggregation of independent towns, each a little democracy, full of religious and educational vigor. In Delaware, John Woolman the tailor was denouncing slavery with all the zeal and arguments of the Garrisons of a century later. These were incongruous elements to be bound into a fagot; but there was a policy being consolidated in England which would presently give them good reason for standing together to secure rights which were more precious than private pet traditions and peculiarities. Newcastle became head of the English government; he appointed the absurd Duke of Cumberland, captain-general of the English army, to the direction of American military affairs; and he picked out an obstinate, ruffianly, stupid martinet of a Perthshire Scotchman, sixty years old and of ruined fortunes, to lead the English forces against the French in America. Braddock went over armed with the new and despotic mutiny bill, and with directions to divest all colonial army officers of their rank while in his service. He was also to exact a revenue by royal prerogative, and the governors were to collect a fund to be expended for colonial military operations. This was Newcastle's notion of what was suitable for the occasion. In the meantime Shirley, persistently malevolent, advocated parliamentary taxation of the colonies and a congress of royal governors; and to the arguments of Franklin against the plan, suggested colonial representation in Parliament: which Franklin disapproved unless all colonial disabilities be removed, and they become in all political respects an integral portion of England. During the discussion, the colonies themselves were resisting the royal prerogative with embarrassing unanimity. Braddock, on landing and finding no money ready, was exceeding wroth; but the helpless governors told him that nothing short of an act of Parliament would suffice; possibly not even that. Taxation was the one cry of every royal office-holder in America. What sort of a tax should it be?— Well, a stamp-tax seemed the easiest method; a stamp, like a mosquito, sucks but little blood at a time, but mosquitoes in the aggregate draw a great deal. But the stamp act was to be delayed eleven years more, and then its authors were to receive an unpleasant surprise.

There was a strong profession of reluctance on both the French and English side to come formally to blows; both sent large bodies of troops to the Ohio valley, "but only for defense." Braddock was ready to advance in April, if only

DEATH OF GENERAL BRADDOCK—WASHINGTON MOVING THE VIRGINIA TROOPS FORWARD

he had "horses and carriages"; which by Franklin's exertions were supplied. The bits of dialogue and comment in which this grizzled nincompoop was an interlocutor, or of which he was the theme, are as amusing as a page from a comedy of Shakespeare. Braddock has been called brave; but the term is inappropriate; he could fly into a rage when his brutal or tyrannical instincts were questioned or thwarted, and become insensible, for a time, even to physical danger. Ignorance, folly and self-conceit not seldom make a man seem fearless who is a poltroon at heart. Braddock's death was a better one than he deserved; he raged about the field like a dazed bull; fly he could not; he was incapable of adopting any intelligent measures to save his troops; on the contrary he kept reiterating conventional orders in a manner that showed his wits were gone. The bullet that dropped him did him good service; but his honor was so little sensitive that he felt no gratitude at being thus saved the consequences of one of the most disgraceful and willfully incurred defeats that ever befell an English general. The English troops upon whom, according to Braddock, "it was impossible that the savages should make any impression," huddled together, and shot down their own officers in their blundering volleys. In the narrow wood path they could not see the enemy, who fired from behind trees at their leisure. Half of the men, and sixty-three out of the eighty-six officers, were killed or wounded. In that hell of explosions, smoke, yells and carnage, Washington was clear-headed and alert, and passed to and fro amid the rain of bullets as if his body were no more mortal than his soul. The contingent of Virginia troops—the "raw American militia," as Braddock had called them, "who have little courage or good will, from whom I expect almost no military service, though I have employed the best officers to drill them":—these men did almost the only fighting that was done on the English side, but they were too few to avert the disaster.

The expedition had set out from Turtle Creek on the Monongahela on the ninth of July—twelve hundred men. The objective point was Fort Duquesne, "which can hardly detain me above three or four days," remarked the dull curmudgeon. No scouts were thrown out: they walked straight into the ambuscade which some two hundred French and six hundred Indians had prepared for them. The slaughter lasted two hours; there was no maneuvering. Thirty men of the three Virginia companies were left alive; they stood their ground to the last, while the British regulars "ran as sheep before hounds," leaving everything to the enemy. Washington did whatever was possible to prevent the retreat from becoming a blind panic. When the rout reached the camp, Dunbar, the officer in charge there, destroyed everything, to the value of half a million dollars, and ran with the rest. Reviewing the affair, Franklin remarks with a demure arching of the eyebrow that it "gave us Americans the first suspicion that our exalted ideas of the prowess of British regular troops had not been well founded."

It was indeed an awakening for the colonists. For all their bold resistance to oppression, they had never ceased to believe that an English soldier was the supreme and final expression of trained and disciplined force; and now, before their almost incredulous eyes, the flower of the British army had been beaten, and the bloody remnant stampeded into a shameful flight by a few hundred painted savages and Frenchmen. They all had been watching Braddock's march; and they never forgot the lesson of his defeat. From that time, the British regular was to them only a "lobster-back," more likely, when it came to equal conflict with themselves, to run away than to stand his ground.

Instead of throwing themselves into the arms of France, however, the colonists loyally addressed themselves to helping King George out of his scrape; and though they would not let him tax them, they hesitated not to tax themselves.

Pennsylvania raised fifty thousand pounds, and Massachusetts sent near eight thousand men to aid in driving the French from the northern border. Acadia's time had come. Though the descendants of the Breton peasants, who dated their settlement from 1604, had since the Peace of Utrecht nominally belonged to England, yet their sentiments and mode of life had been unaltered; Port Royal had been little changed by calling it Annapolis, and the simple, old-fashioned Catholics loved their homes with all the tenacity of six unbroken generations. Their feet were familiar in the paths of a hundred and fifty quiet and industrious years; their houses nestled in their lowly places like natural features of the landscape; their fields and herds and the graves of their forefathers sweetened and consecrated the land. They were a chaste, industrious, homely, pious, but not an intellectual people; and to such the instinct of home is far stronger than in more highly cultivated races. They had prospered in their modest degree, and multiplied; so that now they numbered sixteen thousand men, women and children. During the past few years, however, they had been subjected to the unrestrained brutality of English administration in its worst form; they had no redress at law, their property could be taken from them without payment or recourse; if they did not keep their tyrant's fires burning, "the soldiers shall absolutely take their houses for fuel." Estate-titles, records, all that could identify and guarantee their ownership in the means and conditions of livelihood, were taken; even their boats and their antiquated firearms were sequestrated. And orders were actually given to the soldiers to punish any misbehavior summarily upon the first Acadian who came to hand, whether or not he were guilty of, or aware of, the offense, and with absolutely no concern for the formality of arrest or trial. In all the annals of Spanish brutality, there is nothing more disgraceful to humanity than the systematic and enjoined treatment of these innocent Bretons by the English, even before the consummating outrage which made the whole civilized world stare in indignant amazement.

It is a matter for keen regret that men born on our soil should have been even involuntarily associated with this episode. The design was kept a secret from all until the last moment; but one could wish that some American had then committed an act of insubordination, though at the cost of his life, by way of indicating the detestation which all civilized and humane minds must feel for such an act. The colonists knew the value of liberty; they had made sacrifices for it; they had felt the shadow of oppression; and they might see, in the treatment of the Acadians, what would have been their fate had they yielded to the despotic instincts of England. The best and the worst that can be said of them is that they obeyed orders, and looked on while the iniquity was being perpetrated.

The force of provincials and regulars landed without molestation, and captured the feeble forts with the loss of but twenty killed. The Acadians agreed to take the oath of fidelity, but stipulated not to be forced to bear arms against their own countrymen. General Charles Lawrence, the lieutenant-governor of Nova Scotia, replied to their plea that they be allowed to have their boats and guns, that it was "highly arrogant, insidious and insulting"; and Halifax, another of the companions in infamy, added that they wanted their boats for "carrying provisions to the enemy"—there being no enemy nearer than Quebec. As for the guns, "All Roman Catholics are restrained from having arms, and are subject to penalties if arms are found in their houses."—"Not the want of arms, but our consciences, would engage us not to revolt," pleaded the unhappy men.—"What excuse can you make," bellows Halifax, "for treating this government with such indignity as to expound to them the nature of fidelity?" The Acadians agreed to take the oath unconditionally: "By British statute," they were thereupon informed, "having once refused, you cannot after take the oath, but are popish recusants." Chief-justice Belcher, a third of these British moguls, declared they obstructed the progress of the settlement, and that all of them should be deported from the province. Proclamation was then made, ordering them to assemble at their respective posts; and in the morning they obeyed, leaving their homes, to which, though they knew it not, they were never to return. "Your lands and tenements, cattle of all kinds, and livestock of all sorts, are forfeited to the crown," they were told, "and you yourselves are to be removed from this province." They were kept prisoners, without food, till the ships should be ready. Not only were they torn from their homes, but families were separated, sons from their mothers, husbands from their wives, daughters from their parents, and, as Longfellow has pictured to us, lovers from one another. Those who tried to escape were hunted by the soldiers like wild beasts, and "if they can find a pretext to kill them, they will," said a British officer. They were scattered, helpless, friendless and destitute, all up and down the Atlantic coast, and their villages were laid waste. Lord Loudoun, British commander-in-chief in America, on receiving a petition from some of them written in French, was so enraged not only at their petitioning, but that they should presume to do so in their own language, that he had five of their leading men arrested, consigned to England, and sent as common seamen on English men-of-war. No detail was wanting, from first to last, to make the crime of the Acadian deportation perfect; and only an Irishman, Edmund Burke, lifted his voice to say that the deed was inhuman, and done "upon pretenses that, in the eye of an honest man, are not worth a farthing." But Burke was not in Parliament until eleven years after the Acadians were scattered.

The incident, from an external point of view, does not belong to the history of the United States. Yet is it pertinent thereto, as showing of what enormities the English of that age were capable. Their entire conduct during this French war was dishonorable, and often atrocious. Forgetting the facts of history, we often smile at the grumblings of the Continental nations anent "Perfidious Albion" and "British gold." But the acts committed by the English government during these years fully justify every charge of corruption, treachery and political profligacy that has ever been brought against them. It was a strange age, in which a great and noble people were mysteriously hurried into sins, follies and disgraces seemingly foreign to their character. It was because the people had surrendered their government into alien and shameless hands. They deserved their punishment; for it is nothing less than a crime, having known liberty, either to deny it to others, or for the sake of earthly advantage to consent to any compromise of it in ourselves.

CHAPTER TWELFTH

THE PLAINS OF ABRAHAM AND THE STAMP ACT

THE gathering of soldiers from France, England and the colonies, and the rousing of the Indians on one side and the other, made the great forest which stretched across northern New York and New England populous with troops and resonant with the sounds of war. Those solemn woodland aisles and quiet glades were desecrated by marchings and campings, and in the ravines and recesses lay the corpses of men in uniforms, the grim remains of peasants who had been born three thousand miles away. Passing through the depths of the wilderness, apparently remote from all human habitation, suddenly one would come upon a fortress, frowning with heavy guns, and surrounded by the log-built barracks of the soldiery, who, in the intervals of siege and combat, passed their days impatiently, thinking of the distant homes from which they came, and muttering their discontent at inaction and uncertainty. The region round the junction of Lake George and Lake Champlain, where stood the strongholds of Fort Edward and Fort William Henry, of Crown Point and Ticonderoga, was the scene of many desperate conflicts, between 1758 and 1780; and the wolves of the forest, and the bears of the Vermont mountains, were disturbed in their lairs by the tumults and the restless evolutions, and wandered eastward until they came among the startled hamlets and frontier farms of the settlements. The savagery of man, surpassing theirs, drove them to seek shelter amid the abodes of man himself; but there was no safety for them there, as many a bloody head and paws, trophies of rustic marksmanship, attested. The dominion of the wilderness was approaching its end in America. Everywhere you might hear the roll of the drum, and there was no family but had its soldier, and few that did not have their dead. There were a score of thousand British troops in the northern provinces, and every week brought rumors and alarms, and portents of victory or defeat. The haggard post-rider came galloping in with news from north and west, which the throng of anxious village folks gather to hear. There have been skirmishes, successes, retreats, surprises, massacres, retaliations; there is news from Niagara and Oswego on far away Lake Ontario, and echoes of the guns at Ticonderoga. There are proclamations for enlistment, and requisitions for ammunition; and the tailors in the towns are busy cutting out scarlet uniforms and decorating them with gold braid. Markets for the supply of troops are established in the woods, far from any settled habitations, where shrewd farmers bargain with the hungry soldiery for carcasses of pigs and beeves, and for disheveled hens from distant farmyards; the

butcher's shop is kept under the spreading branches of
the trees, from whose low limbs dangle the tempting wares;
and a stump serves as a chopping-block. Under the shrubbery, where the sun cannot penetrate, are stored home-made
firkins full of yellow butter, and great cheeses, and heaps of
substantial home-baked bread. Kegs of hard cider and
spruce beer and perhaps more potent brews are abroach, and
behind the haggling and jesting and bustle you may catch
the sound of muskets or the whoop of the Indians from afar.
Meanwhile, in the settlements, all manner of industries were
stimulated, and a great number of women throughout the
country, left to take care of their children and themselves
by the absence of their men-folk, went into business of all
kinds, and drove a thriving trade. Lotteries were also popular, the promoters retaining a good share of the profits
after the nominal object of the transaction had been attained. It was well that the war operations were carried
on far from the populous regions, so that only the fighters
themselves were involved in the immediate consequences.
The battle was for the homes of posterity, where as yet the
woodman's ax had never been heard, except to provide defenses against death, instead of habitations for life. Those
who could not go to the war sat round the broad country
hearthstones at night, with the fire of logs leaping up the
great cavern of the chimney, telling stories of past exploits,
speculating as to the present, praying perhaps for the future,
and pausing now and then to listen to strange noises abroad
in the night-ridden sky—strains of ghostly music playing a
march or a charge, or the thunder of phantom guns.

Governor Shirley, who while in France in 1749 had married a French wife and brought her home with him, and
who for a while had the chief command of the king's forces
in America, was in disfavor with the people, who suspected
his wife of sending treasonable news to the enemy; and
having also proved inefficient as a soldier, he was recalled
to England in 1756, and vanished thenceforth as a factor in

American affairs, in which his influence had always been selfish and illiberal, if not worse. Thomas Pownall succeeded him and held his position for three years, when he was transferred to South Carolina. He was a man of fashion, and of little weight. From the shuffle of men who appeared and disappeared during the early years of the war, a few stand out in permanent distinctness. Washington's reputation steadily increased; Amherst, Wolfe and Lyman achieved distinction on the English side, and Montcalm and Dieskau on the French. In 1757, General Loudoun, one of the agents of the despoiling of Acadia, made a professed attempt to capture Louisburg, which had been given back to the French at the last peace; but after wasting a summer in vain drilling of his forces, retired in dismay on learning that the French fleet outnumbered his own by one vessel. The place was bombarded and taken the next year by Amherst and Wolfe, but Halifax was the English headquarters in that region. Before this however, in the summer of 1755, immediately after the defeat of Braddock, an army of New Englanders assembled at Albany to capture Crown Point, where the French had called together every able-bodied man available. William Johnson was commander, and associated with him was Phinehas Lyman, a natural-born soldier. They marched to the southern shore of what the French called the Lake of the Holy Sacrament, but which Johnson thought would better be named Lake George. The army, with its Indian allies, numbered about thirty-four hundred; a camping ground was cleared, but no intrenchments were thrown up; no enemy seemed to be within reach. Dieskau, informed of the advance, turned from his design against Oswego in the west, and marched for Fort Edward, in the rear of Johnson's troops. By a mistake of the guide he found himself approaching the open camp. Johnson sent a Massachusetts man, Ephraim Williams, with a thousand troops, to save Fort Edward. They nearly fell into an ambush; as it was, their party was overpowered by the enemy;

Williams was killed, but Whiting of Connecticut guarded the retreat. During the action, a redoubt of logs had been constructed in the camp; and was strengthened with baggage and wagons. The Americans, with their fowling-pieces, defended this place for five hours against two hundred regular French troops, six hundred Canadians, and as many Indians. Johnson received a scratch early in the engagement, and made it an excuse to retire; and Lyman assumed direction. Dieskau bravely led the French regulars, nearly all of whom were killed; he was four times wounded; the Canadians were intimidated. At length, about half past four in the afternoon, the French retreated, though the American losses equaled theirs; a body of them were pursued by Macginnes of New Hampshire and left their baggage behind them in their haste; but the body of Macginnes also remained on the field. The credit for this battle, won by Lyman, was given by the English government to Johnson, who received a baronetcy and a "tip" of five thousand pounds. It would have been the first step in a series of successes had not Johnson, instead of following up his victory, timidly remained in camp, building Fort William Henry; and when winter approached, he disbanded the New Englanders and retired. The French had taken advantage of their opportunity to intrench themselves in Ticonderoga, which was destined to become a name of awe for the colonists. At the same time that Braddock marched on Fort Duquesne, Shirley had set out with two thousand men to capture the fort at Niagara, garrisoned by but thirty ill-armed men; the intention being to form a junction there with the all-conquering Braddock. The latter's annihilation took all the heart out of the superserviceable Shirley; he got no further than Oswego, where he frittered the summer away, and then retreated under a cloud of pretexts. He and the other royal officials were all this while pleading for a general fund to be created by Parliament, or in any other manner, so that a fund there be; and

DEATH OF GENERAL WOLFE, AT QUEBEC, SEPT. 13, 1759

asserting that the frontiers would otherwise be, and in fact were, defenseless. In the face of such tales the colonies were of their own motion providing all the necessary supplies for war, and Franklin had taken personal charge of the northwest border. But the English ministry saw in these measures only increasing peril from popular power, and pushed forward a scheme for a military dictatorship. In May, 1756, war was formally declared, and England arbitrarily forbade other nations to carry French merchandise in their ships. Abercrombie was chosen general for the prosecution of the campaign in America, and arrived at Albany, after much dilatoriness, in June. Bradstreet reported that he had put stores into Oswego for five thousand men; and that the place was already threatened by the enemy. Still the English delayed. Montcalm arrived at Quebec to lead the French army, and immediately planned the capture of Oswego. In August he took an outlying redoubt, and the garrison of Oswego surrendered just as he was about to open fire upon it. Sixteen hundred prisoners, over a hundred cannon, stores, boats and money were the prize; and Montcalm destroyed the fort and returned in triumph. Loudoun and Abercrombie, with an army of thousands of men, which could have taken Canada with ease, thought only of keeping out of Montcalm's way, pleading in excuse that they feared to trust the "provincials"— who had thus far done all the fighting that had been done, and won all the successes. In spite of the remonstrances of the civic authorities, the British troops and officers were billeted upon New York and Philadelphia. Two more frightened generals were never seen; and the provinces were left open to the enemy's attack. But the Americans took the war into their own hands. John Armstrong of Cumberland County, Pennsylvania, crossed the Alleghanies in September and in a desperate fight destroyed an Indian tribe that had been massacring along the border, burned their town and blew up their powder. In January of 1757,

Stark, a daring ranger, with seventy men, made a dash on Lake George, and engaged a party of two hundred and fifty French. About the same time, at Philadelphia and Boston it was voted to raise men for the service; a hundred thousand pounds was also voted, but the proprietors refused to pay their quota, and represented in England that the Pennsylvanians were obstructing the measures for defense. Franklin, sent to England to remonstrate, was told that the king was the legislator of the colonies. All action was paralyzed by the corruption and cowardice of the royal officials. The pusillanimity of Loudoun, with his ten thousand men and powerful fleet in Nova Scotia, has been already mentioned. In July Montcalm, with a mixed force of more than seven thousand, advanced upon Fort William Henry. Webb, who should have opposed him, retreated, leaving Monro with five hundred men to hold the fort. He refused Montcalm's summons to surrender; Webb, who might still have saved him, refused to do so; he fought until his ammunition was gone and half his guns burst, and then surrendered upon Montcalm's promise of the honors of war and an escort out of the country. But the Indians had got rum from the English stores and passed the night in drunken revelry; in the morning they set upon the unarmed English as they left the fort, and began to plunder and tomahawk them. Montcalm and his officers did their utmost to stop the treacherous outrage; but thirty men were murdered. Montcalm has been treated leniently by history; he was indeed a brilliant and heroic soldier, and he had the crowning honor of dying bravely at Quebec; but he cannot be held blameless in this affair. He had taught the Indians that he was as one of themselves, had omitted no means of securing their amity; had danced and sung with them and smiled approvingly on their butcherings and scalpings; and he had no right to imagine that they would believe him sincere in his promise to spare the prisoners. It was too late for him to cry "Kill me, but spare them!" after the massacre had commenced. It was his duty to have taken measures to render such a thing impossible beforehand. He had touched pitch, and was defiled.

Disgrace and panic reigned among all the English commanders. Webb whimpered to be allowed to fall back on the Hudson with his six thousand men; Loudoun cowered in New York with his large army, and could think of no better way of defending the northwest frontier than by intrenching himself on Long Island. There was not an Englishman in the Ohio or the St. Lawrence Basins. Everywhere beyond the narrow strip of the colonies the French were paramount. In Europe England's position was almost as contemptible. Such was the result of the attempt of the aristocracy to rule England. There was only one man who could save England, and he was an old man, poor, a commoner, and sick almost to death. But in 1757 William Pitt was called to the English helm, accepted the responsibility, and steered the country from her darkest to her most brilliant hour. The campaigns which drove the soldiers of Louis XV. out of America were the first chapter of the movement which ended in the expulsion of the British from the territory of the United States. Catholicism and Protestantism were arrayed against each other for the last time. Pitt was the man of the people; his ambition, though generous, was as great as his abilities; the colonies knew him as their friend. "I can save this country, and nobody else can," he said; and bent his final energies to making England the foremost nation in the world, and the most respected. The faith of Rome allied France with Austria; and Prussia, with Frederic the Great, standing as the sole bulwark of Protestantism on the Continent, was inevitably drawn toward England.

With one movement of his all-powerful hand, Pitt reversed the oppressive and suicidal policy of the colonial administration. Loudoun was recalled; his excuses were vain. Amherst and Wolfe were sent out. The colonies were told that no compulsion should be put upon them; they were expected to levy, clothe and pay their men, but the government would repay their outlay. Instantly they responded, and their contributions exceeded all anticipation. Massachusetts taxed herself thirteen and fourpence in the pound. Provincial officers not above colonel ranked with the British, and a new spirit animated all. On the other hand Canada suffered from famine, and Montcalm foresaw eventual defeat. Amherst and Wolfe, with ten thousand men, captured Louisburg and destroyed the fortifications. At the same time, a great army was collected against Ticonderoga. Nine thousand provincials, with Stark, Israel Putnam, and six hundred New England rangers, camped side by side with over six thousand troops of the British regulars under Abercrombie and Lord Howe. The French under Montcalm had erected Fort Carillon on the outlet from Lake George to Champlain, approachable only from the northwest. It was here that he planned his defense. The English disembarked on the west side of the lake, protected by Point Howe. In marching round the bend they came upon a French party of three hundred and defeated them, Howe falling in the first attack. Montcalm was behind intrenchments with thirty-six hundred men; Abercrombie rashly gave orders to carry the works by storm without waiting for cannon, but was careful to remain far in the rear during the action. The attack was most gallantly and persistently delivered; nearly two thousand men, mostly regulars, were killed; and at the end of the murderous day, Montcalm remained master of the field. Abercrombie still had four times as many men as Montcalm, and with his artillery could easily have carried the works and captured Ticonderoga; but he was by this time "distilled almost to a jelly by the act of fear," and fled headlong at once. Montcalm had not yet met his match.

Bradstreet, however, with seven hundred Massachusetts men and eleven hundred New Yorkers, crossed Lake Ontario and took Fort Frontenac, the garrison fleeing at their approach. Amherst, on hearing of Abercrombie's cowardice, embarked for Boston with over four thousand men, marched thence to Albany and on to the camp; Abercrombie was sent to England, and Amherst took his place as chief. The capture of Fort Duquesne was the first thing planned. Over forty-five hundred men were raised in South Carolina, Pennsylvania and Virginia; Joseph Forbes commanded them as brigadier-general; Washington led the Virginians; John Armstrong and the boy, Anthony Wayne, were with the Pennsylvanians. Washington, who had clad part of his men in Indian deerskins, wanted to follow Braddock's line of march; but Forbes, who had not long to live, though his brain remained clear, preferred to build a road by which ready communication with Philadelphia could be kept up. Washington got news that the Fort had but eight hundred defenders, and a strong reconnaissance was sent forward, without his knowledge, under Major Grant, who, thinking he had the French at advantage, exposed himself and was defeated with a loss of three hundred. The remaining five hundred reached camp in good order, thanks to the discipline which had been given them by Washington. Forbes had decided to advance no further that season—it was then November; but Washington had information which caused him to gain permission to advance with twenty-five hundred provincials, and he occupied intrenchments near Duquesne. Nine days later the rest of the army arrived; and the garrison of the Fort set fire to it at night and fled. The place was entered by the troops, Armstrong raised the British flag, and at Forbes' suggestion it was rechristened Pittsburgh. And there, above the confluence of the two rivers, the city named after the Great Commoner stands to-day. A vast and fertile country was thenceforward opened to the east. After burying the bleaching bones of the men killed under Braddock, a garrison was left on the spot, and the rest of the army returned.

Washington, who had seen five years' arduous service, resigned his commission, and after receiving cordial honors from his fellow officers and the Virginia legislature, married the widow, Martha Custis, and settled down as a planter in Mount Vernon. He was a delegate to the Virginia House of Burgesses and to the Continental Congresses of 1774 and 1775; but it was not until the latter year that he reappeared as a soldier, accepting the command of the Continental forces on the 15th of June, not against the French, but against the English.

In 1759, the genius and spirit of Pitt began to be fully felt. The English were triumphant in Europe, and a comprehensive plan for the conquest of Canada was intrusted for the first time to men capable of carrying it out. Thousands of men were enlisted and paid for by the colonies north of Maryland. Stanwix, Amherst, Prideaux and Wolfe were the chiefs in command. Fifty thousand English and provincial troops were opposed by not more than an eighth as many half-starved Frenchmen and Canadians. Montcalm had no illusions; he told the French Minister of War that, barring extraordinary accidents, Canada's hour had come; but he "was resolved to find his grave under the ruins of the colony." And young General Wolfe had said, on being given the department of the St. Lawrence, "I feel called upon to justify the notice taken of me by such exertions and exposure of myself as will probably lead to my fall." The premonitions of both these valiant soldiers were fulfilled. Wolfe was at this time thirty-two years of age, and had spent half his life in the army. The Marquis de Montcalm was forty-seven when he fell on the Plains of Abraham. Neither general had been defeated up to the moment they faced each other; neither could succumb to any less worthy adversary.

But the first objective point was not Quebec, but Fort Niagara, which, standing between Erie and Ontario, commanded the fur trade of the country to the west. Prideaux, with an adequate force of English, Americans and Indians, invested the place in July, D'Aubry, the French commander, bringing up twelve hundred men to relieve it. Just before the action Prideaux was killed by the bursting of a mountain howitzer, but Sir William Johnson was at hand to take his place. On the 24th the battle took place; the French were flanked by the English Indians, and charged by the English; they broke and fled, and the Fort surrendered next day. Stanwix had meanwhile taken possession of all the French posts between Pittsburgh and Erie. The English had got their enemy on the run all along the line. Gage was the only English officer to disgrace himself in this campaign; he squirmed out of compliance with Amherst's order to occupy the passes of Ogdensburgh. Amherst, with artillery and eleven thousand men, advanced on the hitherto invincible Ticonderoga. The French knew they were beaten, and therefore, instead of fighting, abandoned the famous stronghold and Crown Point, and retreated down to Isle aux Nois, whither Amherst should have followed them. Instead of doing so he took to building and repairing fortifications—the last infirmity of military minds of a certain order—and finally went into winter quarters with nothing further done. Amherst, at the end of the war, received the routine rewards of a well-meaning and not defeated commander-in-chief; but it was Wolfe who won immortality.

He collected his force of eight thousand men, including two battalions of "Royal Americans," at Louisburg; among his ship captains was Cook the explorer; Lieutenant-colonel Howe commanded a body of light infantry. Before the end of June the army stepped ashore on the island that fills the channel of the St. Lawrence below Quebec, called the Isle of Orleans. Montcalm's camp was between them and the tall acclivity on which stood the famous fortress, which had defied capture for a hundred and thirty years. The French outnumbered the English, but neither the physical condition nor the morale of their troops was good. That beetling cliff was the ally on which Montcalm most depended. All the landing-places up stream for nine miles had been fortified: the small river St. Charles covered with its sedgy marshes the approach on the north and east, while on the west another stream, the Montmorenci, rising nearly at the same place as the St. Charles, falls in cataracts into the St. Lawrence nine miles above the citadel. All these natural features had been improved by military art. High up, north and west of the city, spread the broad Plains of Abraham.

Wolfe's fleet commanded the river and the south shore. Point Levi, on this shore, opposite Quebec, was fortified by the English, and siege guns were mounted there, the channel being but a mile wide; the lower town could be reached by the red-hot balls, but not the lofty citadel. After personally examining the region during the greater part of July, Wolfe decided on a double attack; one party to ford the Montmorenci, which was practicable at a certain hour of the tide, and the other to cross over in boats from Point Levi. But the boats grounded on some rocks in the channel; and Wolfe was repulsed at the Montmorenci. Four hundred men were lost. An expedition was now sent up stream to open communication with Amherst; but though it was learned that Niagara, Crown Point and Ticonderoga had fallen, Amherst did not appear. Wolfe must do his work alone; the entire population of the country was against him, and the strongest natural fortification in the world. His eager anxiety threw him into a fever. "My constitution is entirely ruined, without the consolation of having done any considerable service to the state, and without any prospect of it," was what he wrote to the English government. Four days afterward he was dying victorious on the Plains of Abraham.

The early Canadian winter would soon be at hand. The impossible must be done, and at once. Wolfe, after several desperate proposals of his had been rejected by the council

THE PLAINS OF ABRAHAM

of war, made a feint in force up the river, in the hope of getting Montcalm where he could fight him. He scrutinized the precipitous north shore as with a magnifying glass. At last, on the 11th of September, the hope that had so long been burning within him was gratified. But what a hope! A headlong goat-track cleft its zigzag way up the awful steep, and emerged at last upon the dizzy and breathless height above. Two men could scarce climb abreast in it; and even this was defended by fortifications, and at the summit, against the sky, tents could be seen. Yet this was the only way to victory: only by this heartbreaking path could England drive France from the western continent, and give a mighty nation to the world. Wolfe saw, and was content; where one man could go, thousands might follow. And he perceived that the very difficulty of the enterprise was the best assurance of its success. The place was defended indeed, but not strongly. Montcalm knew what daring could accomplish, but even he had not dreamed of daring such as this. Wolfe, with a great soul kindled into flame by the resolve to achieve a feat almost beyond mortal limitations, dared it, and prevailed.

Till the hour of action, he kept his troops far up the stream. By the 13th, all preparations were made. Night came on, calm, like the heart of the hero who knows that the culminating moment of his destiny has arrived. At such a crisis, the mortal part of the man is transfigured by the towering spirit, and his eyes pierce through the veils of things. His life lies beneath him, and he contemplates its vicissitudes with the high tranquillity of an immortal freedom. What is death to him who has already triumphed over the fetters of the flesh, and tasted the drink of immortality? He is the trustee of the purpose of God; and the guerdon his deed deserves can be nothing less noble than to die.

It was at one in the morning that the adventure was begun. Silently the boats moved down the stream, the dark ships following in silence. Thousands of brave hearts beat with heroic resolve beneath the eternal stars. The shadowy cove was gained; Wolfe's foot has touched the shore; as the armed figures follow and gather at the foot of the ascent, no words are spoken, but what an eloquence in those faces! Upward they climb, afire with zeal; Howe has won a battery; upward! the picket on the height, too late aroused from sleep by the stern miracle, is overpowered. With panting lungs man after man tops the ascent and sees the darkling plain and forms in line with his comrades, while still the stream winds up endlessly from the depths below. The earth is giving birth to an army. Coiling upward, deploying, ranging out, rank after rank they are extended along the front of the forest, with Quebec before them. No drum has beat; no bugle has spoken; but Wolfe is there, his spirit is in five thousand breasts, and there needs no trumpet for the battle.

As the last of the army formed upon the rugged field, dawn broke upon the east, and soon the early sunshine sparkled on their weapons and glowed along the ranks of English red. Meanwhile Montcalm had been apprised; his first instinct of incredulity had been swept away by the inevitable truth, and he manned himself for the struggle. Often had he conquered against odds; but now his spirit must bow before a spirit stronger than his, as Antony's before Augustus. And what had he to oppose against the seasoned veterans of the English army, thrice armed in the consciousness of their unparalleled achievement?—Five weak and astounded battalions, and a horde of inchoate peasants. But Montcalm did not falter; by ten he had taken up his position, and by eleven, after some ineffectual cannonading, to allow time for the arrival of re-enforcements which came not, he led the charge. The attack was disordered by the uneven ground, the fences and the ravines; and it was broken by the granite front of the English (three-fourths of them Americans) and their long-reserved and withering fire. The undisciplined Canadians flinched from that certain death; and Wolfe, advancing on them with his grenadiers, saw them melt away before the cold steel could reach them. The two leaders faced each other, both equally undaunted and alert; it was like a duel between them; no opening was missed, no chance neglected. The smoke hung in the still air of morning; the long lines of men swayed and undulated beneath it obscurely, and the roar of musketry dinned terribly in the ear, here slackening for a moment, there breaking forth in volleying thunders; and men were dropping everywhere; there were shoutings from the captains, the fierce crash of cheers, yells of triumph or agony, and the faint groans of the wounded unto death. Wolfe was hit, but he did not heed it; Montcalm has received a musket ball, but he cannot yet die. The English battle does not yield; it advances, the light of victory is upon it. Backward stagger the French; Montcalm strives to check the fatal movement, but the flying death has torn its way through his body, and he can no more. Wolfe, even as the day was won, got his death wound in the breast, but "Support me—don't let my brave fellows see me drop," he gasped out. His thoughts were with his army; let the retreat of the enemy be cut off; and he died with a happy will, and with God's name on his lips. Montcalm lingered, suggesting means by which to retrieve the day; but the power of France died with him. Quebec was lost and won; and human history was turned into a new channel, and no longer flowing through the caverns of mediæval error, rolled its current toward the sunlight of liberty and progress. "The more a man is versed in business, the more he finds the hand of Providence everywhere," was the reply of William Pitt, when Parliament congratulated him on the victory. He had wrought his plans with wisdom and zeal; but "except the Lord build the city, they labor in vain who build it." There have been great statesmen and brave soldiers, before Pitt and Wolfe, and since; but there could be only one fall of Quebec, with all which that implied.

The following spring and summer were overshadowed by an unrighteous war against the Cherokees, precipitated by the royalist governor of Virginia, Lyttleton. An attempt by the French under Levi to recapture Quebec failed, in spite of the folly of the English commander, Murray; Pitt had foreseen the effort, and destroyed it with an English fleet. Amherst, in his own tortoise-like way, advanced and took possession of Montreal; and by permission of the Indian, Pontiac, who regarded himself as lord of the country, the English flag was carried to the outposts. Canada had surrendered; in the terms imposed, property and the religious faith of the people were respected; but nothing was promised them in the way of civil liberty. In discussing the European peace that was now looked for, question was raised whether to restore Canada, or the West Indian island of Guadaloupe, to France. Some, who feared that the retention of Canada would too much incline the colonies to independence, favored its return. But Franklin said that Canada would be a source of strength to England. The expense of defending that vast frontier would be saved; the rapidly increasing population would absorb English manufactures without limit, and their necessary devotion to farming would diminish their competition as manufacturers. He pointed out that their differences in governments and mutual jealousies made their united action against England unthinkable, "unless you grossly abuse them."—"Very true: that, I see, will happen," returned the English lawyer Pratt, afterward Lord Camden, the attorney-general. But Pitt would not listen to Canada's being given up; he was for England, not for any English clique. On the other hand, one of those cliques was preparing to carry out the long meditated taxation of the colonies; and the sudden death of George II., bringing his son to the throne, favored their purpose; for the Third George had character and energy, and not a little intelligence for a king; and he was soon seen to intend the re-establishment of the royal prerogative in all its integrity. As a preliminary step to this end, he accepted Pitt's resignation in October, 1761.

Much to the displeasure of Massachusetts, Thomas Hutchinson, already Judge of Probate, was by Governor Bernard appointed to the Chief Justiceship of the colony; the royalist direction of his sympathies was known. In February, 1761, he heard argument in court as to whether revenue officers had power to call in executive assistance to enforce the acts of trade. The crown lawyer argued that to refuse it was to deny the sovereignty of the English Parliament in the colonies. Then James Otis arose, and made a protest which tingled through the whole colony, and was the first direct blow aimed against English domination. Power such as was asked for, he said, had already cost one king of England his head and another his throne. Writs of assistance were open to intolerable abuse; were the instrument of arbitrary power and destructive of the fundamental principles of law. Reason and the constitution were against them. "No act of Parliament can establish such a writ: an act of parliament against the constitution is void!" These words were the seed of revolution. Hutchinson was frightened, but succeeded in persuading his colleagues to postpone decision until he had written to England. The English instruction was to enforce the law, and the judges acted accordingly; but the people replied by electing Otis to the assembly; and Hutchinson was more distrusted than ever. At the same time, in Virginia, Richard Henry Lee denounced the slave trade; the legislature indorsed his plea, but England denied it. South Carolina was alienated by the same decree, and also by an unpopular war against the Cherokees. In New York, the appointment of a judge "during the king's pleasure" roused the assembly; but the result of their remonstrance was that all colonial governors were instructed from England to grant no judicial commissions but during the king's pleasure. This was to make the Bench the instrument of the Prerogative. A judge acted on questions of property, without a jury, on information furnished by crown officers, and derived emoluments from his own award of forfeitures; and the governor would favor large seizures because he got one-third of the spoils. All the assemblies could do, for the present, was to reduce salaries; but that did not make the offenders any less avaricious. Moreover, the king began the practice of paying them in spite of the assemblies, and reproved the latter for "not being animated by a sense of their duty to their king and country."

James Otis continued to be the voice of the colonies. "Kings were made for the good of the people, not the people for them. By the laws of God and nature, government must not raise taxes on the property of the people without the consent of the people. To tax without the assembly's consent was the same in principle as for the king and the House of Lords to usurp legislative authority in England." For the utterance of these sentiments he was honored by the hearty support of the people, and still more by the denunciations of men of the Hutchinson sort. The ministers were not silent on the popular side. "May Heaven blast the designs, though not the soul," said Mayhew, with Christian discrimination, "of whoever he be among us who shall have the hardiness to attack the people's rights!" King George's answer, as soon as he had concluded the peace with France and Spain, in 1763, was to take measures to terrorize the colonists by sending out an army of twenty battalions to be kept permanently in America, the expenses of which the colonists were to pay. But by enforcing the acts of trade, England had now made herself the enemy of the whole civilized world, and the American colonies would not be without allies in the struggle that was drawing near.

While these matters were in agitation among the white people, the Indians in the north were discovering grievances of their own. Pontiac, an Ottawa chief, and by his personal abilities the natural leader of many tribes, was the instigator and center of the revolt. The English masters of Canada had showed themselves less congenial to the red men than the French had done; they could not understand that savages had any rights which they were bound to respect; while Pontiac conceived that no white man could live in the wilderness without his permission. Upon this issue, trouble was inevitable; and Pontiac planned a general movement of all the Indians in the north against the colonists. The success of the scheme could of course be only momentary; that it attained the dignity of a "war" was due to the influence and energy of the Indian general. His design was of broad scope, embracing a simultaneous attack on all the English frontier forts; a wide coalition of tribes was effected; and though their tactics were not essentially different from those heretofore employed by savages, yet their possession of arms, their skill in their use, and their numbers, made their onslaughts formidable. On several occasions they effected their entry into the forts by stratagem: a tale of misery told by a squaw; a ball in a game struck toward the door of the stronghold; professedly amicable conferences suddenly becoming massacres; such were the naive yet successful ruses employed. Many lives were lost, and the border lands were laid waste and panicstricken; but it was impossible for the Indians to hold together, and their victories hastened their undoing. No general engagement, of course, was fought, but Pontiac's authority gradually abated, and he was finally compelled to go into retirement. His Conspiracy has its picturesque side, but it is not organically related to our history; it was merely a fresh expression of the familiar fact that there could be no sincere friendship between the white and the red: The former could live with the latter if they would live like them; but no attempt to reverse the case could succeed. The solemnity with which the practice of signing treaties of peace with the Indians has uniformly been kept up is one of the curious features of our colonial annals, and indeed of later times. Indians will keep the peace without treaties, if they are kindly used and given liberty to do as they please; but no engagement is binding on them after they deem themselves wronged. They are pleased by the formalities, the speeches, and the gifts that accompany such conferences; they like to exchange compliments, and to play with belts of wampum; and it is possible that when they make their promises, they think they will keep them. They can understand the advantages of trade, and will make some sacrifice of their pride or convenience to secure them. But the mind is never dominant in them; the tides of passion flood it, and their wild nature carries them away. It may be surmised that we should have had fewer Indian troubles, had we never entered into any treaty with them. But thousands of treaties have been made, and broken, sometimes by one side, sometimes by the other, but always by one of the two. And then, punishments must be administered; but if punishment is for improvement, it has been as ineffective as the treaties. The only rational thing to do with an Indian is to kill him; and yet it may fairly be doubted whether complete moral justification could be shown for the killing of any Indian since Columbus landed at San Salvador.—As for Pontiac, a keg of liquor was inducement sufficient to one of his own race to murder him, five years after the failure of his revolt.

Toward the end of September, Jenkinson, Secretary of the Treasury in England, presented the draft for an American stamp-tax—the true authorship of which was never disclosed. This tax was the result of the argument of exclusion applied to the problem, How to raise a permanent and sufficient revenue from the colonies. Foreign and internal commerce taxes would not serve, because such commerce was forbidden by the Navigation Acts. A poll-tax would be inequitable to the slaveholders. Land-taxes could not be collected. Exchequer-bills were against an act of

Parliament. Nothing but a stamp-tax remained, and all persons concerned were in favor of it, the colonists only excepted. Their opinion was that taxation without representation was an iniquity. But they did not perhaps consider that England owed a debt of seven hundred million dollars which must be provided for somehow; and that the interests of the empire demanded, in the opinion of those who were at its head, that the colonies be ruled with a stronger hand than heretofore. George Grenville accepted the responsibility of the act.

The king gave his consent to the employment of the entire official force of the colonies to prevent infringements of the Navigation Acts, and the army and navy were to assist them. There were large emoluments for seizures, and the right of search was unrestricted, afloat or ashore. In order to diminish the danger of union between the colonies, a new distribution, or alteration of boundaries, was adopted, with a view to increasing their number. But the country between the Alleghanies and the Mississippi was to be closed to colonization, lest it should prove impossible to control settlers at such a distance. It proved, of course, still less possible to prevent emigration thither. But all seemed going well, and the Grenville ministry was so firmly established that nothing seemed able to shake it. The fact that a young Virginia lawyer, Patrick Henry by name, had said in the course of an argument against the claim of a clergyman for the value of some tobacco, that a king who annuls salutary laws is a tyrant, and forfeits all right to obedience; and that if ministers fail to fulfill the uses for which they were ordained, the community may justly strip them of their appointments—this circumstance probably did not come to the ears of the British ministry; but it had its effect in Virginia. Grenville, however, was induced by the appeals of some influential Americans in London to postpone his tax for a year, so that the assemblies might have an opportunity to consent to it. By way of tempting them to do this, he sought for special inducements; he revived the hemp and flax bounties; he permitted rice to be carried south of Carolina and Georgia on payment of half subsidy; and he removed the restrictions on the New England whale fishery. He then informed Parliament of his purpose of applying the stamp-tax to America, and asked if any member wished to question the right of Parliament to impose such a tax. In a full house, not a single person rose to object. The king gave it his "hearty" approval. It only remained for America humbly and gratefully to accept it.

First came comments. "If taxes are laid upon us in any shape, without our having a legal representation where they are laid, are we not reduced from the character of free subjects to the miserable state of tributary slaves?" asked Samuel Adams of Boston. "These duties are only the beginning of evils," said Livingston of New York. "Acts of Parliament against natural equity are void," Otis affirmed; and in a lucid and cogent analysis of the principles and ends of government he pointed out that the best good of the people could be secured only by a supreme legislative and executive ultimately in the people; but a universal congress being impracticable, representation was substituted: "but to bring the powers of all into the hands of one or some few, and to make them hereditary, is the interested work of the weak and wicked. Nothing but life and liberty are actually hereditable. . . . British colonists do not hold their liberties or their lands by so slippery a tenure as the will of princes; the colonists are common children of the same Creator with their brethren in Great Britain. . . . A time may come when Parliament shall declare every American charter void; but the natural, inherent rights of the colonists as men and citizens can never be abolished. The colonists know the blood and treasure independence would cost. They will never think of it till driven to it as the last fatal resort against ministerial oppression: but human nature must and will be rescued from the general slavery that has so long triumphed over the species." The immediate practical result was, that the colonists pledged themselves to use nothing of English manufacture, even to going without lamb to save wool. And even Hutchinson remarked that if England had paid as much for the support of the wars as had been voluntarily paid by the colonists, there would have been no great increase in the national debt.

All this made no impression in England. The dregs of the Canadian population were a handful of disreputable. Protestant ex-officers, traders and publicans—"the most immoral collection of men I ever knew," as Murray said—but judges and juries were selected from these gentry, and the Catholics were disfranchised. In New England, boundaries were rearranged, and colonists had to buy new titles. New York, Connecticut, Rhode Island, protested before Parliament against the taxation scheme; Philadelphia at first petitioned to be delivered from the selfishness of its proprietors even at the cost of becoming a royal colony; but later, Franklin advised that they grant supplies to the crown only when required of them "in the usual constitutional manner." George Wythe, speaking for Virginia, remonstrated against measures "fitter for exiles driven from their country after ignominiously forfeiting its favor and protection, than for the posterity of loyal Britons." Yet there were many royalist Americans who were urgent that English rule should be strengthened; and the English Board of Trade declared that the protests of the colonies showed "a most indecent disrespect to the legislature of Great Britain." The king decreed that in all military matters in America the orders of the commander-in-chief there, and under him of the brigadiers, should be supreme; and only in the absence of these officers might the governors give the word. This became important on the occasion of the "Boston Massacre" a few years later. In Parliament, Grenville said that he would never lend a hand toward forging chains for America, "lest in so doing I forge them for myself"; but he shuffled out of the American demand not to be taxed without representation by declaring that Parliament was "the common council of the whole empire," and added that America was to all intents and purposes as much represented in Parliament as many Englishmen. This assertion brought to his feet Barré, the companion of Wolfe at Quebec. He denied that America was virtually represented, and said that the House was ignorant of American affairs. Charles Townshend, who posed as an infallible authority on America, replied that the last war had cost the colonies little though they had profited much by it; and now these "American children, planted by our care, nourished up to strength and opulence by our indulgence, and protected by our arms, grudge to contribute their mite to relieve us from the heavy burden under which we lie."

Barré could not restrain his indignation. In the course of a fiery rejoinder he uttered truths that made him the most loved Englishman in America, when his words were published there. "Your oppressions planted them in America," he thundered. "They met with pleasure all hardships compared with those they suffered in their own country. They grew by your neglect of them: as soon as you began to care for them, deputies of members of this house were sent to spy out their liberties, to misrepresent their actions, and to prey upon them; men whose behavior caused the blood of those Sons of Liberty to recoil within them: men who were often glad, by going to a foreign country, to escape being brought to the bar of justice in their own. They 'protected by your arms'?—They have, amid their constant and laborious industry, nobly taken up arms for the defense of a country whose frontier was drenched in blood, while its interior parts yielded all its little savings to your emolument. And believe me—remember—the same spirit of freedom which actuated that people at first will accompany them still. They are as truly loyal as any subjects the king has; but a people jealous of their liberties,

THE STAMP ACT

and who will vindicate them, if ever they should be violated." But Grenville had gone too far to retreat; the case went against America by two hundred and forty-five to forty-nine; and only Beckford and Conway were on record as denying the power of Parliament to enact the tax. All petitions from the colonies were refused. "We have power to tax them, and we will tax them," said one of the ministers. In the House of Lords the bill was agreed to without debate or dissent. The king, at the time of signing the bill, was suffering from one of his periodic attacks of insanity; but the ratification was accepted as valid nevertheless. Neither Franklin nor any of the other American agents imagined the act would be forcibly resisted in America. Even Otis had said, "We must submit." But they reckoned without their host. The stamp act was a two-edged sword; in aiming to cut down the liberties of America, it severed the bonds that tied her to the mother country.

The prospect before the colonies was truly intolerable. No product of their industry could be exported save to England; none but English ships might enter their ports; no wool might be moved from one part of the country to another; no Bible might be printed anywhere; all hats must come from England; no ore might be mined or worked; duties were imposed on almost every imported article of use or luxury. No marriage, promissory note, or other transaction requiring documentary record was valid except with the government stamp. In a word, convicts in a jail could hardly be shackled more severely than were these two millions of the most freedom-loving and intelligent people on the globe. "If this system were to prevail," remarked Thacher of Boston, "it would extinguish the flame of liberty all over the world."

But it was not to prevail. Patrick Henry had been elected to the legislature of Virginia. His first act was to maintain, in committee of the whole, that the colony had never given up its right to be governed by its own laws respecting taxation, and that it had been constantly recognized by England; and that any attempt to vest such power in other persons tended to destroy British as well as American freedom. In a passionate peroration he warned George III. to remember the fate of other tyrants who had trampled on popular liberties. Otis in Massachusetts suggested the novel idea of summoning a congress from all the colonies to deliberate on the situation. In New York a writer declared that while there was no disposition among the colonies to break with England as long as they were permitted their full rights, yet they would be "satisfied with no less."— "The Gospel promises liberty and permits resistance," said Mayhew. Finally, the dauntless and faithful Christopher Gadsden of South Carolina, after considering Massachusetts's suggestion of a union, pronounced, as head of the committee, in its favor.

In England, meanwhile, the cause of the colonies had been somewhat favored by the willfulness of the king, who, in order to bring his court favorites into power, dismissed the Grenville ministry. There were no persons of ability in the new cabinet, and vacant feebleness was accounted better for America than resolute will to oppress. The king himself, however, never wavered in his resolve that the colonies should be taxed. On the other hand, the colonies were at this time disposed to think that the king was friendly to their liberties. But whatever misapprehensions existed on either side were soon to be finally dispelled.

In August, 1765, the names of the stamp distributors (who were to be citizens of the colonies) were published in America; and the packages of stamped paper were dispatched from England. There was an old elm-tree in Boston, standing near the corner of Essex Street, opposite Boylston Market. On the morning of the 14th of August, two figures were descried by early pedestrians hanging from the lower branches of the tree. "They were dressed in square-skirted coats and small-clothes, and as their wigs hung down over their faces, they looked like real men. One was intended to represent the Earl of Bute, who was supposed to have advised the king to tax America; the other was meant for the effigy of Andrew Oliver, a gentleman belonging to one of the most respectable families in Massachusetts, whom the king had appointed to be the distributor of stamps." It was in vain that Hutchinson ordered the removal of the effigies; the people had the matter in their own hands. In the evening a great and orderly crowd marched behind a bier bearing the figures, gave three cheers for "Liberty, Property and no stamps," before the State House, where the governor and Hutchinson were in session, and thence went to the house which Oliver had intended for his stamp office, tore it down, and burned his image in the fire they kindled with it, in front of his own residence. "Death to the man who offers stamped paper to sell!" they shouted. "Beat an alarm!" quavered Hutchinson to the militia colonel.—"My drummers are in the mob," was the reply; and when Hutchinson attempted to disperse the crowd, they forced him to run the gantlet, in the Indian fashion which was too familiar to New Englanders, and caught him several raps as he ran. "If Oliver had been there he'd have been murdered," said Governor Bernard, with conviction; "if he doesn't resign—!" But Oliver, much as he loved the perquisites of the office, loved his life more, and he resigned before the mob could threaten him. Bernard, with chattering teeth, was ensconced in the safest room in the castle. There remained Hutchinson, in his handsome house in Garden Court Street, near the North Square. Late at night the mob came surging and roaring in that direction. As they turned into Garden Court Street, the sound of them was as if a wild beast had broken loose and was howling for its prey. From the window, the terrified chief-justice beheld "an immense concourse of people, rolling onward like a tempestuous flood that had swelled beyond its bounds and would sweep everything before it.

He felt, at that moment, that the wrath of the people was a thousand-fold more terrible than the wrath of a king. That was a moment when an aristocrat and a loyalist might have learned how powerless are kings, nobles, and great men, when the low and humble range themselves against them. Had Hutchinson understood and remembered this lesson he need not in after years have been an exile from his native country, nor finally have laid his bones in a distant land."

The mob broke into the house, destroyed the valuable furniture, pictures and library, and completely gutted it. The act was denounced and repudiated by the better class of patriots, like Adams and Mayhew; but it served a good purpose. The voice of the infuriated mob is sometimes the only one that tyranny can hear. One after another all the colonies refused to accept the stamp act, and every stamp officer was obliged to resign. Meanwhile the leaders discussed the people's rights openly. The law was to go into effect on November 1st. "Will you violate the law of Parliament?" was asked. "The stamp act is against Magna Charta, and Lord Coke says an act of Parliament against Magna Charta is for that reason void," was the reply. "Rulers are attorneys, agents and trustees of the people," said Adams, "and if the trust is betrayed or wantonly trifled away, the people have a right to revoke the authority that they themselves have deputed, and to constitute abler and better agents. We have an indisputable right to demand our privileges against all the power and authority on earth." Never had there been such unanimity throughout the colonies; but in New York, General Gage, who had betrayed lack of courage under Amherst a few years before, but who was now commander-in-chief, declared he would put down disaffection with a strong hand. There were ships of war in the harbor, and the fort in the town mounted heavy guns. Major James of the artillery was intrusted with the preparations. "I'll cram the stamps down their throats with the end of my sword: if they attempt to rise I'll drive them out of town for a pack of rascals, with four and twenty men!" It was easy to pass a stamp act, and to bring stamped paper into the colonies; but it would take more than Major James, and Governor Colden, and General Gage himself to make the people swallow them. The day of the "Sons of Liberty" was dawning.

CHAPTER THIRTEENTH

THE PASSING OF THE RUBICON

ISSUE was now joined between America and England. They faced each other—the great, historic figure, and the stripling of a century—and knew that the limit had been reached. The next move might be irrevocable. "You must submit to the tax."—"I will not submit." Englishmen, with some few eminent exceptions, believed that England was in the right. If the word of Parliament was not law, what was? If the law it made could be disregarded, what could stand? A colony was a child: children must be kept in subjection. Colonies were planted for the benefit and extension of commerce; if they were permitted to conduct their commerce without regard to the mother country, their reason for existence was gone. The protection of a colony was expensive: why should not the protected one bear a part at least of the expense? If the mother country allowed the colony to fix the amount it should pay, what guarantee could she have that it would pay anything? Could mighty England assume toward little America the attitude of a tradesman, humbly standing at the door with a bill, asking whether it would be convenient to pay something on account? If there were to be condescension, it should not come from America. She clamored for justice; England would be just: but she must first be obeyed. England might forgive the debt, but must insist upon acknowledgment that the debt was due, and upon the right to collect it at pleasure. As for the plea that taxation should postulate representation, it would not bear examination. It might be true that Parliament was theoretically a representative body; but, in fact, it was a gathering of the men in England best qualified to govern, who were rather selected than elected. Many of the commons held their seats by favor of the nobility; the suffrage, as practiced, was a recognition that the people might have a voice in the government of the country; but that voice was not to be a deciding one. It was exercised only by a part of the people, and even then, largely under advice or influence. Many important towns and districts had no representatives. Americans were as well off as these Englishmen; on what ground could they demand to be better off? They must trust to the will of England to secure their advantage in securing her own; to her wisdom, equity, and benevolence. Why should they complain of the Navigation Acts? What more did they want than a market?—and that, England afforded. Why should they feel aggrieved at the restriction on their manufactures? England could manufacture articles better than they could, and it was necessary to the well-being of her manufacturing classes that they should be free from American competition. Did they object to the measures England took to prevent smuggling and illicit dealing?—They had only themselves to blame: was it not notorious that evasions and open violations of the law had for years existed? Did they object to royal governors?—What better expedient was there to keep the two countries in touch with each other— to maintain that "representation" in England which they craved?—whereas, were they to choose governors from among themselves, they would soon drift away from sympathy with and understanding of England. And why all this uproar about the stamp tax? What easier, more equitable way could be devised to get the financial tribute required without pressing hard on any one? If Americans would object to that, they would object to anything; and they must either be abandoned entirely to their own devices—which of course was out of the question—or they must be compelled, if they would not do it voluntarily, to accede to it. Compulsion meant force; force meant a resident English army; and that army must be supported and accommodated by those for whose regulation it was established.

Such was the attitude of men like Lord Chief-justice Mansfield, who spoke on the subject in the House of Lords. He refused to recognize any essential distinction between external and internal taxes; though, as Pitt pointed out, the former was designed for the regulation of trade, and whatever profit arose from it was incidental; while the latter was imposed to raise revenue for the home government, and was, in effect, arbitrarily appropriating the property of subjects without their consent asked or obtained. Pitt disposed of the argument of virtual representation by denying it point-blank; Americans were not in the same position with those Englishmen who were not directly represented in Parliament; because the latter were inhabitants of the kingdom, and could be, and were indirectly represented in a hundred ways. But while opposing the right of Parliament to rob America, he asserted in the strongest terms its right to govern her. "The will of Parliament, properly signified, must forever keep the colonies dependent upon the sovereign kingdom of Great Britain. If any idea of renouncing allegiance has existed, it was but a momentary frenzy. In a good cause, the force of this country can crush America to atoms. But on this ground of the stamp act, I am one who will lift up my hands against it. I rejoice that America has resisted. In such a cause, your success would be hazardous.

America, if she fell, would embrace the pillar of the state, and pull down the constitution along with her."

The Lords passed the bill against a minority of five. In the Commons, where Burke ardently spoke in favor of the tax, the majority was even greater. "It was decided that irresponsible taxation was not a tyranny but a vested right; that Parliament held legislative power, not as a representative body but in absolute trust: that it was not and had never been responsible to the people." This was the new Toryism, which was to create a new opposition. The debate aroused a discussion of popular rights in England itself, and the press began to advocate genuine representation. Meanwhile, it looked ill for the colonies. But a law which is only engrossed on parchment, and is not also founded in natural truth and justice, has no binding power, even though it be supported by the army and navy of England. Humanity was on the side of America, and made her small numbers and physical weakness as strong as all that is good and right in the world. All appearances to the contrary notwithstanding, there is nothing real but right. Had America fought only for herself, she would have failed.

The instances of mob violence in the colonies at this period were not to be classed with lawless outbreaks in countries which have a government of their own. The colonies were subjected to a government which they did not elect or approve; and the management of their affairs consequently reverted inevitably and rightly to the body of the people themselves. They had no officers and no organization, but they knew what they wanted; and having in view the slowness of inter-communication, and the differences in the ideas and customs of the several colonies, the unanimity of their action in the present juncture is surprising. When their congress met in New York on the 7th of October, 1765, their debate was less as to principles than as to the manner of their declaration and enforcement. The watchword, "Join or die," had been started in September, and was taken up all over the country. Union was strength, and on union all were resolved. The mob had put a stop to the execution of the law; it now rested with the congress to settle in what way and on what grounds the repeal of the law should be demanded. Against the people and the congress were arrayed the royal governors and other officials, and the troops. The former deluged the home government with exhortations to be firm; the latter waited the word to act, not without misgivings; for here were two million inhabitants, a third or fourth part of whom might bear arms.

Should the congress base its liberties on charter rights, or on natural justice and universal reason?—On the latter, said Gadsden of South Carolina; and the rest acceded. "I wish," Gadsden had said, "that the charters may not ensnare us at last by drawing different colonies to act differently in this great cause. There ought to be no New England man, no New Yorker, known on the continent, but all Americans." It was a great truth to be enunciated at that time. There were statesmen less wise in this country a hundred years later. The Duke of Choiseul, premier of France, and one of the acutest ministers that ever lived, foresaw the independence of America, and even so early began to take measures having in view the attitude of France in that contingency.—In the congress, Otis advocated repeal, not of the stamp act alone, but of all acts laying a duty on trade; and it was finally agreed to mention the latter as grievances. Trial by jury was stipulated for instead of admiralty jurisdiction; taxes should be imposed only by colonial legislatures, representation in Parliament being impracticable. One or two of the delegates feared to sign the document embodying these views and demands; whereupon Dyer of Connecticut observed that since disunion in these matters was fatal, the remaining delegates ought to sign them; and this was done, only Ruggles and Ogden, of Massachusetts and of New Jersey respectively, declining. By this act the colonies became "a bundle of sticks which could neither be bent nor broken." At the same time, Samuel Adams addressed a letter to Governor Bernard of Massachusetts. "To suppose a right in Parliament to tax subjects without their consent includes the idea of a despotic power," said he. "The stamp act cancels the very conditions upon which our ancestors, with toil and blood and at their sole expense, settled this country. It tends to destroy that mutual confidence and affection, as well as that equality which ought to subsist among all his majesty's subjects: and what is worst of all evils, if his majesty's subjects are not to be governed according to the known and stated rules of the constitution, their minds may in time become disaffected."

On the 1st of November, the day when the act was to go into effect, Colden, governor of New York, "resolved to have the stamps distributed." The army and navy professed themselves ready to support him. But the population rose up in a body against it, with Isaac Sears as leader. "If you fire on us, we'll hang you," they told Colden. Torchlight processions, with the governor's effigy burned in a bonfire composed of his own carriages, right under the guns of the fort in which he had taken refuge, followed. Colden capitulated, and even gave up the stamps into the custody of the people. Similar scenes were enacted in the other colonies. The principle of "union and liberty" became daily more deeply rooted. If England refused to repeal the act, "we will repeal it ourselves," declared the colonists. John Adams said that the colonies were already discharged from allegiance, because they were "out of the king's protection" —protection and allegiance being reciprocal. The Sons of Liberty became a recognized organization. The press printed an admonition to George III., brief but pithy: GREAT SIR, RETREAT, OR YOU ARE RUINED. Otis maintained that the king, by mismanaging colonial affairs, had practically abdicated, so far as they were concerned. Israel Putnam, being of an active turn, rode through Connecticut to count noses, and reported that he could raise a force of ten thousand men. Meanwhile the routine business of the country went on with but slight modification, though according to the stamp act nothing that was done without a stamp was good in law. But it appeared, upon experiment, that if the law was in the people it could be dispensed with on paper. And wherever you went, you found a population smilingly clad in homespun.

Would England repeal the act? The House of Lords voted in favor of enforcing it February, 1766. In the Commons, General Howard declared that if it were passed, rather than imbrue his hands in the blood of his countrymen, he would sheathe his sword in his own body. The House divided two to one against the repeal. The king said he was willing to modify, but not to repeal it. On the 13th Franklin was summoned to the bar. He showed why the colonies could not and would not pay the tax, and that unless it were repealed, their affection for England, and the commerce depending thereon, would be lost. Would America pay a modified stamp duty?—he was asked; and bravely replied, "No: never: they will never submit to it." But could not a military force carry the act into effect?— "They cannot force a man to take stamps who chooses to do without them," was the answer. He added that the colonists thought it hard that a body in which they were not represented should make a merit of giving what was not its own but theirs. He affirmed a difference between internal and external taxation, because the former could not be evaded, whereas articles of consumption, on which the duty formed part of the price, could be dispensed with at will. "But what if necessaries of life should be taxed?" asked Grenville, thinking he had Franklin on the hip. But the American sage crushingly replied, "I do not know a single article imported into the colonies but what they can either do without it, or make it for themselves."

In the final debates, Pitt, called on to say whether,

should total repeal be granted, in compliance with American menaces of resistance, the consequence would not be the overthrow of British authority in America, gave his voice for repeal as a right. Grenville, on the other hand, thought that America should learn that "prayers are not to be brought to Cæsar through riot and sedition." The vote for repeal, and against modified enforcement, was two hundred and seventy-five to one hundred and sixty-seven. The dissenting members of the Lords signed a protest, because, should they assent to the repeal merely because it had passed the lower house, "we in effect vote ourselves useless." This suggests the "Je ne vois pas la nécessité" of the French epigrammatist. The Lords took themselves too seriously. Meanwhile, Bow bells were rung, Pitt was cheered, and flags flew; the news was sent to America in fast packets, and the rejoicing in the colonies was great. Prisoners for debt were set free, there were illuminations and bonfires, and honor was paid to Pitt, Camden, Barré, and to the king, who was eating his heart with vexation at having been compelled to assent to what he called "the fatal repeal."

The British government, while repealing the law, had yet affirmed its sovereign authority over the colonies. The colonies, on the other hand, were inclined to confirm their present advantage and take a step still further in advance. They would not be taxed without representation; why should they submit to any legislation whatever without representation? What right had England to enforce the Navigation Acts? The more the general situation was contemplated and discussed, the plainer to all did it appear that union was indispensable. The governors of most of the colonies were directing a treacherous attack against the charters; but bold students of the drift of things were foreseeing a time when charters might be superseded by independence. Patriots everywhere were keenly on the watch for any symptoms of a design on Parliament's part to raise a revenue from America. The presence and quartering of English soldiers in the colonies was regarded as not only a burden, but an insinuation. It was moreover a constant occasion of disturbance; for there was no love lost between the people and the soldiers. But, that there was no disposition on the people's part to pick quarrels or to borrow trouble, was evident from their voluntarily passing resolutions for the reimbursement of persons, like Hutchinson, who had suffered loss from the riots. If England would treat them like reasonable creatures, they were more than willing to meet her half way. It is probable that but for the royal governors, England and America might have arrived at an amicable understanding; yet, in the ultimate interests of both countries, it was better that the evil counselors of the day should prevail.

Townshend, an able, eloquent, but entirely untrustworthy man, devoted to affairs, and of insatiable though unprincipled ambition, proposed in Parliament to formulate a plan to derive a permanent revenue from America. This Parliament has been described by historians, and is convicted by its record, as the most corrupt, profligate and unscrupulous in English annals. William Pitt, who had accepted the title of Lord Chatham, and entered the House of Lords, was nominally the leader, but his health and failing faculties left him no real power. Shelburne, Secretary of State, was moderate and liberal, but no match for Townshend's brilliancy. The latter's proposal was to suspend the legislature of New York, as a punishment for the insubordination of the colony and a warning to others; to support a resident army, and to pay salaries to governors, judges and other crown officers, out of the revenue from America; to establish commissioners of the customs in the country; to legalize general writs of assistance; to permit no native-born American to hold office under the crown; and to make the revenue derivable from specified taxes on imports. The tax on tea was among those particularly mentioned. This was the scheme which was to be substituted for the repealed stamp tax; the colonies had objected to that as internal; this was external, and, though Townshend had refused to admit any difference between the two, he now employed it as a means of bringing the colonies to terms. The measure was received with acclaim by Parliament, though it was contrary to the real sentiment of the English nation. The king was charmed with it. Townshend died soon after it was passed, at the age of forty-one; and the king called on Lord North to take his place; a man of infirm will, but able, well-informed and clear-minded, with a settled predisposition against the cause of the people. He was as good an enemy of America as Grenville himself, though a less ill-natured one.

But, viewing this period broadly, it is manifest that the finest brains and best hearts, both in England and America, were friends to the cause of liberty. America, certainly, at this critical epoch in her career, produced a remarkable band of statesmen and patriots, perfectly fitted to the parts they had to play. The two Adamses, Gadsden, Franklin, Otis, Patrick Henry, Livingstone of New York, John Hancock, the wealthy and splendid Boston merchant, Hawley of Connecticut, and Washington, meditating upon the liberties of his country in the retirement of Mount Vernon, and unconsciously preparing himself to lead her armies through the Revolution—there has never been a company of better men active at one time in any country. Just at this juncture, too, there arose in Delaware a prophet by the name of John Dickinson, who wrote under the title of The Farmer, and who formulated an argument against the new revenue law which caught the attention of all the colonies. England, he pointed out, prohibits American manufactures; she now lays duties on importations, for the purpose of revenue only. Americans were taking steps to establish a league to abstain from purchasing any articles brought from England, intending thus to defeat the operation of the act without breaking the law. This might answer in the case of luxuries, or of things which could be made at home. But what if England were to meet this move by laying a duty on some necessary of life, and then forbid Americans to manufacture it at home? Obviously, they would then be constrained to buy it, paying the duty, and thus surrendering their freedom. From this point of view it would not be enough to evade the tax; it must be repealed, or resisted; and resistance meant war.

Unless, however, some action of an official character were taken, binding the colonies to co-operation, it was evident that the law would gradually go into effect. The Massachusetts assembly, early in 1768, sent to its London agent a letter, composed by Samuel Adams, embodying their formal protest to the articles of the revenue act and its corollaries. At the same time, they sent copies of the statement to the other colonial assemblies in the country, accompanied with the suggestion that all unite in discontinuing the use of British imported manufactures and other articles. The crown officers, for their part, renewed their appeal to England for naval and military forces to compel obedience and secure order.

The king and the government inclined to think that force was the remedy in this case. It was in vain that the more magnanimous called attention to the fact that an army and navy could not compel a man to buy a black broadcloth coat, if he liked a homespun one better. Inflammatory reports from America represented it as being practically in a state of insurrection. A Boston newspaper, which had published a severe arraignment of Governor Bernard, was tried for libel, and the jury, though informed by Hutchinson that if they did not convict of high treason they "might depend on being damned," brought in a verdict of acquittal. The Adams letter was laid before the English ministry and pronounced to be "of a most dangerous and factious tendency," and an injunction was dispatched to the several colonial governors to bid their assemblies to treat it with contempt, and if they declined, to dissolve them. Gage was ordered to enforce tranquillity. But the colonial resistance had thus far been passive only. The assemblies now declared that they had exclusive right to tax the people; Virginia not only agreed to the Adams letter, but indited one even more uncompromising; Pennsylvania and New York fell into line. A Boston committee presented an address to Bernard asking him to mediate between the people and England; he promised to do so, but at the same time sent out secret requests to have regiments sent to Boston. Divining his duplicity, John Adams, at the next town meeting, formulated the people's resolve to vindicate their rights "at the utmost hazard of their lives and fortunes," declaring that whosoever should solicit the importation of troops was "an enemy to this town and province." The determination not to rescind the principles stated in the Samuel Adams letter of January was unanimous. Lord Mansfield thereupon declared that the Americans must be reduced to entire obedience before their alleged grievances could be considered. Camden confessed that he did not know what to do; the law must be executed: but how? "If any province is to be chastised, it should be Boston." Finally, two regiments and a squadron were ordered to Boston from Halifax. Samuel Adams felt that the time was now at hand either for independence or annihilation, and he affirmed publicly that the colonists would be justified in "destroying every British soldier whose foot should touch the shore." In the country round Boston, thirty thousand men were ready to fight. A meeting was called in Faneuil Hall, and it resolved that "the inhabitants of the Town of Boston will at the utmost peril of their lives and fortunes maintain and defend their rights, liberties, privileges and immunities."—"And," said Otis, pointing to four hundred muskets which had been collected, "there are your arms; when an attempt is made against your liberties, they will be delivered." Bernard,

www.ingramcontent.com/pod-product-compliance
Lightning Source LLC
Chambersburg PA
CBHW032016220426
43664CB00006B/265